MANAGING PUBLIC ENTERPRISES

The Institute for Research on Public Policy
Published in cooperation with
the Institute for Research on Public Policy
Montreal, Canada

MANAGING PUBLIC ENTERPRISES

Edited by
W. T. Stanbury and Fred Thompson

PRAEGER SPECIAL STUDIES • PRAEGER SCIENTIFIC

HD
62.35
·M36
1982

Library of Congress Cataloging in Publication Data

Main entry under title:

Managing public enterprises.

"Published in cooperation with The Institute for
Research on Public Policy, Montreal, Canada."
Based on two conferences sponsored by the Institute
for Research on Public Policy and the University of
California, Los Angeles.
Includes index.
1. Government business enterprises—Management.
I. Stanbury, W. T.   II. Thompson, Fred, 1943-
III. Institute for Research on Public Policy.   IV. Uni-
versity of California, Los Angeles.
HD62.35.M36   1982   350.009′2   82-9038
ISBN 0-03-061977-7   AACR2

Published in 1982 by Praeger Publishers
CBS Educational and Professional Publishing
a Division of CBS Inc.
521 Fifth Avenue, New York, New York 10175 U.S.A.

© 1982 Praeger Publishers

23456789   052   987654321

Printed in the United States of America

ACKNOWLEDGMENTS

In the preparation of this volume we have been assisted by a number of individuals and organizations whose contributions we are pleased to acknowledge. The chapters herein were originally presented as papers at two conferences on managing public enterprises in Vancouver, British Columbia, and Los Angeles in August and September of 1981. The conferences were jointly sponsored by the UCLA Extension, Continuing Education in Management, Labor, and Business, and the Institute for Research on Public Policy. We are deeply indebted to Warren Pelton and Bud Huizinga of UCLA and Donald Wilson of IRPP for their work in organizing the conferences. Warren Pelton, in particular, deserves special mention, as the conferences were his idea and he initiated the process that resulted in this volume.

For the Vancouver conference we wish to record our special appreciation of the efforts of Melanie Dobben, Louise Gerrais, and Susan Burns. We wish to do the same for the outstanding work done by Tori Esherich for the conference at UCLA.

Although all the papers and comments presented at the conference have not been included in this volume, we want to thank all who gave us the benefit of their thoughts on managing public enterprises. We would, in particular, like to acknowledge the help and counsel given us by Charles Summer of the University of Washington, a true gentleman and a scholar.

Our work was greatly aided by Kathy Welton and Susan Goodman, our editors at Praeger, and Doreen Ferrazzara, our copyeditor; Ruth Ann Crowley, who helped in so many ways; and the secretarial staff at the University of British Columbia. All were most accommodating under difficult conditions.

Finally, we wish to thank all the contributors to this volume. We are very proud of what they have done.

CONTENTS

LIST OF TABLES AND FIGURES

INTRODUCTION

This volume is justified by the belief that imperfect knowledge about things that matter is more useful than even fairly complete knowledge about things that do not. It was in a sense inspired by Ralph Turvey's observation that organizational purposes and objectives and managerial strategy and effectiveness are the key determinants of performance in public enterprises.[1] However, as very little is known about these topics, economists have chosen to direct their attention to those upon which they can make authoritative pronouncements—pricing and investment policy.[2] This behavior has persisted despite common knowledge that, in the absence of prior specification of organizational purpose,[3] such pronouncements have very little practical applicability.

Consequently, we have sought to bring some of the best thinking available to bear on questions of purpose, performance, and strategy in public enterprise, both to indicate what we know and to direct later researchers toward some issues that appear to be of fundamental importance. Of course, we do not know as much as we would like about the management of public enterprise, but neither are we wholly ignorant. At a minimum, we are able to ask the right questions.

In this volume we focus on public enterprises primarily in the United States and Canada. The logic behind this decision rests upon the observation that, from the standpoint of their employment of this instrument of government intervention,[4] the two countries are reasonably similar.[5] Hence comparisons are possible. At the same time, there are enough differences in the scope of services supplied by public enterprises, the patterns of political control, and the structures of the industries in which they operate to make comparisons between the two countries interesting.

1

ORGANIZATION OF THE VOLUME

The chapters that follow are grouped according to three broad themes. These are: purpose, performance, and strategy. Part I addresses the purposes of public enterprises. William G. Shepherd provides from an economist's perspective an overview of the purposes of public enterprise and also shows how their performance might be assessed in Chapter 1. He asks what valid purposes they can serve and, so far as possible, answers that question. Arie Y. Lewin, in Chapter 2, tells us what objects are actually pursued by state-owned enterprises in Western Europe. In addition, he examines some of the practical problems involved in measuring the performance of such enterprises. In Chapter 3 Larry Pratt looks in detail at a single, highly politicized public enterprise—Petro-Canada—and analyzes the roles state oil companies play in achieving "national objectives" and what role they play vis-à-vis their private-sector counterparts. In addition, Pratt offers an assessment of Petro-Canada's performance since it began operations in 1976. In Chapter 4, T. M. Ohashi tells us what can be done with public enterprises that have outlived their public purposes and the decision is made to "privatize" them.

Part II studies the performance of public enterprises. Douglas W. Caves and colleagues assess the relative performance of Canadian and American railways as measured by total factor productivity in Chapter 5. This permits direct comparison of public and private enterprises operating in a reasonably competitive environment (CN and CP in Canada) with private enterprises operating in a highly regulated one (the United States). T. D. Heaver and W. G. Waters II study public enterprise under competition in Chapter 6, with a comment on Canadian railways. William A. Jordan in Chapter 7 presents an assessment of the airline industry, comparing public and private enterprises operating in a regulated environment (Canada and Australia) with private firms operating in a more competitive one (the United States). George W. Hilton in Chapter 8 attempts to explain the highly unsatisfactory performance of railway passenger service in the United States (Amtrak) and concludes that its performance reflects mutually inconsistent objectives. Finally, in Chapter 9, Catherine Eckel and Aidan Vining show how joint private and government ownership can promote improved performance and how governments can clarify their objectives with respect to public enterprises.

Part III reflects our belief that, from a strategic viewpoint, the problems of management in both public and private enterprises are fundamentally alike. What do we mean by strategic viewpoint? First, following Charles Summer,[6] strategic management is a matter of managing evolutionary adaptation. Second, the ultimate basis of successful adaptation is seen in the fact that public and private enterprise organizations come into being, grow, decline, or die. Every organization must compete for support in a complex, frequently harsh, environment with only limited financial and managerial resources. By support we mean not only support from customers (i.e., sales revenue) or from the public treasury, but political support as well. Third, the key task of top management is to ensure there is a "comprehensive alignment" of all the competencies of the organization. This means logically relating a set of external competencies (products or services directed to market or clients or constituency segments) to the complex network of internal competencies of the organization (physical capital, organizational structure, control system, personnel skills, technology or operating procedures, and so forth). Fourth, successful alignments are produced by a long, often slow, process of development. In some ways the process is analogous to the process of mutation in the biological theory of evolution, although the rate of adaptation varies considerably. There is no way to simply wave a magic wand to produce the complex network of external and internal competencies required for survival.

Part III, therefore, deals with problems of strategic adaptation and task alignment in four major public enterprises: the Tennessee Valley Authority (Allan G. Pulsipher, Chapter 10), Canadian National Railways (John Gratwick, Chapter 11), Hydro-Québec (Georges Lafond, Chapter 12), and the U.S. Postal Service (Christopher H. Lovelock and Charles B. Weinberg, Chapter 13).

MAJOR THEMES

One of the most significant ideas running through this volume is that ownership per se may not matter all that much. Enterprises, whether owned by governments or by individuals in the private sector, have to respond to their environments. Where growth and survival require responsiveness to political demands, public enterprises do, in fact, accommodate themselves to the opportunities and risks created by government action and initiatives. So do private enterprises. George Eads argues, for example, that in the United States the new social regulation of the 1970s fundamentally altered the nature of top management in several industries.[7] When government began to tell companies how to organize production processes, where to locate, and how to design products, cope with waste and by-products, and to select employees, Eads claims that companies downgraded traditional operational skills (e.g., marketing, finance, production) in favor of political and legal skills that could be employed to influence the regulatory regimes in which they operated. This, he concludes, has very likely had a significant negative effect on productivity.

Certainly, during the 1970s a remarkable politicization of business occurred in the United States.[8] Now, not only the losers in competitive market transactions are to be found seeking favors in Washington and the state capitals. Many firms have developed a capacity to deal with bureaucrats and politicians, to monitor and even to influence the design and enforcement of regulatory standards. This capacity is reflected in increased government relations staffs, Washington offices, and the investment of millions of dollars in "public affairs."[9]

In a number of industries (e.g., coal mining, chemical products, and so forth), it is clear that survival and growth are contingent upon management's ability to cope with government.[10] The competitive advantage accruing to those firms with the financial and managerial resources to adapt to the new regulatory regimes—for the most part larger, more technologically sophisticated enterprises—is significant. It is overwhelming for those firms that have the capacity to influence the shape and content of the regulatory regimes to which they and their competitors are subject. (Generally, newer firms that have grown up with regulation seem particularly advantaged in adapting to new environments, but older industries learn to adapt too.) It would, of course, be surprising if this politicization—the pursuit of a distinctive competency to influence government—failed to reduce productivity and the dynamic responsiveness to customer wants and preferences. This is precisely what Jordan (Chapter 7) observes: passenger air carriers, both public and private enterprises, in a highly regulated environment are characterized by higher costs and lower productivity than are carriers in a less politicized (regulated) environment.

Of course, one might expect that where growth and survival required responsiveness to the opportunities and risks created by competitive markets, private enterprises will evaluate their strengths and weaknesses in the light of trends in their markets and the activities taken by their competitors and adapt accordingly. So do public enterprises. Caves et al. (Chapter 5) plausibly demonstrate that both publicly owned and privately owned railways in the less regulated, more competitive Canadian environment outperform, by a wide margin, their private but highly regulated American counterparts. We might note that this example (the Canadian railways) provides some support for Shepherd's speculation that one of the potentially useful roles for public enterprise is the enforcement of competition in oligopolistic or duopolistic markets.

Were the two railroads in Canada private enterprises, we strongly suspect that they might collude or at least "closely coordinate" their behavior. Public monopoly would also have real drawbacks. But in this case, they engage in active rivalry, not only with each other but also with other modes of transport as well.

Just as the threat of hostile takeovers may be assumed to influence the behavior of private sector managers, it is possible that the threat of "privatization" may be an equally effective spur where managers of public enterprises are concerned.[11] Here, however, we would note that although it is widely believed that left-wing regimes tend to take over high-performing private enterprises, while centrist regimes are predisposed to nationalize failures, the papers in this volume provide little if any confirmation of this conventional wisdom. It seems as though profitability or the lack thereof is not a very useful criterion for a government takeover or for the conversion from public agency (e.g., government department) to public enterprise.[12] Furthermore, it appears that it takes a long time to turn mismanaged organizations around—this conclusion is suggested by the case of both the Canadian National Railways and the U.S. Post Office.[13]

It also appears that once government action has turned an enterprise around or the public purpose that led to the creation of the public enterprise has been achieved, there is a problem of how to get rid of it. This is so not only because the mechanics of "divestiture" are not well explored, but also because of the incentives created for management. Just as it may be counterproductive to make high-performing private enterprises targets for takeover by the state,[14] it may be equally counterproductive to threaten successful public managers with divestiture. We note that of the managers of public enterprises writing in this volume, only those now operating in highly politicized environments saw privatization as a threat rather than an opportunity (and even a few of those were ambivalent).

In this vein, Eckel and Vining (Chapter 9) make a very interesting argument for jointly owned enterprises. Since they are to achieve certain valid public purposes, such enterprises might well be more responsive than private enterprises and, at the same time and in certain environments, less prone to politicization than purely public enterprises.

Two other trends should be noted. First, much of the growth in the scope and scale of public enterprises likely to occur in the near future will result from the conversion of existing public agencies (e.g., departments) into public enterprises. Second, governments will be less likely to "guarantee" new or existing public enterprises against threats from potential entrants. At the same time, it seems likely that public enterprises will be given greater freedom to develop new products and explore new markets.[15]

These trends, however, raise a number of questions that have not been answered. First, between direct public provision and provision by a public enterprise, is the latter always the dominant institutional arrangement where goods and services are marketed to customers? It has been suggested by Shepherd (Chapter 1) that this is the case, except where the core activity performed by the public agency is collective purchasing. Of course, since the principal justification of collective purchasing is reducing transaction costs associated with interaction with the ultimate service supplier, the actual delivery of the service need not be performed by the purchasing agent (e.g., trash collection).[16] Unfortunately, this suggestion is not based either on rigorous analysis or hard evidence.

Second, what should the role of profits be? Nearly everyone acknowledges that profit is highly visible and sensitive to small changes in performance. As such it effectively performs the "scorecard" function of performance measurement and thereby serves to motivate managers to make the "right" decisions. In structurally competitive markets, economic logic tells us that these decisions are, in fact, the right decisions. However, as Shepherd explains, where public enterprise is a natural monopoly, the appropriate maximand is revenue maximization (at least in some cases) and not profit maximization.[17] But what does it mean to ask a firm to maximize revenue? One obvious point is that assets should be carried on the organization's books at replacement cost rather than at purchase price. But beyond this rather obvious point, the fact is we do not know what is implied by revenue maximization.

Third, how do we get public enterprises to be responsive to public demands without telling them exactly what to do, how to do it, and who can do it? That is, how do we make them responsive without bureaucratizing them? Shepherd provides the usual answer given by economists: pay them a per-unit subsidy, based upon actual performance. But does this mean that all participants in the industry as well as potential entrants should be eligible for the same per-unit subsidy? Certainly, in some cases, such a regime can promote effective competition between public and private enterprise. The case of the Canadian railways appears to demonstrate that. Furthermore, per-unit subsidies tend to promote the development and use of accrual, responsibility, and program accounts as well as Ramsey pricing. The problem is that we do not know where such a regime is appropriate.[18] Furthermore, many of the objectives[19] sought by government through the public enterprise appear to defy the design of simple per-unit subsidies.

These, therefore, are the kinds of questions raised by this volume. We hope what follows will be interesting enough to inspire some attempts to answer them.

NOTES

1. Ralph Turvey, ed., Public Enterprise: Selected Readings (Baltimore: Penguin Modern Economics Series, 1968), p. 7.

2. See, for example, Ralph Turvey, Economic Analysis and Public Enterprise (London: Allen and Unwin, 1971); Alec Nove, Efficiency Criteria for Nationalized Industries (London: Allen and Unwin, 1973); R. Rees, Public Enterprise Economics (London: Weidenfeld and Nicholson, 1976); Michael G. Webb, The Economics of Nationalized Industries: A Theoretical Approach (London: Thomas Nelson and Sons, 1973); and G. R. Faulhaber, "Cross-Subsidization: Pricing in Public Enterprise," American Economic Review 65 (1975):966-77.

3. One recent volume that focuses on the origins and objectives of individual public enterprises is Allan Tupper and G. Bruce Doern, eds., Public Corporations and Public Policy in Canada (Montreal: The Institute for Research on Public Policy, 1981).

4. An examination of why governments choose one instrument of intervention (e.g., public enterprise) over others (e.g., taxes, expenditures, regulation, "tax expenditures," loans/ guarantees) is explored in M. J. Trebilcock et al., The Choice of Governing Instrument (Ottawa: Minister of Supply and Services, 1982), and in M. J. Trebilcock et al., The Choice of Governing Instrument: Some Applications, Regulation Reference Report no. 12 (Ottawa: Economic Council of Canada, July 1981).

5. It appears that the comparability of the two countries in respect to the scope and coverage of government regulation is greater. See W. T. Stanbury and Fred Thompson, "The Scope and Coverage of Regulation in Canada and the United States; Implications for the Demand for Reform," in Government Regulation: Scope, Growth, Process, ed. W. T. Stanbury (Montreal: The Institute for Research on Public Policy, 1980).

6. This formulation follows the keynote presentation made by Charles Summer at the second of the two conferences on managing public enterprises held in Los Angeles, September 10-11, 1981, and entitled "Strategy Formulation in Public Enterprises." It is no exaggeration to suggest that the analytical framework for the papers presented in the last section of this volume was provided by Summer. The interested reader will be well served by reference to his Strategic Behavior in Business and Government (Boston: Little, Brown, 1980).

7. George Eads, Business Week, December 11, 1981, p. 4.

8. This phenomenon is not limited to the United States. In Canada, the extent of government intervention expanded greatly in the 1970s as measured by the level of expenditures, regulatory activity, "tax expenditures," and public enterprise. The federal government moved to "bail out" Chrysler Canada Ltd. and Massey Ferguson, the twelfth largest corporation in Canada in terms of sales. There appears to have been a tremendous growth in expenditures by business on lobbying and other representational activities, although this is hard to document.

9. Mobil's public affairs department, for example, has a budget of $21 million. See Alexander Stuart, "What Makes Mobil Run," Fortune, December 14, 1981, p. 95.

10. See, for example, Bruce Ackerman and William Hassler, Clean Coal, Dirty Air (New Haven: Yale University Press, 1981); Robert A. Leone and John E. Jackson, "The Political Economy of Federal Regulatory Activity: The Case of Water-Pollution Control," in Studies in Public Regulation, ed. Gary Fromm (Cambridge, Mass.: M.I.T. Press, 1981), pp. 231-76.

11. Generally see T. M. Ohashi and T. Roth, eds., Privatization: Theory and Practice (Vancouver: The Fraser Institute, 1980.

12. We would note, however, that in both Canada and the United States, the post office has been transformed from a department of the federal government to a crown corporation whose rates are subject to cabinet approval (in Canada) and to a public enterprise subject to an independent regulatory agency (in the United States).

13. See Caves et al. (Chapter 5) and Gratwick (Chapter 10) on CN and Weinberg (Chapter 11) on the U.S. Post Office. On the latter, see also John T. Tierney, Postal Reorganization: Managing the Public's Business (Boston: Auburn House, 1981); and Roger Sherman, ed., Perspectives on Postal Service Issues (Washington, D.C.: American Enterprise Institute, 1980).

14. For example, between 1976 and 1981 Petro-Canada, owned by the federal government, made three large acquisitions (Atlantic Richfield Canada, Pacific Petroleums, and Petrofina Canada Inc.)—all were successful, privately owned firms. See Pratt, Chapter 3 in this volume.

15. The most obvious examples are postal services and state oil companies. In the case of telecommunications, governments in Canada and the United States are dismantling the regulatory barriers around privately owned enterprises. (The United States is pursuing this policy more enthusiastically than is Canada.)

16. See, for example, E. S. Savas, Privatizing the Public Sector (New York: Chatham House, 1982).

17. See William Niskanen, Bureaucracy and Representative Government (Chicago and New York: Aldine Atherton, 1971), chaps. 9-11; J. C. Panzer and R. D. Willig, "Free Entry and Sustainability of Natural Monopoly," Bell Journal of Economics 8, no. 1 (1977): 1-22.

18. See the discussion in Shepherd, Chapter 1 in this volume.

19. See the list provided by Lewin, Chapter 2, Table 2.2 in this volume.

I

THE PURPOSES OF
PUBLIC ENTERPRISES

1

PUBLIC ENTERPRISES:
PURPOSES AND PERFORMANCE

William G. Shepherd

This chapter interprets some of the recent academic literature on the economic criteria for public enterprise. The lessons are based on a richer understanding of experience than was the case in the 1960s. Moreover, there have been offered some interesting new concepts that could illumine several of the most stubborn problems of public enterprises. Yet the new treatments have only provided a marginal advance on the earlier discussions.

The main criteria for public firms have been long established, and so they will be restated as the first step. Then I will consider how to fit social elements into the performance of commercial operations. The problems of controls, as applied by governments or other groups, will be discussed next. Then specific forms and causes of possible influences in public enterprises will be presented. The problem of sustainability is given a rather long treatment. Finally, the appraisal of performance will be discussed briefly.

BASIC ECONOMIC CRITERIA[1]

Simple Analysis

We need to start with a simple analysis, in order to show where the more complex points fit in. A public enterprise carries

I am grateful to Barton L. Lipman for research assistance with this chapter. I have also benefited from discussions with Harry Trebing and David Sappington about some of the issues.

on production of some kind, using inputs to create outputs. The simple diagram in Figure 1.1 relates this activity to the economic values of the inputs and outputs. Inputs are bought at prevailing prices, in amounts which the firm chooses so as to meet its own objectives. The inputs are processed using technology chosen by the firm in line with its view of efficient production. Then the outputs are sold at prices that generate the firm's total revenue. If total revenue exceeds total cost, there is profit, as shown in equation 1, where P is output price, Q is quantity, i is an output, and j is an input.

$$\text{Profit} = \text{Total Revenue} - \text{Total Cost}$$

$$\text{Profit} = \sum_{i=1}^{n} (P_i \cdot Q_i) - \sum_{j=1}^{m} (p_j \cdot q_j) \tag{1}$$

If costs exceed revenue, the financial losses must be covered from some other source, commonly by a subsidy from the government.

FIGURE 1.1

Basic Features of the Firm

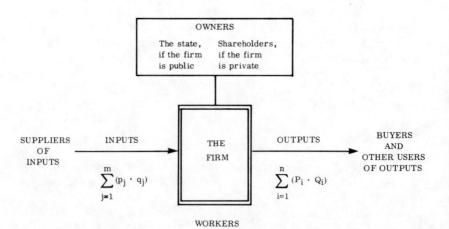

The firm may exert some monopsony power on its input suppliers, thereby reducing the price of the inputs. Or the firm may be required to pay more than the prevailing input prices, especially when governments intervene to make public firms pay higher wages so as to achieve social justice or merely to avoid a strike.

The public firm may also exert monopoly power in selling outputs, so as to raise prices and increase its profits. At the extreme, the firm will choose the monopolist's profit-maximizing prices, with possibly a high degree of price discrimination. But conversely, the firm may choose, or be required from outside, to set lower prices in order to serve some "public" purpose.

In short, the public firm's economic choices may be made indeterminate by a mixture of monopsony, monopoly, and social elements. The social elements may affect both the prices of inputs and outputs and the quantities of inputs and outputs. These elements may be fitted into the firm's actions either by the firm's voluntary choices or by force from outside.

The firm's profits (positive or negative) are a rate of return on its capital, as expressed in equation 2, where k is an item of capital.

$$\text{Rate of Return} = \frac{\sum\limits_{i=1}^{n} (P_i \cdot Q_i) - \sum\limits_{j=1}^{m} (p_j \cdot q_j)}{\sum\limits_{k=1}^{o} (P_k \cdot Q_k)} \qquad (2)$$

The firm's assets are accumulated by past investment decisions. Ideally the efficient asset collection exists at each point, but actual amounts may deviate from the ideal. If so, the accounts can be adjusted to write off "dead" capital. Then the firm's profitability will reflect only the economically productive capital assets.

The rate of return is naturally of special concern because it is widely compared both to the profitability of capital in private firms and to the cost of capital to this firm. Ultimately the public enterprise's rate of return needs to bear some relationship to the true cost of capital.

Social efficiency is reached where output prices are set in line with social marginal costs, and investments are made to the levels where the marginal social rate of return equals the opportunity cost of capital. These rules have become platitudinous by repetition, but they do describe the core of efficient conditions. Defining and measuring the quantities is often difficult, and causes many decisions to be taken in a fog of uncertainty and controversy. Even when the crucial values are known, it may be difficult to align them, or there may be outside pressures to depart from them. Yet the broad lines of efficient decisions are often known pretty well, within reasonable margins of error. Politics then often disturbs choices from outside, or the firms may pursue deviant policies for their own internal reasons.

I will return later to these equations to point out the individual biases in choices that may be caused by deviating from competitive-market choices. But first we need to consider the role of social elements.

Social Elements

I would now stand back from the details of actual public enterprises and consider the social purposes that may be served. Of course, the usual competitive market goals may be sought; the internal minimization of cost, the setting of prices at both marginal cost and minimum average cost, the rapid adoption of innovations, and the like. But those can be provided by private firms, under appropriate market conditions and, if necessary, antitrust supervision. Public enterprises may be used for such cases if the society simply prefers a public to a private basis.

Usually, however, a public firm has some degree and form of social elements—special purposes that market choices would not provide. Some of the main types of such social elements are summarized in Table 1.1, but the list is far from complete. A virtual infinity of social elements can be defined, and public firms can serve many of them. Each may need differing treatments by the public firm, using prices, quantities, types of innovation, or other special actions.

The elements of publicness are usually matters of degree, varying continuously. The social elements are often small, and often a public firm will have several of them, in varying degrees. Yet the choice between private and public enterprise tends to be abrupt: the enterprise is either public or private.[2] That can be seen back in Figure 1.1. The private firms' owners are the shareholders, as provided by the issuance of voting stock. Sever that one link—convert all voting stock into bonds—and the firm becomes a public firm. Actually, nonprivate categories also include so-called "third-sector" firms, such as charitable units (hospitals, Red Cross), cooperatives, worker-owned firms, and others.

Still, firms are commonly treated as being all private or all public. Yet the public element ranges from large to small. Ideally,

TABLE 1.1

Leading Reasons for Adopting Public Enterprise

---

1. Social preference. A society (city, state, or country) may simply prefer public to private control, especially for certain prominent sectors.

2. Inadequate private supply. A new industry or project may seem too large and risky for private firms to invest in. They will demand government guarantees or grants, and possibly other subsidies. It may seem wiser to put the public cost under direct public ownership. Such cases are often controversial. A backlog of them is usually on tap at any time, each with its backers and beneficiaries. Only a few will justify public support.

3. Salvaging firms. The public often "rescues" failing firms by buying out their capital and supporting their rehabilitation. There are always new candidates for such residuary treatment. Some are valid. But they tend to burden the public with sick industries that absorb large subsidies.

4. Exerting competition. One firm in an oligopoly may be made a public enterprise and then run aggressively as a "pace setter." This can reduce prices, improve efficiency, and stir innovation. Alternatively, the public firm may provide indirect "yardstick" competition in utility sectors. For example, a public electricity system may achieve lower costs than private firms, thereby putting pressure on the private firms to do better.

5. Inner nature of the firm. Public firms may modify the power structure and working conditions of private management. Such changes may be significant even if they do not magically transform the social content of the firm as much as the workers had hoped.

6. External impacts. Public firms may allow for outside social harms or benefits that private firms ignore. There may be a structural disequilibrium (for example, shrinking railroads) with transitional social impacts, or a continuing social benefit that justifies continuing subsidy. In the extreme, the service may be a pure public good calling for a full subsidy.

7. Sovereignty. A country may take over the local branches of large international firms in order to neutralize their power. When the country is small and the private firm is big, the action may be necessary for the country's political stability.

8. Incomplete supply to needy users. Universal coverage of some services (for example, good housing, primary education, health care) is often regarded as part of a "good" society. Private firms may supply only the more lucrative groups of customers, leaving needy groups unprovided. Public programs may be the most efficient way to give complete coverage on a fair and decent basis.

Source: Compiled by the author.

instead, the degree of publicness of a public firm would be fitted precisely to the social element. A small social element could result in a small degree of publicness.

Publicness itself involves several elements, not just one. Table 1.2 lists the main elements, of which public ownership is the most conventional, but not always the most important. These are not just hypothetical dimensions. Actual public firms vary along them, as Table 1.3 indicates for just the United States. Examples from other countries would increase the variety even more.

TABLE 1.2

Criteria Defining Public Enterprises

Condition	Possible Range of Variation

Degree of subsidy
  Current
  Capital
	From total subsidy to, to generation of
	  large profits by, the enterprise

Degree of public control	From nil to complete
Ownership	From nil to completely public
Management	From wholly private to wholly public
Degree of monopoly	From nil to pure monopoly
Geographical scope	From local to national

Source: Compiled by the author.

One could not say that the varieties shown in Tables 1.2 and 1.3 neatly fit the social elements listed in Table 1.1. Some cases do, but other cases stray far from them. One point I wish to stress here is that the elements are often complex and that fitting them properly within the public firm's whole set of economic choices will often be a sophisticated task.

Another point is that public enterprises are by no means confined to utility sectors, nor should they be routinely granted monopoly status. Nor should they necessarily fit the older British public corporation mold: completely publicly owned, drawing capital only from the treasury,[3] aiming toward zero profits, and possibly requiring substantial subsidies. Instead, public enterprise can be created in virtually any form, in any sector, in any degree of publicness (along several dimensions), and following a variety of behavioral criteria.

TABLE 1.3

Selected Public-Enterprise Activities in the United States,
by Approximate Degree of Control and Subsidy

Degree of Public Sponsorship	Degree of Effective Public Control		
	Slight Control	Partial Control	Full Control
No Subsidy	Port of New York Authority	State liquor stores	Municipal utilities (water, sewage)
	Federal Reserve Board	National land management	AEC enrichment plants
	FHA housing program	Amtrak	U.S. Government Printing Office
	Tennessee Valley Authority	SBA programs (including minority support)	Social Security
	Performing arts centers	FAA programs	Municipal parking facilities
	Sports stadiums	Airports	Municipal transit
	Public housing	Highway construction and maintenance	Federal courts
	Medicare	State courts	Public law
	Medicaid	Local courts	Child-care programs
	Public universities	Federal maritime program	Primary education
	Military R&D contracting	Mental hospitals	
	Veterans Administration hospitals	State and local law enforcement agencies	
	Weapons purchasing and management	Prisons	
		Corps of Engineers	
		Census Bureau	
Full Subsidy			

Source: Compiled by the author.

In short, public enterprise offers a variety of forms and choices that need to be fitted to the true public needs. The very narrowness of private enterprises limits their suitability to certain market situations in which social elements are minor. When social elements are large and/or complex, public enterprise offers an array of tools to accommodate them. But fitting the public firm to the public purposes is not easy. Public firms need to be carefully designed, and changes in the social elements may require frequent adjustments in the forms and guidelines for the enterprises.

SOCIAL AND COMMERCIAL OPERATIONS[4]

Public Burdens

The tasks are all the harder because the public firms are not free to meet them in a vacuum. Instead, the enterprises operate within a setting that may itself create some problems as well as solve others. The typical setting is shown in Figure 1.2. Of course all firms (public and private) operate among these political and economic conditions: private firms learn to deal with, or manipulate, the various interest groups and public agencies. But for public firms the pressures are often unusually strong.

The setting affects public firms on two planes: the imposition of social burdens and the attempts to control them. On both planes the setting can distort the outcome away from the social optimum. Only the first plane will be discussed here, saving the second for later.

Social elements do not just exist as an exogenous given for the public firm. Usually the social element could be met by a variety of methods, some within the public firm but others by government action outside the firm. Whether the public firm should have the burden of a given social element is often an open issue. For example, transport service to small towns may not be commercially viable, even though it is regarded as socially important. The solution may be either continued provision by the public railroad firm, with or without a subsidy, or increasing bus and trucking services, with or without a subsidy. The former method with no subsidy imposes financial burdens, while the latter method relieves the public railroad of the burden entirely. The literature offers many such examples where the social element can be provided by direct government actions or imposed on public firms, and if imposed on the firms, the activity may or may not be subsidized by the government.

In short, social elements are often endogenous to the government's actions. A government can always escape burden by loading

FIGURE 1.2

The Setting of a Typical Public Enterprise

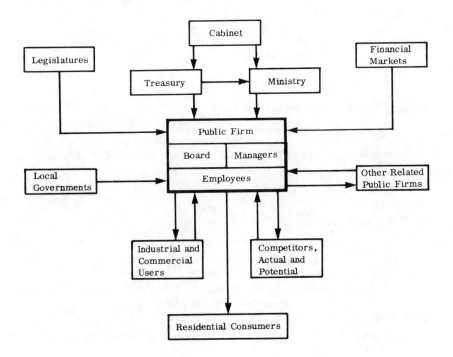

them on public firms, rather than taking direct action. And governments can cause financial stress by refusing full subsidies to the firms for carrying the social elements. In the extreme, a government can cause virtually any degree of financial stress for the public firms that it wishes.

The social elements therefore may exist objectively, but practical politics may distort them. They can be met efficiently by public firms only within a larger setting where the government is efficiently performing its own tasks. Where governments are biased, economists need to allow for the bias in assessing the public firms' choices.

Serving Social and Commercial Goals

There are two polar concepts for reconciling the social and commercial objectives of public firms. One separates the commercial and social elements for explicit treatment, while the other does not.

Separating the Social Elements

If the enterprise engages mainly in commercial activities (selling outputs at going prices in markets), then the social elements may be a relatively small and separable set of activities. Ideally, these social elements can be kept separate in decisions and accounts. The strictly commercial choices can be left undisturbed, to be guided by conventional profit criteria. The social elements can be treated by cost-benefit methods and financed by direct public subsidies, if necessary.

This basis has become the standard economist's approach. It leaves the mass of decisions to be done autonomously. Only a minor element needs to be supervised and paid for publicly. Efforts to apply it are widespread, and meet some success. Indeed, such a separation is inevitably the first step toward a rational treatment.

Yet there are difficulties. The social elements are usually controversial. Moreover, as noted, they are often endogenous rather than exogenous. Identifying them objectively is therefore often difficult or virtually impossible. Even if they are known, the subsidy for them needs to be designed with great care. A full subsidy of indefinite duration may strongly affect incentives for efficiency, not only in the social element but also in related commercial activities. An optimal subsidy may usually be smaller than the full social cost and have a schedule for phasing out as the social need changes. Yet those conditions need to be fitted to various features of the social element, often in complex ways.

The design of optimal subsidies is one of the leading unsolved problems in public enterprises. The literature on it so far is slight. Perhaps it will attract some of the younger analysts.

Not Separating the Social Elements

Pending such an advance, separate subsidies have a weak basis. Therefore the opposite concept has been widely adopted. There may be some effort to judge how heavy the social burdens on the public firm are, which then leads to an approximate view of what degree of total profits or subsidy the firm should aim for. Then the firm is left largely on its own in reaching specific decisions about social and commercial activities. The result is a degree of cross-subsidizing among the public firm's parts.

This issue, which I first treated some 20 years ago in the case of the British Coal Board,[5] has gotten increased attention in recent discussions about U.S. telephone systems under regulation. In fact, it is a widespread phenomenon, as in postal pricing, railroad operations, public broadcasting, city bus lines and subways, and so forth. It is especially important in "social enterprises" such as hospitals, universal medical programs, courts, and education, where the social elements are large and pervasive. Part of the enterprise's very purpose will be to cover the unprofitable activities within the complete system.

Such a large social element should not cause abandonment of the conventional tests for economic efficiency. Even the most highly "social" enterprise is still using costly inputs to produce valuable outputs, as in Figure 1.1. The real differences are no private ownership and profit-maximizing goals, and users do not pay a price to cover the entire costs of their services (nor perhaps even any of the costs). An attempt to distinguish the social and commercial elements is always needed, as part of a rational treatment. Otherwise, "social elements" can become a vague excuse for irrational and sloppy decisions and for bloated costs.

But once social elements are as clear as possible, then a pooled financing of them may be as effective as a pretense at separation and direct subsidies. Many public enterprises—probably the great majority—operate on this basis, some with a high degree of social efficiency. Yet the conditions for optimizing the results under this approach are not known. This is a second frontier for analysis.

The discussion so far has been exceedingly broad. Simple truths can be stated precisely, but their applications involve infinite varieties of special cases and conditions. Several leading issues will be dealt with more specifically later. But first we need to review the stresses that arise between public firms and their supervising government agencies.

CONTROLS AND ACCOUNTABILITY

The creation of a public firm does not in itself assure, or even define, the best social outcome. The solution must often be formulated and guided from outside. It must always at least be monitored, for public firms can deviate widely from the public interest.

This is the "accountability" problem. It is highly complex, but there has been little thorough analytical study of it.[6] It does have important economic aspects. As with public regulation of private firms, there is difficulty in allocating cause and effect— that is, assigning the responsibility for the economic outcomes— between the public firm and the government that supervises and influences it.

There is usually a natural conflict between outside account- ability and internal flexibility and innovation by the public enterprise. This opposition is not complete. Yet outside controls commonly do cause rigidity and chill the ability of the public enterprise to adapt and create.

The basic condition is one of bilateral monopoly between the public enterprise and the government that owns and supervises it. The interests of the firm are not necessarily congruent with those of the government and/or the larger public interest that the govern- ment supposedly represents. Each side—firm and government— has specific motivations, inner conditions, and outside constraints of its own. Each also has a version of the public interest that it regards itself as serving, along with its own internal interests. The actual outcomes will reflect the mutual adjustment of these conditions. The outcomes also reflect the particular structure and economic setting of the public enterprise.

The typical setting of a public firm involves a degree of "regulation" and also some competitive elements. Therefore, the public enterprise is commonly not exempt from the familiar condi- tions of regulation and antitrust. Often it will be deeply involved with them. For example, the U.S. Postal Service is regulated, in some degree, and it faces competition—and vertical bargaining power—in parcels and other operations.[7] Informally or formally, nearly all public enterprises are regulated.[8] And nearly all face— or would face, if it were not officially excluded—competition on all

or part of their activities. Once again: public enterprise is a substitute for private ownership, not for the other regulatory and antitrust policy treatments.

In addition, there will often be interdependencies and external
effects. The supervising public authority will seek to integrate the
public firm's operation with other conditions and objectives, some
of which arise in other public firms (e.g., among transit units in a
city). This often involves a degree of shadow pricing and complex
"coordination"—of merging some operations of the public firms
within larger objectives.

Usually the public enterprise is surrounded by interest groups,
including various parts of the government itself. The public enterprise is naturally likely to respond to all the pressures upon it.
In turn the government agencies will seek to change the form and
setting of the public enterprise as their own interests evolve.

Most public enterprises have a degree of continuity in their
top officers and staff members exceeding that of their official supervisors and regulators. Most top government officials are in and
out within two or three years, while the heads of public firms rise
in the ranks and stay in office long enough to know—and control—
the ropes. This can be partly offset by the fact that the upper civil
servants in the government agencies also tend to last. Therefore,
the relative continuity and cohesion within the two sides can vary
and may often be about equal. Still, a public enterprise typically
contains a strong and continuing set of interests over which the
supervising agency—because of its own inner flux—often is able to
exert relatively little control.

The Role of Accounts

Control is usually based on the actual accounts of the enterprise and an informal interaction process. There are many of the
same difficulties that arise under public regulation of private firms
and, indeed, under attempts by antitrust authorities to investigate
and treat monopoly conditions. For all these policies, the enterprise's accounts are usually very important. They reveal to the
outside, on a tangible basis, what the enterprise has done. Such
exposure forces the enterprise to bring its activities—or, at least,
those that are shown in the accounts—at least partially in line
with what the supervising agency and other outside powers wish to
occur. This pressure works by anticipation, as well as retrospectively. Therefore, the accounts themselves—financial, physical,
and other—are a powerful device by which the supervising agency
exerts control.

Yet the accounts are inherently narrow, even if—as never happens—they comprehensively present every relevant fact about the public firm's activities. They show only what has occurred, not what might have occurred, or what might occur in the future. They do not present the range of social choices and trade-offs that society has had in the past and has now for the future. To that extent the accounts do not convey the genuine conditions for full social choices. Nor can they give a sufficient basis for evaluating what has happened. This is true even if the accounts are utterly complete and accurate.

In practice, the accounts often are incomplete, inaccurate, and have a checkered emphasis. Usually the financial aspects are treated as central in the enterprise's accounts. The commercial kinds of asset, income, profits, and pricing data take up most of the attention, and they are given as the main outcome of the enterprise's activity. This gives a basis for beginning to evaluate certain financial performance criteria. Even these data are controversial, since costs, depreciation, and productivity pose sophisticated measurement problems. Financial performance can be misrepresented in many ways—honestly or otherwise—by the choice of accounting definitions and methods. In any event, these magnitudes are often much too narrow to present the whole range of social effects of the public firms.

Accounts also include physical and social activities. The physical employment, production, allocation, and other outcomes naturally need exposure. In addition, the pollutions, interactions, and other social effects of company activity are also part of an adequate social reckoning. However, these are rarely reported fully or objectively. Also, such data suffer from representing only what has happened, without a full basis for comparing the possibilities. They also can be given in ways that slant their results or—as is often the case—simply omitted. Social effects are especially difficult to render in concrete measures, and they may be deliberately biased by the managers of the enterprise to fit their own purposes. Routinely, understandably, the enterprises will state their accounts so as to make their performance seem as good as possible. This is routine in the explanations that the firms give of their yearly results. These often match the tone, direction, and thinness of the annual reports of private companies. One understands why this happens: managers are human, and outside criticism is often unfairly hostile. Still, the fact remains that the accounts are often incomplete.

In general, the public enterprise's control over information about it is critical. Even when outside investigation is intense and sophisticated, the enterprise can influence the range and quality of what it must tell. The accounting requirements themselves often become a sensitive issue, part of the bilateral bargaining process between the firm and the supervising public agencies.

Fundamentally, full disclosure by the public firm is not efficient in any case. The enterprise's very being is premised on its carrying out social purposes without the full participation or expenditure of effort by the government itself. Therefore, outside review is bound to be partial. This usually tends to keep supervision of the more sensitive items from being complete. Instead, outside review tends to become periodic and fitful, rather than steady and thorough. To repeat, the thinness of outside supervision is both desirable (so as not to inhibit the firm) and subject to abuse.

The Conditions Affecting Accountability

There are certain bilateral monopoly conditions in which each side has special advantages and powers. On the side of the public enterprise itself there are several factors. First is the control of data on its own operations and plans. As noted, this can be not only thorough but purposive and manipulated to maximize the firm's independence and security.

A second power is, paradoxically, the firm's ability to fail or otherwise impose a variety of costs upon the government. The firm's failure itself causes stress and a loss of public support for the government because the officials share responsibility for performance. Short of failure, the firm can still impose a drain on funds and public resources, or it can impose other kinds of difficulties upon the government. These can grow large, as a share of public expenditure and budgeting. Such problems cater to the widespread fears—groundless or otherwise—that public enterprises are increasingly drawing on public resources. Like public regulators of private firms in the United States, supervisors of public firms can be injured if their wards are seen to perform poorly.

Third, a public enterprise often can simply outlast the minister who is endeavoring to impose special authority upon it. To this extent, the firm has added bargaining strength.

As for the supervisors of public enterprises, they have three specific advantages. First, they have control over finances. It is widely believed that the public agencies' control over capital to the public firm may be a critical element of control because if the public firm can—or must—go to private markets for capital, it becomes more independent of control by public authorities. To that extent, the power of the purse may be great. Indeed, many public enterprises—especially those that are subsidized chronically in some degree—are heavily dependent upon their financial sources. Yet this is strongest only for the more conventional types of public firms. When a public firm is not capital-intensive and required to fund large loans, it may be nearly or entirely free of this element of control.

Of course, private-market influences can be as restrictive as public-agency ones, and so a public firm's shift to private bond markets may simply exchange one set of outside controls for another. Many conventional public firms that rely on private capital markets are subject to very tight commercial restraints indeed. These limits are not so tight for the other types of firms whose needs for capital—beyond what they can raise from their own cash flows—are relatively small.

Second, the government usually has other powers. These include the powers of appointment, of setting salaries, and of other kinds of sanctions. Some of these are political, taking the form of public reproofs, controversies, or assertions, rather than of directions or orders. But they can often be quite effective as economic levers on the firm, in forcing or inducing public firm managers to take the desired actions. Accounts may be a central vehicle for detailed supervision of the firm. But the supervisors have other, cruder tools, some of them very powerful indeed, in dealing personally with the managers.

Third, agencies usually have more authority when they supervise more than one public firm. This is clear from the parallel experience in regulating private firms, where one commission may find itself dealing only with one company. In such cases mutual dependence or even passivity by the commissions is a common result. By contrast, an agency that deals with three or five or even more public enterprises is often relatively free to take a tough line with one or the other of them, since it is not so dependent on any particular one.

These are only some of the conditions that influence the bilateral-monopoly outcome between public agencies and the public firms that they attempt to supervise. They are sufficient, however, to show that the optimum package of controls and results depends very much on the conditions of the specific case. Solutions that would give the optimal accountability for a public firm in a utility industry with structural problems of adjustment may be quite different from solutions for a financial public firm or a social enterprise. Therefore, one begins with a full appreciation of the variety of possibilities, rather than trying to settle on one or even several types of public supervision as being best.

Perhaps the most common criticism about public enterprises
has been that they cause inefficiency, both internal cost slackness
and allocational inefficiency between the public firms and the rest
of the economy. The main specific criticisms are summarized in
Table 1.4. Each point relates to an item in equation 2, the rate-
of-return equation. All of the criticisms refer to genuinely logical
possibilities, but each has been denied in real cases. For example,
public firms are repeatedly said to use too much capital because
their target rates of profit are too low, thus increasing the quantity
of output and of needed capacity, and because they obtain capital
funds at costs below the opportunity costs of the capital (as shown
either by private-market rates or by the governments' cost of
capital). Indeed there is a general sense that public firms often
try to invest their way out of difficulties.

However, the effect is a matter of degree. It will be strong
only if there is high elasticity of output demand and of the firms'
demand for capital. If instead the elasticities are low, then the
excess margin of investment will be small. When netted out
against the possible social benefits of lower prices and higher capacity, the social costs of excess investment may be small. Therefore each case needs an individual appraisal. In one done on the
National Coal Board during 1950-63, the distortion did not emerge
as large. In the case of British electricity investment before 1968,
rather more overinvestment did appear to occur.[9] Yet that excess
partly reflected the general optimism about scale economies and
nuclear power, not just a low-price, low-interest mechanism.

Moreover, the possible overinvestment may be smaller than
the excess investment encouraged by the conventional rate-base
regulation of private utilities (the Averch-Johnson effect).[10] One
always needs to compare public enterprises to the practical alternatives, not just to some ideal model. In this matter, it is not
clear a priori which of the two possible expansions is likely to be
most severe because the Averch-Johnson effect is well established
and probably not small.

The reader may easily supply other instances of possible distortions, as noted in Table 1.4. For another example, U.S. postal
rates are said to depart from the true marginal costs of various
service classes.[11] That could cause sharp distortions in the volumes of those mail classes, especially toward restricting first
class mail while overexpanding the carrying of bulk mails. These
are old issues. Recently some economists have complained that
postal rates do not even fit the inverse elasticity rate—the Ramsey
pricing rule,[12] which is simply price discrimination. Whatever
the true degree of distortion, much of it is forced upon the postal
service by congressional policy.

TABLE 1.4

Specific Directions of Possible Inefficiency
in Public Firms

Inefficiency	Source(s)	Consequence(s)
Internal inefficiency	Low rate-of-return targets	Input quantities are too large.
Exploitation of the firm by suppliers	Low rate-of-return targets. Intervention to force higher wages.	Input prices too high, including wages too high, and capital prices too high.
Underpricing of outputs	Low rate-of-return targets. Intervention to restrain output prices. Failure of the firm to use monopoly power where justified.	Output prices too low.
Overproducing of outputs	Output prices too low; significant elasticity of demand.	Output quantities too large.
Inefficient price structure	Output prices do not fit marginal costs; or they deviate from the Ramsey inverse-elasticity rule.	An inefficient bundle of outputs. Excessive output at peak-load times.
Overinvestment	Low rate-of-return targets. Interest costs to the firm kept too low, either explicitly or because of risk guarantees.	Investment amounts too large.

Source: Compiled by the author.

These general points can lead to fruitful reviews of many specific cases. So far they are only tendencies whose strength depends on elasticities and whose social costs have rarely been shown precisely.

SUSTAINABILITY AND COMPETITION

These points bring us to the new "sustainability" literature that has been written mainly by Bell System economists concerned about excessive competition in the regulated telephone sector. In a series of rigorous articles, W. J. Baumol, Robert D. Willig, and others[13] have suggested strongly that discriminatory prices (Ramsey prices) are the best practical outcome for utilities, and that competition would interfere with such prices and therefore is harmful. The argument is highly abstract and has not been challenged.[14]

Willig and others have also applied it to public firms. That step is natural and convincing to some observers because public enterprise has been subject to so little theoretical analysis. Also the sustainability ideas are exclusively about multiproductive natural monopolies, which is what public enterprise is widely believed to be confined to. Sustainability, therefore, may be the new set of answers for public enterprise. Those answers are, again: price discrimination is efficient, and competition should be prevented. Sustainability, therefore, offers public firms a rationale for virtually a free hand in charging what the traffic will bear and keeping out competition. There are other fascinating side points, but these are the two main lessons. These points will now be given a closer analysis, focusing on their relevance for public firms. First, I will set the stage by defining some basic concepts. The analysis begins with the natural-monopoly case but then extends to consider natural competition. Although public firms are discussed here, much of the discussion applies equally well to regulated private firms.

The Setting

Conventional Natural Monopoly

The conventional publicly owned and/or regulated monopoly is defined by conditions of demand and cost.[15] If market demand is small relative to economies of scale, as in Figure 1.3, there is the simple case of natural monopoly. Demand may intersect with average cost in the declining part, as does D_1, or just where average cost reaches its minimum, as does D_2. In either case, competition could not survive. The monopolist will prefer to set one monopoly price such as P_M, earning monopoly profits as shown. It will also try to segment the market and set discriminatory prices, in line with customers' varying demand elasticities.[16] That can yield higher profits.

FIGURE 1.3

Simple Natural Monopoly under Regulation

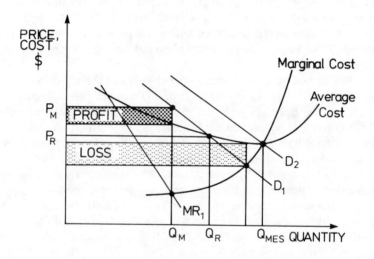

Under public control, the monopoly (public or private) is usually given a public franchise as the exclusive supplier, and it is then supposed to hold price down to average cost—at P_R (R for regulation) for demand of D_1. Ideally, price would be set equal to marginal cost. But with a demand of D_1, marginal-cost pricing would cause financial deficits, as shown. That long-familiar analytical problem requires a "second-best" solution. Some analysts still consider it to be the utility problem, inexorably imposing difficult choices.

But that often need not be so. Demand may grow to D_2 or beyond, or costs may evolve toward smaller scale economies, or both may occur. A properly planned growth path for the utility will keep the firm's capacity in line with demand, so that demand intersects the average cost curve at its minimum, as does D_2 in

Figure 1.3.[17] Then price can equal marginal cost while yielding zero or positive profits: the problem of the deficit disappears. Moreover, cost variations in multiproduct firms (including demand fluctuations between peak and off-peak times) can call for a structure of prices in line with the marginal costs. Under common conditions, this array of prices can still yield sufficient profits.

The franchised firm bears the responsibility for service in two senses: First, it must extend service to all who meet the going price. That is the conventional "common carrier" duty. Second, the firm is also supposed to guarantee all customers a reliable service: its capacity will be adequate and assured. Because customers have to rely on this supplier, their activities come to depend on continuous, ample supply from it. A service failure therefore imposes severe costs, and it imperils the firm's retention of its franchise.

In the ideal static case (with D_2 in Figure 1.3), perfect regulation forces price just down to average cost, permitting just adequate profits. In practice the results may deviate slightly or sharply from this ideal result.

Room for Competition and the Cross-over
Zone of Market Share

Now consider the advent of possible competition. Demand may shift out beyond the given declining part of the average cost curve, or new technology may reduce minimum efficient scale, or both changes may occur in parallel. Where demand intersects the flat average cost curve, there can occur the "first-best" output level, with price equal to marginal cost and no excess profits. Call that level Q_I (I for industry output). Between MES and Q_I, there is now what I will call room for competition. That "room" may be of any degree, from small to large, depending on costs and demand.

Figure 1.4 illustrates two interesting cases. First, with demand D_3 there is some slight room for competition (MES to Q_{I3}), but the original monopolist's market share (M_O) will continue at over 50 percent. I will define such cases—where M_O remains between 50 and 100 percent of the market—as natural quasi monopoly (it is also frequently called a "dominant firm" case). The new room for competition (between MES and Q_{I3}) may, of course, be captured by the established monopolist, rather than by new entrants. The actual market share taken by new entrants is indeterminate: other conditions will influence it. Though natural quasi-monopoly conditions make some competition possible, they do not assure that competition will actually emerge, nor that it will be effective.

FIGURE 1.4

Varying "Room for Competition"

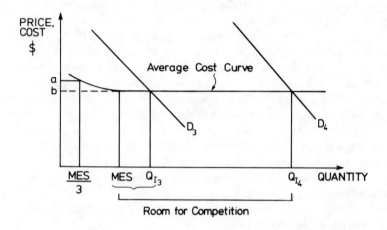

Second, further relative demand growth may give natural oligopoly, as illustrated by demand curve D4. There is now room for four equal-size firms, and competition could become severe. Yet this tight oligopoly might instead develop collusion, either tacit or direct. And the original monopoly may, as before, be able to capture all or part of the output above MES for itself, with M_O staying as high as 100 percent.

Finally, if the demand and cost shifts go still further, then natural competition may emerge, with an even larger ratio of Q_I to MES. Many efficient firms might be able to coexist, and price will be driven down to average cost. The original monopolist may find it hard to retain a high market share; yet conceivably its M_O could still remain high.

The spectrum therefore contains all degrees, from pure monopoly to quasi monopoly, oligopoly, and full competition.[18] Evidently, the shift from traditional natural-monopoly regulation to natural competition is a large one. It presumes a radical relative shift of demand and of scale economies. Any lesser shift, say to Q_I at double the level of MES, will leave a high degree of market power even if M_O is held strictly to MES. Deregulation will need to be a careful, complex sequence—dealing with pricing, entry, mergers, and other aspects—so as to fit and use the growing room for competition. No easy, quick deregulation is possible.

The shift toward competition involves what may be called a cross-over zone, defined in terms of the market share of the established firm, M_O. As M_O declines across that range, effective regulatory constraint will be replaced by the constraints of a competitive market.

The cross-over zone of M_O is not a unique level of market share. It depends on other firms' market shares and on the height of barriers to further entry. The literature on market structure and performance suggests that the zone usually lies between about 60 and 30 percent of the market.[19] With an M_O of 60 percent or higher, competition cannot be fully effective; but when M_O is below 30 percent and entry barriers are low, competition usually is fully effective.

The benefits of effective competition are the same as those for ideal public firm choices: prices aligned with costs, X-efficiency, and innovation. If M_O remains above the cross-over zone, then competition is inadequate and public control needs to be retained.

Related to the cross-over zone is the concept of minimum efficient market share. It is the M_O value that provides an optimum balance between the gradient of the average cost curve below MES, and the efficiency and innovation benefits of competition.[20] The cost gradient is commonly defined as the cost penalty from being only one-third the size of minimum efficient scale, as a percent of minimum cost. That point is illustrated in Figure 1.4 at MES/3, where average cost of a is about 15 percent above the lowest attainable cost b. The cost gradient is:

$$G = (a - b)/b$$

MES does not set a rigid lower border on M_O. If the cost gradient is low, then setting M_O below MES will raise cost only slightly, while the added competition may yield much more X-efficiency and innovation. The relationship between M_O, MES, and G is complex, but Figure 1.5 illustrates its basic form. The diagonal line is the lower limit on optimal M_O if the cost gradient is infinite. But as the gradient decreases, the optimum M_O declines relative to MES. The exact contours of Figure 1.5 are an important research topic, both in general and for regulatory economics.

Core Services

Most public firms contain certain operations that are regarded as, or merely claimed to be, the essential core or network that makes the whole system's service possible. Other services are adjacent: ancillary, normal, or ordinary, in some sense.

FIGURE 1.5

Low Cost Gradients Increase the Range of Possible
Competition, Even When MES May Be High

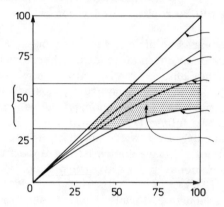

Core services are not uniquely defined. They may be those
that have the greatest relative economies of scale. Often they share
joint costs of production. But scale economies and joint costs are
neither necessary nor sufficient. Core services may simply be regarded as the unifying or crucial part of the system. For example,
telephone officials may regard intercity switching and transmission
(rather than local telephone switching) as the real core of their system, essential to its unified operations. Several other instances of
core services are given in Table 1.5.

Core operations are often controversial, for the established
firms have an interest in contending that the core is large, even if
it is not. Core services are usually the main part in any argument
that the existing monopolist needs to be protected. If there are no
core outputs, then it does not matter who supplies which outputs.
And if consumers value them less than their costs, then such outputs can be omitted altogether.

I am not urging the importance nor even the existence of core
outputs. But since the recent sustainability analysis is predicated
on core outputs, it is important to consider them explicitly. Although at this stage they have not been fully defined, we can perhaps
analyze their general role.

TABLE 1.5

Possible Core Services

Sector	Possible Core Services	Presently Provided by
Airlines, air freight	Airports Flight guidance systems Reservations systems	Public agencies Federal Aviation Authority Each airline
Trucking, intercity buses	Highways and roads	Public agencies
Broadcasting of radio and television	Spectrum allocation controls	Federal Communications Commission
Satellite communications	Satellite launching systems	National Aeronautics and Space Administration
Telephones	Local switching and loops	Telephone companies
Postal service	Local delivery routes Local sorting	Postal System Postal System
Electric power	Local distribution Regional pooling	Electric firms (private and public) By agreement among electric systems
Banking	Check clearing	Federal Reserve System

Source: Compiled by the author.

Separability

The crucial question is how separable the utility's services are. If they are closely mingled—with joint production and high overhead costs, often called economies of scope—then their provision will require a single unified multiproduct monopolist.[21] But if instead production and costs can be cleanly separated for each output, then each can be treated as in a separate market. Products with natural-monopoly conditions can be separated from the rest, and competition can be applied just where it is appropriate.

The degree of separability is often unclear, particularly to outside observers. Technology is usually not transparent, especially for complex monopoly systems such as telephones. Moreover, separability is often not just a technical given. The firm may be able to control the degree of separability among its output in two different ways. First, it can select the technologies that have the largest element of joint production and overhead cost, avoiding the more highly separable ones. And second, it can conduct its operations and cost accounting in ways that make the joint costs and overhead costs seem as large as possible.

When that occurs, the recorded marginal costs for individual outputs will be minimized, giving the utility the widest discretion in its pricing actions—and in its pricing reactions to new competitors. The utility has an interest in minimizing the apparent degree of separability, so as to make its monopoly control of most or all services seem necessary. Often the firm has wide discretion in doing so. The result can be to overstate sharply the true degree of economies of scope within the utility "system."

Where true economies of scope are large, there may exist a set of true core services. (Yet even so, they may be a peripheral subset of outputs, interrelated but a minor part of the whole set of outputs.) If core services are separable from the rest, they can be provided by the utility or separately by some other unit—perhaps by a separate public agency (such as the public provision of airports and Federal Aviation Agency flight guidance systems).

At any rate, core services (if they do exist as such) can often be quite separate in provision and pricing from other outputs of the sector. If public policy succeeds in maximizing that separability, then the viability of competition in quasi-monopoly settings will be enhanced. Table 1.5 indicates that separability can be complete. Core services in several sectors (airlines, air freight, trucking, and banking) are provided separately from the firms themselves.

Since core services do not necessarily have large scale economies, they need not create natural monopoly. Competition may be possible, and firms may be able to proliferate, each with its own core services. Airline reservations systems are an example of that: each airline is able to provide itself with the core system.

Core conditions may change or fade away, as technology develops. There have been marked reductions of core conditions in a variety of sectors. Indeed, the series of recent deregulation in various U.S. markets has been mainly following the shrinkage or disappearance of core conditions. Therefore the public-firm multiproduct monopoly bears a burden of proof to demonstrate that its claimed core conditions and complementarities of production do exist—and that they are unavoidable by alternative technological choices. Otherwise outsiders, with their limited knowledge of technology and internal company conditions, may be unable to find the true conditions, be led to underestimate separability, and therefore be maneuvered so as to limit competition unnecessarily.

Joint Costs and Entry

These concepts help to redefine the role of joint costs in the face of entry by low-cost firms. Consider the simplest case, with two outputs 1 and 2 produced jointly by monopolist A. There are separable marginal costs for each output, plus some shared overhead cost.

Now let a new firm appear, able to produce output 1 at less than its marginal cost to the monopolist. At that point, the output ceases to possess the economic attribute of a joint product with output 2. As a joint product, it can no longer survive. Therefore output 1 will henceforth be produced only with the new method by the new firm B—and/or by the existing monopoly firm A. The former joint costs now must be assigned by firm A solely to output 2. Whether to produce output 2 depends on the demand conditions. If consumers are not willing to pay the combined cost, then either the output is to be discontinued, or the overhead costs are (partly or wholly) written off, reflecting the new true cost of output 2. Firm A suffers a loss of asset value, but this is merely the efficient outcome of technological progress in producing output 1.

In this way, innovation in producing individual outputs may reduce the breadth of the monopolist's offerings, unless the monopolist preempts entry by adopting the new technology first. The innovation may force up the monopolist's apparent costs on the remaining outputs. Yet the shift of overhead cost to output 2 is part of an efficient assimilation of new technology. Only by letting it happen under the threat or reality of entry can the innovation (by either firm) be assured. The monopolist's financial injury is inevitable. In practice, of course, the injury can be lightened or avoided, if the monopolist is farsighted and progressive, so that it avoids mistaken commitments to doomed technology.

The Responsibility for Service

Under conventional policies, the franchised firm has borne exclusive responsibility for service. Any shrinkage of that domain of responsibility seems to challenge the firm's exclusive role as well as the interests of customers. New competition is therefore often resisted for being likely to undermine reliable service. Yet eliminating or diluting that exclusive responsibility for service is necessary, if competition is to become effective. In virtually all

industries (regulated and unregulated), goods and services are provided steadily and reliably by several or many competitors, even
though no one firm is required to accept any formal responsibility
for service. Competition and profit-seeking induce an adequate
supply to be forthcoming. Of course there may be occasional
lapses in supply. But such lapses also occur occasionally in exclusively "responsible" utilities.[22] The idea of absolute responsibility of franchised utilities for service is largely a myth. Accordingly, competition's dilution of formal responsibility is merely a
matter of degree. Only in extreme cases of certain emergency
services is absolute responsibility possible and perhaps desirable.

Furthermore, customers can usually adjust so as to be less
reliant on utility service. Industrial customers often have their
own reserve power sources to tide over electricity failures.
Families can adjust their consumption habits and appliances so as
to be less vulnerable. Such adjustments to lighten the future impacts may impose higher costs, but the net rise in costs may be
small.

In short, we already live in a world of partial service responsibility. Competition may increase reliability, not reduce it. Even
if reliability is reduced, the costs are finite and may be small.

The Sustainability Analysis

With these points in mind, we can now consider the question
of sustainability. The term has been coined and advanced variously
by Baumol, Bailey, Willig, and Panzar (BBWP) and others associated with the Bell System.[23] Despite some variation in analyses,
they offer similar views and conclusions. Their analysis would
reverse certain concepts of regulated firms, and it suggests a
strict public policy against competition. It would also be highly
relevant to public firms in monopoly or quasi-monopoly positions.

Assumptions

The main assumptions of BBWP analysis are given in the
left-hand side of Table 1.6. Regulation is assumed by BBWP to
be "ideal": omniscient and all-powerful. Optimal prices and outputs are known and enforced. This result holds even if the firm is
a multiproduct producer with complex joint-production and overhead costs.

Under natural-monopoly conditions (assumption 2) and ideal
regulation, the firm offers the ideal set of products at Ramsey
prices that maximize consumer surplus.[24] Since there is unlimited reselling of products (assumption 3), the monopolist can set

only one price for each product. BBWP analysis does not consider the nature or relative importance of those various products (core or adjacent, large or small volume). Nor does BBWP analysis permit the firm or new entrants to vary the products as the action proceeds. By assumptions 5 through 8, the monopolist is completely exposed to entry, without advantages, frictions, or barriers. Nor by the Cournot-Nash assumption (number 9) is the monopolist expected to retaliate at all against entrants, or even to threaten to respond.

Results

The results under regulation are assumed to be "ideal," maximizing consumer surplus. Because of the cost conditions, strict marginal-cost pricing will cause the firm to run financial deficits. Therefore, prices can do no better than to fit some second-best pattern. For the multiple output use, BBWP analysis proposes Ramsey prices, a discriminatory multiproduct price structure. Prices are set short of full monopoly price discrimination by some uniform ratio. Such prices may well maximize consumer surplus when a deficit is otherwise inevitable.[25]

Ramsey prices may even arise voluntarily if a utility faces a moderate degree of entry, according to BBWP. A "weak invisible hand" may tend to give Ramsey prices, by the monopolist's voluntary choice. This outcome should also maximize static consumer surplus.

However, if an entrant can and is permitted to produce a subset of products at lower than the Ramsey prices for those products, the utility's price vector is said by BBWP to be no longer "sustainable." The costs of the other products and overhead costs cannot be covered by the Ramsey prices. Therefore low-price entry can reduce consumer welfare, and it imperils the utility's existence. Still other harms have also been suggested, including "wasteful entry" and "destructive innovation." The lessons would also apply to public firms.

Evaluation

In appraising this many-sided analysis, one begins with the assumptions. I will discuss them as a group and then consider several of them individually.

Assumptions. The main BBWP assumptions appear to be self-defeating: they contradict the reality that the analysis is intended to clarify. The right side of Table 1.6 summarizes actual conditions in regulated firms, based on the rich literature on these subjects. At the static level, assumptions 2, 4, and 10 are doubtful in most cases. Assumptions 1, 3, and 5 through 9 are radically inaccurate.

TABLE 1.6

Assumptions for the Baumol, Bailey, Willig, and Panzar Sustainability Analysis

BBWP Assumptions	Common Conditions in Real Sectors
1. <u>Regulation is ideal</u>. Regulators' information and powers are complete, and their actions impose ideal results without any friction or delay. The monopolist produces the socially ideal set of products, under regulation. The monopoly earns zero excess profits.	1. Actual regulation is usually imperfect, incomplete, and lagged. The firm has wide discretion in product offerings. Profits are often well above zero.
2. <u>Costs</u>. For the single-product firm, there are large economies of scale. For multiple-product firms, there are high joint and overhead costs.	2. Cost conditions vary, in both scale economies and joint costs.
3. <u>Reselling</u>. All products can be freely resold among customers, so that only one price can be set by the monopolist for each product.	3. Reselling is usually not feasible, except for certain limited products. Price discrimination is usually possible.
4. <u>Nature of the products</u>. First, no distinction is made between core and adjacent goods. All are treated as if they were core products. Second, the monopolist's and entrants' goods are identical items; no variation is permitted, either at the start or as events unfold. Third, the social value of goods is reflected only in demand conditions (including consumer surplus).	4. The products vary, both among core and adjacent services and between the established firm's products and entrants' products. Social values often go beyond demand conditions.

42

5. <u>Technology is transparent</u> (both the existing conditions and possible future choices). It is as completely known and accessible to entrants as it is to the monopolist. The regulators also have complete knowledge of present and alternative future technologies.

6. <u>Friction in adjustments.</u> There are none. Changes are instantaneous.

7. <u>Barriers to entry.</u> There are none (other than those created by scale economies or joint costs in the multi-product case). Barriers to entry by low-cost firms can only be provided by actions of the regulators.

8. <u>Competitive advantages of the monopolist (in knowledge, financial ties, customer loyalty, experience, etc.).</u> There are none.

9. <u>Responses or preemptive actions by the monopolist.</u> There are none, and the entrant expects none to be made (by the Cournot-Nash assumptions).

10. <u>X-efficiency and innovation.</u> The monopolist is expected to optimize them under perfect regulation.

5. Actual and alternative technologies are often complex and incompletely known to outsiders.

6. Frictions and irreducible lags in adjustments are often large.

7. Barriers to entry are often large and have many sources.

8. The monopolist often has large advantages over entrants.

9. The monopolist typically responds sharply to new entry, and entrants usually expect retaliation by price or other actions.

10. Monopoly effects on innovation often remain. Also, the side effects of regulation itself often raise costs and enlarge investment (the cost-plus and rate-base effects).

<u>Note:</u> Static analysis.
<u>Source:</u> Compiled by the author.

Baumol, Bailey, Willig, and Panzar have indicated at some points that their analysis is an "exercise," not pretending to deal with real sectors. Certain assumptions (especially number 9) are needed to make the analysis tractable. Yet the results have been presented as if they have relevance, and they are gaining acceptance as being important, if not conclusive. Therefore, one must judge the relation of the BBWP analysis to reality. As Table 1.6 indicates and as I will discuss more thoroughly, it is slight.

Pricing Criteria. In the single-output case, BBWP analysis focuses on natural monopoly conditions, where Q_I is less than MES (Figure 1.4). Setting price at marginal cost will cause a financial deficit, and so some second-best result is needed. New competition would reduce the established firm's output and force a higher price, perhaps putting the firm in deficit.

But if Q_I exceeds MES, so that there is room for competition, then sustainability is no longer in question. Prices can be at cost, while all firms—established and entering—are viable. In short, BBWP sustainability analysis adds little to well-established conclusions about the single-output case.

As for multiple products, the sustainability issue arises when economies of scope prevail throughout. Then joint production and overhead costs are extensive, and all outputs have marginal costs below average costs.

Yet if Ramsey prices are not required, the BBWP analysis loses its force. That can occur if enough of the firm's outputs have rising marginal costs that lie above average cost. Examples include peak-load outputs, which are common among utilities because of fluctuating demand. In other directions, too, marginal costs may be above average costs, for regulated firms typically provide a variety of services outside the central set of joint-cost products.[26] There is often room for competition in many of the regulated firm's services. Therefore, the need for comprehensive Ramsey prices is a peculiar special case, rarely found among regulated firms.

Even where Ramsey prices are appropriate throughout, they will cease to be the welfare criterion for those outputs where the new entrant is able to set its price below the original firm's marginal cost. Then joint cost ceases to be joint, and it applies only to the remaining output (as noted above). The former monopolist may need to write off the joint cost and adopt a new set of prices. It is optimal to accept this entry, even if it renders the Ramsey prices unsustainable.

Sustainability therefore needs protecting only where the entrant's price falls in the band between the original firm's average and marginal cost, and where no marginal costs are above average costs. This is a limited and perhaps small problem. Moreover, it is one of degree, not of absolutes. Entry may require adjusting the Ramsey prices, but perhaps by little. Any loss of consumer surplus may be slight. BBWP analysis has neglected the question of degree, instead discussing only if sustainability exists or not. That has implied a more ominous effect of entry: that the firm's very existence is unsustainable. Why would BBWP give the problem such extended analysis if it did not have serious effects of that sort?

Yet the effect may instead be trivial. A robust established firm—dominant in its markets and with a wide range of pricing and strategic choices—merely adjusts one or several of its prices, or lets an entrant replace one of its products. [27]

Logic versus Matters of Degree. The whole topic is one of degree as well as logic. As for logic, the sustainability literature has first adopted a strange version of the regulated firm. It has treated competition as a threat to a price vector, and suggested that the firm's viability and existence will be in danger. But that matters only if the social losses exceed the competitive improvements in efficiency, innovation, and other directions. Those matters of degree depend on the cost functions, demand conditions, and other relationships.

New competition may usually cause some degree of adjustment of relative prices, minor rather than large or decisive. The resulting efficiency losses, if any, may be trivial, sizable, or large.

BBWP analysis provides no guidance on that, nor does it permit us to weigh the quantitative effects, or whether core or adjacent goods are involved. This is the obvious line for research, but BBWP analysis instead treats "sustainable" as merely a yes-no issue.

Sustainability is no guide to the really difficult issues in the main areas of public enterprise. Public firms might like to hide behind sustainability but that would almost always be inappropriate. The main lessons go the other way, toward competition and marginal cost pricing. I have recently shown that the degree of competition has increased in the U.S. economy. [28] Public enterprises can expect to join this trend, facing more competition in their own markets. The continuing move toward marginal-cost pricing also offers important gains in efficiency.

APPRAISING PERFORMANCE

Though competition and marginal cost are not universal answers, they are the most general guidelines available. Competition provides a stimulus to efficiency and to innovation. It also presses prices toward costs. It need not be perfect in order to provide the main benefits. Therefore monopoly is an aberration that should be avoided whenever possible. As for marginal-cost pricing, it properly bases choices upon opportunity costs.

Competition and marginal cost are the starting point for appraising the performance of public firms. Beyond that there are no simple tests. Performance is a composite of many parts, some subtle and obscure. Yet difficult though they are to do, appraisals of public firm performance are necessary. Otherwise, public enterprises are left merely to polemics and political pressures.

A good appraisal will involve measurements of costs and technological progress. These can then be compared normatively with the costs and innovations that might reasonably have been expected. To do that, comparisons with a benchmark are needed. Engineering studies may help occasionally, but comparative studies using other firms are the most promising. Public firm A in industry X can be compared with private firms in the same industry; or with private and public firms in industry X in other countries or regions; or with private and public firms in similar industries in the same or other countries.[29] Such comparative studies have been few so far, and of course they will rarely give conclusive answers. But they can provide normative comparisons based on reality rather than just on theoretical norms.

Such normative comparisons are a research frontier. There is a still larger frontier: explaining why public enterprises have good or bad performance. There are some general explanatory lessons in the literature. But they are primitive and have had little success in specific cases. Why, for example, has the British Steel Corporation done so poorly (as it seems) and Renault so well (as it seems)? Perhaps we can begin developing the methods for reaching such explanations.

NOTES

1. This section is drawn partly from W. G. Shepherd and Associates, Public Enterprise: Economic Analysis of Theory and Practice (Lexington, Mass.: D. C. Heath, 1976), pp. 40-45.

2. Editors' note: Jointly owned enterprises are discussed by Eckel and Vining in Chapter 9 of this volume.

3. See, for example, W. A. Robson, Nationalized Industry and Public Ownership, 2d ed. (London: Allen and Unwin, 1962). More recent discussions of British public enterprises can be found in Richard Pryke, Public Enterprise in Practice (New York: St. Martin's Press, 1972), and The Nationalized Industries (London: Martin Robertson, 1981).

4. Parts of this section draw on W. G. Shepherd, "Public Enterprise in Western Europe and the United States," in The Structure of European Industry, ed. H. W. deJong (The Hague: Martinus Nijhoff, 1981).

5. See W. G. Shepherd, Economic Performance Under Public Ownership (New Haven: Yale University Press, 1965).

6. But see Annmarie Hauck Walsh, The Public's Business: The Politics and Practice of Government Corporations (Cambridge, Mass.: M.I.T. Press, 1978); Christopher D. Foster, Politics, Finance, and the Role of Economics: An Essay on the Control of Public Enterprise (London: Allen and Unwin, 1971); and David Heald, "The Economics and Financial Control of U. K. Nationalized Industries," Economic Journal 90 (June 1980):243-65.

7. See Roger Sherman, ed., Perspectives on Postal Service Issues (Washington, D.C.: American Enterprise Institute, 1980); and Alan L. Sorkin, The Economics of the Postal System (Lexington, Mass.: D. C. Heath, 1980).

8. Editors' note: In Canada, many of the largest public enterprises are directly regulated. See, for example, Allan Tupper and G. Bruce Doern, eds., Public Corporations and Public Policy in Canada (Montreal: The Institute for Research on Public Policy, 1981); John Baldwin, The Regulatory Agency and the Public Corporation (Cambridge, Mass.: Ballinger, 1975).

9. See Ralph Turvey, Optimal Pricing and Investment in Electricity Supply (London: Allen and Unwin, 1968).

10. Harvey Averch and Leland Johnson, "Behavior of the Firm under Regulatory Constraint," American Economic Review 52 (1962):1052-69. See also Alvin Klevorick, "The Optimal Fair Rate of Return," Bell Journal of Economics and Management Science 2 (1971):122-53.

11. See note 7.

12. Frank Ramsey, "A Contribution to the Theory of Taxation," Economic Journal 37 (March 1927):47-61.

13. The main papers are John C. Panzar and Robert D. Willig, "Free Entry and the Sustainability of Natural Monopoly," Bell Journal of Economics 8 (Spring 1977):1-22; J. C. Panzar and R. D. Willig, "Economies of Scale in Multi-Output Production," Quarterly Journal of Economics, August 1977, pp. 481-94; W. J. Baumol, Elizabeth E. Bailey, and Robert D. Willig, "Weak Invisible Hand Theorems on the Sustainability of Prices in a Multiproduct Natural Monopoly," American Economic Review 67 (June 1977): 350-65; W. J. Baumol, "On the Proper Cost Tests for Natural Monopoly in a Multiproduct Industry," American Economic Review 67 (December 1977):811-22; Robert D. Willig, "Multiproduct Technology and Market Structure," American Economic Review 69

(May 1979):346-51; R. D. Willig and W. J. Baumol, "Intertemporal Unsustainability," manuscript, 1980; and Elizabeth E. Bailey, "Contestability and the Design of Regulatory and Antitrust Policy," manuscript, 1980.

14. The only previous published review of sustainability has been by Vinson C. Snowberger, "Sustainability Theory: Its Implications for Governmental Restriction of Entry," Quarterly Review of Economics and Business 18 (Winter 1978):81-89. It is a brief summary of his "Efficiency, Sustainability, and Ramsey-Optimality of a Multi-Product Regulated Monopoly," Contractor's Report (Washington, D.C.: Office of Telecommunications Technology, Executive Office of the President, September 1977), and deals only with the earlier papers. See also W. G. Shepherd, "Competition and Sustainability," in De-regulation, ed. W. Sichel (Ann Arbor: University of Michigan Graduate School of Business, 1982).

15. See Alfred E. Kahn, The Economics of Regulation, 2 vols. (New York: Wiley, 1971); W. G. Shepherd and Clair Wilcox, Public Policies Toward Business, 6th ed. (Homewood: Irwin, 1979); James C. Bonbright, Principles of Public Utility Rates (New York: Columbia University Press, 1961); James R. Nelson, Marginal Cost Pricing in Practice (Englewood Cliffs, N.J.: Prentice-Hall, 1964); and F. M. Scherer, Industrial Market Structure and Economic Performance, 2d ed. (Chicago: Rand McNally, 1980).

16. On price discrimination, see Fritz Machlup, The Political Economy of Monopoly (Baltimore: Johns Hopkins University Press, 1952); Joan Robinson, The Economics of Imperfect Competition (London: Macmillan, 1933); Kahn, The Economics of Regulation; and Scherer, Industrial Market Structure.

17. See Shepherd and Wilcox, Public Policies Toward Business; W. G. Shepherd, The Treatment of Market Power: Antitrust, Regulation, and Public Enterprise (New York: Columbia University Press, 1975); and Nelson, Marginal Cost Pricing.

18. For analysis of the complexity of these conditions, see Scherer, Industrial Market Structure; and W. G. Shepherd, The Economics of Industrial Organization (Englewood Cliffs, N.J.: Prentice-Hall, 1979).

19. These issues are reviewed in Scherer, Industrial Market Structure; Shepherd, The Economics; and Shepherd, The Treatment of Market Power. Dominant firms (with M_O above 50 percent) usually diverge sharply from competitive conditions. Antitrust policy has used 60 percent as a threshold for defining monopoly power; the criterion used in Great Britain is 30 percent. See Scherer, Industrial Market Structure; and Shepherd and Wilcox, Public Policies. There is no sharp border line, and other factors (such as entry barriers) can affect monopoly power. Yet market shares and market power are positively related.

20. See Scherer, Industrial Market Structure; and W. G. Shepherd, "Economies of Scale and Monopoly Profits," in Industrial Organization Research, ed. J. Craven (under review, 1982).

21. On cost conditions, the classical sources include J. M. Clark, Studies in the Economics of Overhead Costs (Chicago: University of Chicago Press, 1923); and W. Arthur Lewis, Overhead Costs (London: Allen and Unwin, 1948). See also Scherer, Industrial Market Structure.

22. Occasional strikes, overloads, and weather catastrophes are reluctantly accepted by regulators and customers, despite the utility's formal absolute obligation (as in New York telephone service during 1969-70 and the blackouts of 1965 and 1979). Regulatory penalties are applied carefully, often lightly and forgivingly. Franchises are rarely revoked, even for inept utilities. See Kahn, The Economics of Regulation; and Bonbright, The Principles of Public Utility Rates.

23. In addition to the references in note 8 above, see W. J. Baumol and David F. Bradford, "Optimal Departures from Marginal Cost Pricing," American Economic Review 60 (June 1970):265-83; G. R. Faulhaber, "Cross-subsidization: Pricing in Public Enterprises," American Economic Review 65 (December 1975):966-77; and Edward E. Zajac, Fairness or Efficiency (Cambridge, Mass.: Ballinger, 1978).

24. Frank Ramsey's 1927 note on taxation (see note 12) provided a simple rule for minimizing the impact of taxes. The BBWP analysis has adapted this rule for the ceiling-cost, inevitable-deficit case of a public utility.

25. Static consumer surplus is not an ultimate criterion of social welfare. It may not be a well-defined maximand. Also, there may be other social values not included in consumer surplus.

26. Such mixed sectors are discussed in Kahn, The Economics of Regulation; Bonbright, The Principles of Public Utility Rates; Shepherd, The Treatment of Market Power; Almarin Phillips, ed., Promoting Competition in Regulated Markets (Washington, D.C.: Brookings, 1975); and many other sources.

27. The literature on the complex conditions of entry has grown to a large volume. See J. S. Bain, Barriers to New Competition (Cambridge, Mass.: Harvard University Press, 1956); Scherer, Industrial Market Structure; Michael W. Klass and William G. Shepherd, eds., Regulation and Entry (East Lansing: Michigan State University Institute of Public Utilities, 1976); W. G. Shepherd, "Entry as a Substitute for Regulation," American Economic Review 63 (May 1973):98-105; Kahn, The Economics of Regulation; and Phillips, Promoting Competition.

28. W. G. Shepherd, "The Trend of Competition in the U.S. Economy, 1939 to 1980," working paper, 1982.

29. <u>Editors' note</u>: See the papers by Caves et al., Chapter 5, and Jordan, Chapter 7.

2

PUBLIC ENTERPRISE, PURPOSES AND PERFORMANCE: A SURVEY OF WESTERN EUROPEAN EXPERIENCE

Arie Y. Lewin

INTRODUCTION

Traditional policy instruments employed by governments as a means of managing national economies include regulation, subsidies, tax concessions, licenses, "voluntary agreements," tariff protection, nontariff barriers, and government-guaranteed loans. State ownership of enterprises—the ownership of the production of goods and services by the state—is increasingly recognized as a new political and economic policy tool available to government for the purpose of directing the economy, achieving higher levels of efficiency, equalizing incomes, redistributing resources between regions, and achieving other goals a government considers important. Regardless of a country's size, political leaning, or degree of development, its government is involved in business.

State-owned enterprises (SOEs) are no longer confined to traditional fiscal monopolies such as tobacco, saccharine, liquor, and matches; natural monopolies such as electricity, railroads, and other public utilities; agricultural marketing boards; a few holdings inherited from the monarchs of the times such as the Gobelin factories in France; or enterprises obtained through punitive nationalization (e.g., Renault and Berliet of France). [1]

The economic impact of SOEs has been growing rapidly. The contribution of SOEs to the gross national product was 22 percent in Austria, 26 percent in Italy, and more than 11 percent in Great Britain. In the Federal Republic of Germany, SOEs contributed 11 percent of the value added, and in France, 12.7 percent. Overall, SOEs in Europe account for 10 to 25 percent of total value added and for 20 to 45 percent of total national investments. [2]

51

By any yardstick, the growth rate of SOEs is impressive. In terms of sales, the average annual growth of SOEs in the Fortune list of the largest non-U.S. corporations between 1957 and 1976 was 21.8 percent as against 14.9 percent for private firms in the same list. In terms of assets, the corresponding figure is 25.4 percent per annum versus 16.0 percent. In terms of numbers, SOEs have grown substantially in countries like Canada and France and the United Kingdom. More than half of the 500 "crown corporations" that exist in Canada today were created between 1970 and 1975. In France, the number of subsidiaries of SOEs is estimated to have multiplied from 266 to almost 650 in the last two decades.

Table 2.1 summarizes the significance of state-owned enterprises in the economies of Austria, Belgium, Denmark, France, Germany, Italy, the Netherlands, and the United Kingdom. It is clear that SOEs dominate many strategic sectors such as banking, energy, public transport, communications, airlines, aerospace, oil production, and sometimes forestry, iron, steel, chemicals, textiles, shipbuilding, automobile and truck manufacturing, and financial institutions. These enterprises are producers of basic goods and services that are widely used by other industries. They are also important—and sometimes monopsonistic—customers. In the United Kingdom, for example, the total plant and machinery purchases of the six largest nationalized industries accounted for approximately one-third of the total U.K. industry expenditures in plant and equipment. These purchases were concentrated on a small range of capital goods such as power-generating transmission and distribution equipment, mining machinery, and telecommunications equipment. The investment of state-owned enterprises is generally much larger than their share in total value added. In many countries the investment expenditures of the public sector represent more than half of the total capital investment in those countries.

In the period prior to World War II and during the postwar reconstruction era, much of the growth of SOEs had been fueled by large and sustained investments in infrastructure industries such as telephones, electricity, and transportation. The growth of SOEs appeared to slow down during the 1960s. This was due to a combination of factors: much of the growth came from manufacturing industries where the share of SOEs was much smaller; most countries' antiinflationary policies included price freezes for coal, gas, electricity, transportation, and water, and the resulting deficits dampened new investment; and SOEs operating in declining industries (e.g., coal) rationalized their operations by reducing output and employment.

In the 1970s, primarily after the energy crisis induced by the Organization of Petroleum Exporting Countries (OPEC), governments increased their intervention in the economy, including an expanded role for SOEs. There are at least three reasons for this increase. First, aid to high-technology industries (e. g. , aerospace and computers) in the form of tax concessions, subsidized loans, grants, or direct state ownership was increased. Second, in an attempt to reduce the pressures on employment caused by structural changes in declining industries (e. g. , shipbuilding and textiles), governments have come to the aid of private firms. Early in the 1970s Italy, France, and the United Kingdom established special SOEs to help firms in "temporary difficulties" through loans and equity. In some cases, the government had to acquire a firm simply because it could not pay previous government loans and nationalization was the only feasible solution to save public funds. Third, as private investment dwindled, the size of public investment increased and the large public enterprises created the growth sectors.

Western European countries differ in their cultural heritage, the traditional role of government in society, the degree of congruence between business interests and public goals as perceived by the government, their economic structure, and their economic problems. State ownership in these countries is a fact of life. It is more than a question of ideology—it is a pragmatic response to the problems of a complex interdependent world.

MOTIVES FOR THE CREATION OF STATE-OWNED ENTERPRISES

In general, there has been a shift in public opinion regarding the appropriate role of the state in economic affairs. The extent and the character of the shift to what Yair Aharoni has called a "no-risk society"[3] have varied from one country to the next, but most governments are now seen as responsible for the management of the economy in order to achieve growth, prevent unemployment, or promote regional development. The demands of the public for a larger role of government meant more intervention in the working of the market economies. Governments found it necessary to slow down and control the inevitable process of economic adjustment. Left unchecked to market forces, the adjustment process might have created politically intolerable high unemployment and unacceptable human hardship. In part, government tried to solve these problems through the establishment of state-owned enterprises.

In addition, the increased interdependence of the world economies has further diminished the effectiveness of traditional macroeconomic tools. In Europe this interdependence has intensified because of the European Economic Community (EEC) and other inter-

TABLE 2.1

The Significance of State-Owned Enterprise Involvement by Country and Sector

	Market Share			
	80-100% (monopoly)	40-80%	20-40%	5-20%
Austria	Post & telecommunications Railroads Ports & airports Electricity Gas Mining Metallurgy Airline	Water Chemicals Oil processing Foodstuffs Beverages	Electrical goods Steel construction Motor vehicles	Machinery Textiles Paper Agriculture Forestry
Belgium	Post & telecommunications Railroads Ports & airports	Electricity Gas	Textiles Coal Steel	
Denmark	Post & telecommunications Electricity Railroads Ports & airports	Steel		
France	Post & telecommunications Electricity Railroads Ports & airports Armaments Tobacco & matches Gas Coal Aerospace	Cars Banks Steel Chemicals Shipping	Insurance Oil refining	Domestic appliances

Country				
Germany	Post & telecommunications Railroads Ports & airports Alcohol Electric power	Aluminum Iron ore Car production Electricity Gas Banks Insurance	Hollow glass Oil production	Coal & lignite Crude oil Crude steel Pig iron Shipbuilding Chemicals
Italy	Post & telecommunications Electricity Gas Railroads Ports & airports Water Tobacco	Steel Shipping Shipbuilding Iron Aerospace Chemicals Banks Aluminum	Car production Mining Petroleum products	Food & beverages
Netherlands	Post & telecommunications Electricity Railroads Ports & airports Banks	Gas Car production	Steel Shipbuilding	
United Kingdom	Post & telecommunications Electricity Gas Water Coal Railroads Aerospace Shipbuilding	Ports & airports Motor industry Steel	Oil production Chemicals	

Source: Compiled by the author.

national agreements. As a result there is a tendency on the part of governments to seek additional policy options. One such option is state ownership of enterprises as an instrument of social, political, and economic policy.

State ownership can also have strong ideological overtones. These are not limited to Communist countries or to any political ideology. There are those on the Left who perceive private ownership of the means of production as the source of all evil and inequity. For them, state ownership is an end in itself, an integral part of the efforts to achieve a better and just society. At the other extreme, any government intervention in the workings of economic markets is perceived to be wrong, evil, and leading to an excessive and dangerous concentration of power. Government is assumed to be corruptible and should not run a business because it cannot do so efficiently. These divergent beliefs and conflicting ideologies influence the policies and behavior of government.

The initial impetus behind nationalization of industry in the United Kingdom and France after World War II was the belief of Socialists that the state should take over "the commanding heights of the economy" and operate them for the benefit of the entire economy rather than the benefit of a small set of private owners. The Labour Party in the United Kingdom developed its nationalization program during the 1930s, covering the postal service, telephone and telegraph, coal, electricity and gas, transportation, iron and steel, and heavy engineering, which was implemented after Labour came to power in 1945. In France, nationalization of the electricity, banking, coal, insurance, and transportation industries was implemented after World War II as part of the Socialist plan to initiate a new economic and social order. More recently, President Mitterrand of France was elected on a Socialist platform calling for nationalization of the remaining private banks and the new "commanding heights," e.g., telecommunications, aerospace. [4]

Right-wing governments have also justified nationalization, but for reasons opposite to those of the Socialists. In the 1920s and 1930s, Mussolini's Fascist government in Italy took over sectors of industry for the purpose of building the nation into an international power that would become the focus of all citizens' personal identities. Nazism and Fascism used nationalization to complement private enterprise and build a strong "capitalistic" economy.

Another important motivation for the creation of SOEs has been to use them for maintaining an industry that the private sector seemed unable to sustain. Both Germany and Italy nationalized the railroads to assure continued service when they were not economically viable. In the United Kingdom, the Conservative government reversed its free enterprise policy to nationalize Rolls-Royce and the

Upper Clyde Shipbuilders yards when both firms incurred losses as a result of poor management.

SOEs have been used to promote the development of the poorer, less industrialized regions in each country. Italy's effort to develop the Mezzogiorno (by requiring its SOEs to place 80 percent of new investment in plant and 60 percent of total investment in the region) is a premier example. Germany has granted loans through publicly owned banks to SOEs that invest or locate in the "incentive region" of the country.

Sometimes, the objective in creating the state-owned firm has been to ensure that the national industry would not be dominated by foreign-owned enterprises. Keeping up with the rapidly increasing costs and complexity of the technology underlying such industries as aircraft, aerospace, nuclear energy and weapons, computers, telecommunications, and microelectronics was beyond the means of the private sector companies comprising these industries in France, the United Kingdom, Italy, and other countries. Reluctant nevertheless (for reasons of national prestige) to forfeit all progress in these areas to the United States and the Soviet Union, European countries have sought ways to remain abreast of the two superpowers in both development and production of high-technology products.[5] Often the reaction to the "American challenge" was the establishment of state-owned enterprises in order to merge weak and diffused local firms, circumvent acquisitions of local firms by U.S. multinationals, or foster technological development and ensure that a technological know-how be maintained and enhanced. France, Germany, the Netherlands, and the United Kingdom also sponsored a variety of high-technology projects by creating joint transnational SOEs to share the costs and risks involved and to counteract the U.S. multinational threat (e.g., Airbus Industries).

Although there are differences in timing and political ideologies of the governments in power in each of the countries reviewed, there are many similar motivations for the establishment of SOEs. In short, there is no clear pattern to explain why state-owned enterprises came about in mixed economies. Case studies of the origins of individual SOEs suggest many additional motives for their creation:

Political retaliation (e.g., Renault and Berliet)
Historical accident (e.g., potash and ammonia production in France)
Promote political and ideological tenets (e.g., redistribution of
    wealth)
Balance social and commercial costs and benefits (e.g., railroads)
Exploit profits from scarce resources (oil, coal) or commodities
    made artificially scarce (fiscal monopolies)
Redistribute wealth and employment

Provide a "window in the industry"
Preserve declining industries
Boost exports, curtail imports, and improve the balance of payments
Control strategic industries
Provide investment in infant industries (aerospace)
Protect domestic industries
Cross-subsidize downstream industries
Encourage regional development
Control inflation
Promote national security and national prestige
Reduce dependence on foreign technology and raw materials
Improve productivity
Provide leadership in mixed industries
Foster high-risk and/or high-technology industries

DEFINITIONS AND DATA

Despite many efforts, and the work of the European Economic Community and the European Centre for Public Enterprises, the definition of what is and is not a public enterprise has yet to be agreed upon. No standard set of figures is available for the countries reviewed in this chapter. The figures cited herein, inasmuch as they are measures, must be treated with care.

Definitional problems arise in delineating the specifics of "public" versus "private" and "enterprise" versus other activities. "Public," in most studies of the topic, refers to those enterprises in which the state, either directly or indirectly, has a controlling interest, usually defined as ownership of 50 percent or more of the voting shares. State control, however, may be exercised with less than 50 percent of the voting shares.

In Germany, for example, the government denationalized some of the large industrial undertakings inherited from the Third Reich. In 1958, 83 percent of Preussag was sold to 200,000 small shareholders; in 1961, 60 percent of the shares in Volkswagen were sold to approximately 1,200,000 private persons; and in 1965, 74 percent of the shares in VEBA, the largest industrial concern in the Federal Republic, were disposed of in the form of "people's shares" to some 2,600,000 persons. The official aim of these actions was to promote savings and the widest possible distribution of shares among the population. Indeed, special terms of purchase were offered to persons with modest means. As a result, the German government does not have a controlling interest in any one of these large industrial concerns. However, since most of the shares are widely dispersed, the remaining large blocks of shares held by the government are sufficient to influence the direction of these firms. For example, such influence is clearly visible in connection with development and capital investment in the "incentive regions."

Government may control a firm through the firm's dependence on the government. Thus, if the firm's only client is the state, it will have less discretion over its actions than if it had a larger number of customers. For example, the "affermage" system in France and the use of concessions are arrangements used by many local authorities for public transportation, garbage collection, street cleaning, and so forth.

Local authorities also participate in the share capital of private firms. In France, the sponsoring ministries require that the local authority will own at least 10 percent of the voting shares. In the United Kingdom, no such minimum exists. In all countries, statistics about the size of such participation do not exist in any usable form.

The boundary lines between "public" and "private" are often hard to establish for different reasons. The shipbuilding industry suffered a severe crisis in the late 1970s as the yards competed fiercely for a share of the rapidly declining orders. Some governments rescued the private firms and guaranteed continued employment through nationalization (e.g., Sweden and the United Kingdom). Others granted large subsidies to the private firms on the condition that they not significantly curtail employment. The German government increased the amount of aid to developing countries that agreed to purchase German-built ships. The French government did not nationalize its shipyards. With the sanction of the EEC commission, the French government set up a $1 billion fund for ailing industries, mainly for the aid of shipyards. In reality, the "assistance" plan provided subsidies of approximately 25 percent to shipbuilders.

In Germany, aid to ailing firms sometimes took the form of governmental guarantees (e.g., Ruhrkohle) or mergers arranged by large federal or provincially owned banks. In Italy, the bailout of Montedison, the giant aluminum and chemical firm, was arranged by both state holding concerns—IRI and ENI—and state-owned banks. Two-thirds of the shares in this company are now in public hands, but it was decided to give most of these shares to the state-owned banks "in order to preserve for Montedison the appearance of a prevalently private company." Since the major financial institutions in France, Italy, and the Federal Republic of Germany are state owned, shareholdings and loans granted by these institutions may be used to aid firms in difficulty (or otherwise) without officially adding such firms to the list of SOEs.

It is difficult to define "enterprise." First, many business activities are carried out directly by the government through its budget. Second, integral parts of the government have separate budgets, for example, the post and telephone services in France, Italy, and the Federal Republic of Germany. In some countries, the national opera and/or the theaters are state-owned enterprises; in others, they are classified as part of the general government. Hospitals are seen as either business enterprises or as social services.

In the official statistics SOEs are defined differently by different sources, none of which are inclusive. In the United Kingdom, for example, only the so-called "nationalized industries" appear in the national income accounts (GNP) as part of the public sector, while the more than 80 firms owned and controlled by the state-owned National Enterprise Board are classified as private sector activities.

Certain countries publish statistics only for the public enterprises owned or controlled by the national government. However, at least as many firms are owned by the provincial states or local governments. For example, Volkswagen is 20 percent owned by the federal government of Germany, and 20 percent by the state of Lower Saxony.

The French statistics, for example, do not include subsidiaries of SOEs in the figures for public enterprises. Much of the increase in the activities of SOEs in France has been through subsidiaries and their subsidiaries. Until recently, Germany did not include the public financial institutions or the economic activities of firms in which they did not have majority ownership in their official statistics. Thus, in electric power, the production of the leading firm, RWE (40 percent of total German production), was not included in the official statistics because the German municipalities owned only 31.2 percent of the shares. Nevertheless, through plural voting shares, the municipalities have control of the company. [6]

The principal public enterprises in terms of size and resources used are easier to identify. As this review relies on published data, the statistics cited are those available from public sources. Herein SOEs are defined to include all public undertakings, regardless of their legal structure, that appear to carry on activities of business character. However, the reader is reminded that the statistics cited necessarily rely on official statistical sources, and seem to severely underestimate the size of the SOE sector broadly defined. At this stage, a more rigid definition of SOEs seems both elusive and undesirable in view of the variety of legal and organizational forms encountered in various countries.

TAXONOMY OF STATE-OWNED ENTERPRISES

State-owned enterprises can be categorized by their economic objectives, types of economic activities (e.g., production, distribution, financial, or services), organizational forms (e.g., government departments, autonomous agency of civil servants, public corporation or its subsidiaries, or joint stock corporation), and the structure of the market in which they operate (e.g., monopoly with or without legal barriers to entry, oligopoly, or competitive). The following are the major categories that seem to be meaningful and useful:

Economic Objectives
    Revenue generation
    Regulation
    Equitable distribution of wealth and income among regions
    Improvements of terms of trade
    Reduction of dependency on foreign technology or source of inputs
    Promotion of national security
Types of Economic Activities
    Production
    Distribution
    Financial
    Service
Organizational Forms
    Government department
    Autonomous agency of civil servants
    Public corporation, created by a special act, and subsidiaries
        of a public corporation
Market Structure
    Monopoly with legal barriers to entry by competition
    Monopoly without legal barriers to entry by competition
    Oligopoly
    Competitive

SOEs usually encompass some combination of the preceding categories. One of the basic characteristics of an SOE is the multiplicity of its objectives and the variety of stakeholders that have legal right to intervene in its affairs. It is clear that, in comparison to a market economy, the problems of performance evaluation and social control become much more complex and difficult. This complexity arises from the multiple, and often conflicting, social and economic objectives, the range of institutional arrangements, and the market structures in which SOEs operate.

SOCIAL CONTROL

Most SOEs are hybrids, attempting to achieve traditional economic goals in the marketplace while subject to satisfying a variety of political pressures and demands to which they are exposed. Consequently, the management of an SOE must be especially sensitive to its political and social environment when it makes resource allocation decisions. Thus, for example, political considerations can and have affected strategic decisions such as location of factories, levels of employment, pricing policies, codes of ethics, capital investments, and personnel selection.

The ownership by the state of the means of production does not necessarily imply control over the internal decision making of the firm. State ownership, however, does make moot the question of social and political legitimacy of an SOE, since the property rights are vested in the state and the SOE is expected to incorporate the public's welfare in its decision making.

The motivation of the state to exercise control over its SOEs goes beyond property rights and the desire to satisfy public expectations. The dependence of the state on the outcome of economic decisions (production, employment, and investments) in the private sector is assumed to decrease as the contribution of SOEs to GNP increases. In other words, as the public sector becomes more self-sufficient economically, the less crucial becomes the economic performance of the private sector and the greater the perceived abilities of governments to control social, political, and economic destinies.

In reality, however, such control has been almost impossible to achieve. Furthermore, the growth and diversity of SOEs has meant that, in addition to its traditional functions of supervising the market economy, the state has also assumed the role of an active participant. It is expected to juggle conflicting roles. It is expected to act as the disinterested arbiter, yet through its SOE it is partner and competitor of the participants in the market. Consequently, SOEs achieve economic advantages in the market. Such advantages are often not in the best interest of the state and society. The increasing number of SOEs, their size and complexity, has created new problems of governance, coordination, and control. Indeed, the issue of the social control of SOEs coupled with the associated problems of management accountability, performance evaluation, and relationship to the private sector has probably emerged as the central issue involving SOEs in their relationship to society.

Unlike pure market economies which have built-in means for evaluating the financial performance of firms, evaluating the performance of SOEs is much more complex. The performance of SOEs is measured along a multitude of different dimensions. In addition to traditional measures of profitability and growth, such factors as employment, regional development, and investment in technology are often considered. Thus, the overall evaluation of performance becomes difficult and provides the managers of SOEs many opportunities to influence the way in which they will be evaluated. Furthermore, the more subjective the evaluation of the enterprise becomes, the greater the discretion and freedom of action by the management.

The sources and means of financing SOEs also contribute to the ambiguity of evaluating their performance. The potential for financing through the state, at below-market interest rates, frees SOEs from control of the capital markets. To the extent that the state as an owner/investor of its SOEs does not develop a clear set of preferences and sanctions analogous to those that apply in the private sector, a failure in social control of the SOEs will occur. This increases the degree of managerial independence and discretion in running the enterprise.

As in the case of the large U.S. corporations, the exercise of economic power by the managers of SOEs associated with unforeseen societal consequences has raised the issue of accountability in the case of SOEs. It has become a widespread matter of concern to governments in Western Europe and in developing countries. In several countries there has been political dissatisfaction with the conduct and performance of SOEs and with the structures of their governance and control. In several cases this criticism has resulted in interventions and changes in the structure of relationships between government and the SOEs. For example, Sweden created a state holding company, Statsfortag, which was given complete oversight over most of the SOEs in Sweden. Statsfortag is expected to represent the government in the role of owner-investor and to buffer Swedish SOEs from the direct influence of government departments. The establishment of OIAG in Austria, IRI in Italy, and the National Enterprise Board (NEB) in the United Kingdom were motivated by similar considerations, and most recently the idea of a state holding company was suggested in Canada. [7] As the experiences of the United Kingdom and Italy suggest, it is not clear whether the concept of a state holding company can resolve the conflicting issues involving social control, managerial autonomy, and accountability (performance evaluation).

Now that SOEs have become major social and economic institutions in Western Europe, it is not surprising that governments are focusing greater attention on the unanticipated consequences that have arisen. Foremost among them is the problem of social control.

ACCOUNTABILITY AND PERFORMANCE EVALUATION

Evaluating the performance of state-owned enterprises is a subject of increasing concern. Although the managers of SOEs, various oversight bodies, academic researchers, and numerous study commissions recommend that SOEs be judged on the basis of profitability or rate of return on investment, it is clear that in most instances such measures are meaningless. In all mixed industrial economies, political considerations affect performance evaluation. The higher the incidence of unemployment, the greater the pressure of SOEs to hire or avoid reductions in their labor force. In the case of SOEs that are major employers, labor agreements are often directly negotiated with the government and not with the management of the enterprise. As a result, many SOEs are overstaffed. This is a problem that managers of SOEs complain about repeatedly. By all accounts, overstaffing is prevalent in many sectors, including airlines, railways, electricity generation, coal mining, shipbuilding, steel, automobiles, textiles, chemicals, and postal services.

SOEs have incurred substantial losses due to political pressures to freeze prices. The inclination to direct SOEs to restrain their prices is most likely to occur during major labor contract negotiations, prior to elections, or when inflationary pressures are most severe. Such price freezes amount to cross-subsidization by basic industries (e.g., coal, electricity, gas, transport) of downstream industries. The governments of Belgium, France, Italy, and the United Kingdom have preferred to subsidize the losses rather than face the adverse political reactions that result from the rising prices of consumer products and services.

As major purchasers, SOEs can be directed to, in effect, subsidize domestic enterprises by preferring local suppliers, and thereby increase their costs. Governments provide their SOEs funds (capital grants and loans) or other incentives to locate new plants and equipment in depressed or underdeveloped regions. Often such investments cannot be justified commercially but are undertaken purely for political reasons. Government policies regarding SOEs in high-technology industries (aerospace, electronics, computers, nuclear power) are often determined on the basis of national prestige or contribution to military strength. SOEs are often required to undertake high-risk projects (e.g., the Airbus) with the tacit understanding that, if the project fails, the government would cover the costs (as in the case of the Concorde).

SEPARATING SOCIAL COSTS

Thus, because SOEs are used to achieve social and political objectives as well as economic goals, it is next to impossible to separate out the costs associated with various objectives. Furthermore, it is often in the interest of government to disguise the true cost of social welfare programs. As a result, separating the costs of regional development undertaken through SOEs, subsidization of downstream industries, provision of services "in the national interest," and maintaining employment from the necessary costs required to operate the enterprise often becomes a meaningless exercise.

The principle of measuring enterprise performance on the basis of profitability after full compensation for social costs has several advantages, however. Economic and social costs would have to be properly accounted for and disclosed publicly. The management of SOEs would have more explicit knowledge of the criteria by which their performance would be evaluated. Thus, in theory at least, the costs and benefits of social programs would be made public and competing alternatives could be evaluated.

The two most common methods of compensation involve subsidization of incremental costs and provision of "endowment" capital. Neither method solves the underlying problems of determining how much compensation enterprises deserve or distinguishes between economic and social activities. The major reason is that both government policymakers and managers of SOEs often are motivated to finance so-called social activities within the enterprises by cross-subsidization. Furthermore, financially self-sufficient SOEs are often motivated not to seek compensation from the government for the social activities they perform.

Italy, France, and the United Kingdom have experimented with multiyear contracts that represent an exchange of commitments between the government and the management of an SOE regarding financing, pricing, labor productivity, and other important variables that can be used to evaluate performance. For example, the "contrat de programme" for the period 1971-75 between the French government and EDF (which generates electric power) committed the enterprise to carry out an acceptable investment program, realize an 8 percent rate of return on investment, stay within a debt/equity ratio ceiling, increase the ratio of net income/sales by 1 percent, and achieve a 5 percent growth rate in total factor productivity. In return, the government granted the enterprise greater freedom from intervention in its operations, allowed it to return profits above the target rate, gave it the liberty to set prices within the average ceiling determined by government and the autonomy necessary to establish new subsidiaries, provided loan guarantees, and agreed to compensation for performing specified social obligations. Most recently, the contrat de programme between the French government and the SNCF provided explicit compensation for all extra burdens including construction and maintenance of lines so that the railway can compete on even terms with private trucking companies.

Contracts, however, are difficult and time-consuming to negotiate. Commitments often have not proved durable because changes
that inevitably occur in the political or economic environment require renegotiation. Finally, it is not clear that the managers of
SOEs are very concerned about honoring such contracts because of
their belief that an SOE will not be allowed to go bankrupt.

Measuring Reported Profits

The accounting measurement of economic performance is by
itself a complex problem. In the case of SOEs it is complicated by
additional factors. Profitability can be affected by the allocation of
depreciation charges and other costs. British Rail, for example, is
profitable on its freight operations (and its intercity passenger service). However, it incurs substantial losses on short haul lines,
which are kept in service for social and political reasons. They
are cross-subsidized by the freight operations. In 1980 the British
government changed the cost allocation formula, requiring freight
operations to cover 64 percent (instead of 30 percent) of total depreciation and tracking costs. Clearly the arbitrary altering of the
cost allocation formula will affect reported profits.

Pricing policies also affect reported profits. For SOEs that
occupy monopoly positions, the level of profits is directly related
to the prices that are determined with the concurrence of the government. British Gas, for example, was prevented from raising
its prices in the period April 1977 to June 1979. The result was a
15 percent drop in gas prices in real terms. Subsequently, the
Conservative government allowed prices to rise 27 percent and the
firm became profitable.

The net income (after subsidies) of the largest Western European state-owned firms (excluding utilities, transportation companies, and financial institutions) is shown in Table 2.2 for the
years 1974-79.

It is clear that the petroleum and coal sector (with the exception of ENI) has been consistently profitable. In the metals and
heavy engineering group only VOEST-Alpine (Austria) seems to be
consistently profitable (Volkswagenwerke has been profitable since
1976). In the aerospace group, three firms—British Aerospace,
Messerschmidt-Bolkow-Blohm (Germany), and SNECMA (France)—
are consistently profitable, and in chemicals the Dutch firm DSM
and Enterprise Minière et Chimique have been consistently profitable. It is important to note that these are reported profits after
subsidies. Without information as to the level of subsidies and
capital grants it is very difficult to interpret the reported profits
of these SOEs.

The capital structure of SOEs also affects their reported profits. The majority of SOEs have very low equity capitalization and consequently high debt to equity ratios. Each country, however, provides capital grants, loans, and other financing in various ways. Italian SOEs receive "capital donations" free of interest and other costs, but they are expected to return to the government 64 percent of their profits in the form of dividends. A similar situation exists in the United Kingdom with regard to "public dividend capital." In addition, SOEs have access to loans from state-owned financial institutions at favorable rates or they incur debt that in effect is guaranteed by the state. Furthermore, each government has on many occasions (e.g., British Steel, British Leyland, Salzgitter, Ruhrkohle, IRI, ENI, CII-Bull, and more) written off or forgiven debts in addition to providing various operating subsidies.

Measuring the performance of state-owned financial institutions is a separate problem. Publicly owned banks in France, Italy, and the Federal Republic of Germany, when ranked in terms of their deposits or assets, are ranked in the top 30 banks in the world. Yet, as a group, state-owned banks rank far below privately owned banks in terms of their capital-to-assets ratio. This may suggest that state-owned banks are managed less prudently and/or their managers feel that the government would not let them go bankrupt. In any event, the ability to operate with much lower capital-to-asset ratios might account for their high ranking in terms of assets and rate of return on investment.

One attempt at rating the performance of selected Western European SOEs on three indicators of commercial performance (within limits set from the outside) and on a measure of social contribution (as compared to costs) was that by William G. Shepherd.[8] It is interesting to note that of 33 SOEs evaluated by Shepherd only two (ENI, National Coal Board) were rated as having made "large" social contributions, whereas the majority (20) were rated "marginal" or "negative." In terms of commercial performance measures it would appear that, on the whole, the 33 SOEs studied by Shepherd are performing well. Only British Steel received a rating of "poor" on the efficiency of its operations. In addition, Alfa Romeo and PTT (France) received a "poor" rating on their investments and choice of technology. These evaluations, as Shepherd notes, are extremely subjective and exclude a large number of enterprises for which data were not available. A comparison of firms evaluated by Shepherd for which profitability measures are shown in Table 2.2 reveals many discrepancies. For example, it is difficult to justify "excellent/good" commercial ratings for Renault and ENI or "fair" for British Leyland.

TABLE 2.2

Net Income (or Loss) of the Largest Western European State-Owned Firms
(in thousands of dollars)

Industry	Fortune 500 Rank 1979	1974	1975	1976	1977	1978	1979
Metals and Heavy Engineering							
British Steel (UK)	50	170,455	171,867	(541,209)	(164,727)	(797,597)	(600,796)
Cockerill (Bel)	110	18,139	(107,480)	(49,816)	(202,697)	(227,625)	(122,423)
Halsider (It)	96	50,413	(110,654)	(159,609)	(446,619)	(411,236)	(309,730)
Salzgitter (Ger)	89	20,503	6,567	(18,517)	(40,119)	(48,272)	(1,997)
Statsforetag Group (Swed)	127	16,869	(25,555)	1,091,735	(145,827)	(113,638)	45,000
Svenska Varv (Swed)	336	—*	—	—	(414,509)	541,485	98,724
Svenskt Stal (Swed)	386	—	—	—	—	(18,534)	(6,882)
VIAG (Ger)	160	23,684	(17,170)	16,096	14,071	(9,606)	25,325
VOEST-Alpine (Aust)	86	—	—	—	—	25,872	50,367
Motor Vehicles							
Alfa Romeo (It)	207	(89,432)	(178,632)	(102,632)	(169,839)	(149,506)	(109,920)
BL Ltd. (UK)	52	156,318	(283,359)	61,205	(90,562)	(72,329)	(306,632)
Renault (Fr)	10	7,261	(128,702)	—	4,070	2,222	241,520
Volkswagenwerke (Ger)	8	(312,585)	(63,971)	399,164	179,759	275,671	371,534
Volvo (Swed)	65	23,769	1,907	14,465	44,329	69,042	97,161

Industry / Company	Rank						
Aerospace							
Aerospatiale (Fr)	137	(76,569)	(113,816)	(129,902)	(91,045)	(19,238)	1,956
British Aerospace (UK)	178	40,421	31,441	34,649	51,364	54,786	86,844
Messerschmidt-Bolkow-Blohm (Ger)	277	—	4,073	4,014	4,353	13,370	24,024
Rolls-Royce (UK)	219	—	—	(16,538)	25,503	13,746	(133,475)
SNECMA (Fr)	376	—	10,578	22,419	19,333	15,195	15,527
VFW-Fokker (Ger)	—	—	2,383	(2,089)	(67,949)	275	—
Chemicals							
Charbonnage de France (Fr)	77	(2,573)	(138,769)	(158,132)	(40,907)	(40,957)	18,249
DSM (Neth)	51	192,995	56,935	49,980	44,961	11,809	44,446
Enterprise Miniere et Chimique (Fr)	245	42,770	13,987	18,639	33,644	—	22,988
Montedison (It)	33	173,602	(183,912)	(195,019)	(514,686)	(312,733)	(22,193)
Petroleum and Coal							
BNOC (UK)	43	—	—	—	—	(5,839)	28,859
BP (UK)	2	1,140,177	369,202	324,615	530,797	853,057	3,439,582
CFP-Total (Fr)	6	294,457	168,472	34,731	27,373	60,305	1,137,282
Elf-Aquitaine (Fr)	19	238,229	199,875	340,108	358,974	332,336	1,310,132
ENI (It)	4	(91,256)	(134,869)	(37,026)	(249,391)	(367,892)	89,040
National Coal Board (UK)	61	(315,777)	0	11,382	47,164	36,696	(36,671)
OMV (Aust)	152	13,153	3,902	8,301	8,110	16,555	19,616
Saarbergwerke (Ger)	134	(10,157)	—	5,059	12,100	—	—
VEBA (Ger)	37	12,118	(24,333)	(7,389)	(50,080)	25,872	50,367

*Data not available.

Source: Compiled from Annual Directory of Largest Industrial Corporations Outside the U.S., _Fortune_ (August/September issues).

In short, assessing performance of public enterprises, and especially making comparative analyses among different enterprises, is a very difficult task. In addition to measuring profits, rate of return, or flow of funds, SOEs are evaluated in a "broader context" of attaining social goals and aiding the political aspirations of the country. Comparison between countries is difficult because of differences in institutional arrangements, accounting conventions (on inflationary adjustments, depreciation, financial charges, foreign exchange losses, unfunded liabilities, subsidies, and so on), and the incomplete disclosure of the financial relationship between the enterprise and the state.

Setting Target Rates of Return

The United Kingdom and (to some extent) France have experimented with the use of target rates of return. The targets are determined after a process of "consultation" between the enterprise management and the government. The consultation process is supposed to take account of the range of social and economic goals as well as strategic opportunities.

The targets are expected to serve as guidelines for assessing performance. In practice, however, it is not clear what purpose they serve. Target rates of return are calculated on performance after subsidies. Thus the greater the negotiated compensation for social costs, the more attainable the target. Achievement of the targets also depends on economic conditions and government policy on pricing. Table 2.3 summarizes the experience of the United Kingdom with financial targets and their results. It is clear that only monopolistic enterprises achieved or exceeded their targets in some years. The failure to reach their targets may be due to external events such as directives from the government to freeze prices. It is also clear that such enterprises as the railways, the post office, and coal (all of which were rated by Shepherd average or good) hardly ever achieve their targets and thus the negotiated subsidies often have to be increased. Since failure to achieve targets does not appear to be associated with any severe consequences, it would seem that financial targets are of little practical value.

Flow of Funds Analysis

A rough measure of enterprise performance can be obtained from an analysis of the flow of funds between the government and the enterprise. When a state-owned enterprise is not able to cover

TABLE 2.3

Selected Nationalized Industry Financial Targets and Results in the United Kingdom

Enterprise	Years	Target	Result	Achievement
GPO (All)	1963–67	8.0%	7.6%	95%
Telecommunications	1963–67		8.0	100
	1968–69	8.5	8.4	98
	1970	9.6	9.8	102
	1971	10.0	8.6	86
	1972		6.9	69
	1972–76	No targets		
	1976–78	6.0[a]		
Post Office	1963–67		1.8	90
	1968–72	2% on revenue expenditure	loss	_[b]
	1972–78	No targets		
	1978–80	2% on turnover[c]		
Electricity	1962–66	12.4	12.0	96
	1967	12.4	11.7	94
	1968	12.3	13.0	105
	1969–73	7.0	4.8	69
	1973	No targets		93
Gas	1962–66	10.2	9.8	96
	1967	10.2	7.7	76
	1968	10.2	10.9	107
	1969–73	7.0	6.5	
	1973	No targets		
Steel	1963–68	No targets		
	1973	8.0	6.8	85
	1974		8.9	111
Railways	1963–68	Break–even as soon as possible	Losses of £120–£155m p.a.[d] (1,037–1,339m)	_[b]
	1969	No targets		
	1970	£17m p.a. surplus	£+ 9.5m (83m)	56
	1971		−15.4m (−133m)	_[b]
	1976	Break–even reinstated		
Coal	1963–67	Break–even	1963 £0.7m (6m) 1964 £0.5m (4.3m)	
	1968	No targets		
	1969–71	Break–even		
	1971	Break–even waived		

[a]This target is in real terms, i.e., both depreciation and mean net assets values are at replacement costs.

[b]Negative.

[c]After both historic and supplementary depreciation and interest charges.

[d]p.a. = per annum.

Source: Compiled by author.

all its costs through self-generated revenues, it will require government assistance. The implication is that the needed resources are diverted from other uses. Such a redistribution of resources may or may not be socially desirable. However, it may be useful to measure the extent of revenue self-sufficiency and the degree to which tax revenues are required to sustain the various state enterprises.

In measuring revenue self-sufficiency, it should be noted that an SOE can incur heavy losses (at least in the short run) without having a negative cash flow. For example, a Mediobanca survey of Italian SOEs showed that accumulated deficits between 1968 and 1975 totaled 3,975 billion lire, accounting for 54.4 percent of total depreciation charges for the period. Not funding pension liabilities is another accounting stratagem. In the long run, however, accumulated negative cash flows will require government help. Such assistance has taken the form of writing off government debt (e.g., in the United Kingdom, Italy, France), or providing capital grants to enterprises (such as public dividend capital in the United Kingdom or Fondi di Donazioni in Italy). In Germany the government waived the dividend payments from Salzgitter, VIAG, and the post office during periods of financial crisis.

In theory, however, it should be possible to construct a flow of funds statement between the government and its enterprises. Government outflow of funds consists of the issuance of additional share capital to the enterprises and the granting of loans to the enterprises from the treasury or through state-owned financial institutions. The outflow of funds would also include subsidies granted to the enterprises to cover either operating deficits or specific costs. In addition, there might be special allocation of investment funds earmarked for specific investments demanded by the government. On the inflow side, government could receive from the enterprises royalty payments for concessions, dividends, interest payments, and payments for direct and indirect taxes.

The United Kingdom is the only country for which such a consolidated funds flow statement has been constructed. Table 2.4 summarizes the net borrowing requirements of the nine nationalized industries in the United Kingdom. It is clear that over the five years, the nationalized industries (excluding the National Enterprise Board and the corporations under its control) were directly dependent on the government for more than £5700 million in net capital and revenue funding. In addition, more than £1600 million net capital was borrowed from nongovernmental sources. However, this debt is effectively guaranteed by the U.K. government. Since 1975 the dependence of the nationalized industries on the government has increased significantly.

TABLE 2.4

Net Impact on Public Sector Borrowing Requirement of Nine
Nationalized Industries in the United Kingdom
(£'000 million)

	1961–65	1966–70	1971–75
Capital			
Net borrowing from government	2.71	4.86	5.86
Capital transfers		0.15	0.69
Capital write-offs	(1.02)	(1.53)	(1.19)
	1.69	3.48	5.36
Revenue[a]			
Subsidies and compensation	0.72	0.92	3.83
Interest, dividend, and tax payments to government	(1.36)	(2.66)	(4.66)
Capital write-offs (equivalent to subsidies)	1.02	1.53	1.19
	0.38	(0.21)	0.36
Net impact on central government funds	2.07	3.27	5.72
Net borrowing from nongovernment sources[b]	0.04	(0.08)	1.65
Net impact on public sector borrowing requirement	2.11	3.19	7.37

[a]Excluding national insurance contributions.
[b]Equivalent to public corporations' direct contribution to
public sector borrowing requirement.
Source: NEDO Report 1976.

No similar detailed official statistics are publicly available
for the other Western European countries, or in the United Kingdom
for the firms controlled by the NEB. In Germany the web of financial relations between public enterprises (federal, provincial, and
local), the federal government, municipalities, and provincial state
governments is so complex that a complete funds flow analysis for
the public enterprise sector is an almost impossible task.

Flow of funds analysis can provide insights into the total economic impact of state-owned enterprises. To be most useful, such
statements need to be constructed for each enterprise. It is clear

that not all enterprises in the countries reviewed are a drain on public funds. However, it is clear that the aggregate of interest payments, dividends, and taxes from state-owned enterprises (profitable and unprofitable) to government does not cover their needs for capital, operating subsidies, and so on. Most of the financial problems, and the major share of all public subsidies, are accounted for by the railways, other public transportation, coal, aerospace, post office, and (more recently) steel, automobiles, and shipbuilding. There is no evidence, however, that SOEs operating in competitive industries such as petrochemicals or banking are self-sufficient in terms of their requirements for working capital.

IMPLICATIONS FOR THE UNITED STATES

It cannot be said that government ownership of enterprises has not been practiced in the United States. A 1945 General Accounting Office (GAO) Reference Manual of Government Corporations lists 49 federal government corporations that were chartered between 1929 and 1945. In the 1980 Budget of the United States Government, at least 54 federal enterprises of one form or another are listed with budget authority of $62 billion. Furthermore, at the state and local levels government enterprises abound. Yet few among policymakers, or the public at large, realize the extent to which public ownership and control pervades the free enterprise system of the United States. Except for several spectacular interventions (e.g., Conrail, Amtrak, and the Chrysler "bail-out"), government participation in the private sector in the form of public enterprises goes virtually unnoticed. Clearly there is a need for a comprehensive understanding of the history, motivation, role, and impact of government enterprises (federal, state, and local).

The focus of such research should be government competition with private business firms. It should have the objectives of developing insights into the respective roles of private and public enterprises in a democratic society, and outline a contingency theory for selecting the appropriate policy instrument (e.g., regulation, subsidies, loan guarantees, state ownership, reconstruction finance corporation, and so forth) for directing national or regional economies.[9]

The role of state-owned enterprises in international trade and their impact on the ability of U.S. enterprises to compete in domestic and international markets is also not well understood by policymakers or by the public. State-owned enterprises in industrialized Western economies compete directly with U.S. private enterprises in such industries as oil, petrochemicals, steel and other primary metals, automobiles, airlines, aerospace, shipping, shipbuilding, transportation equipment, banking and finance, textiles, and more. The negotiations on landing rights in the United States, the studies by the U.S. International Trade Commission of competition in the automobile and steel industries, bank regulations, and various international trade negotiations demonstrate a lack of appreciation for how other countries position their state-owned enterprises to compete with U.S. enterprises. Thus the luxury of being able to forego profits, the seemingly limitless source of capital at very favorable terms, the ability of having one state-owned enterprise cross-subsidize another, and preferential placement of orders are just a few of the stratagems employed by other countries that place U.S. enterprises at a competitive disadvantage.

The declining state of the automobile, pulp and paper products, lumber and wood products, chemicals, machinery and equipment, and steel industries, among others, suggests that the inability of the United States to compete is approaching a critical stage. Public ownership of enterprises may itself become an important public policy issue of the 1980s. Of immediate concern, however, should be the need to coordinate international trade agreements and the development of a comprehensive U.S. policy on international trade that will ensure the ability of U.S. industry to compete on equal terms.

Similarly, it is necessary to examine whether antitrust laws (which, for example, forbid pooling of research and development) and regulatory burdens place American industry at a competitive disadvantage, and how to counteract the easy access of state-owned enterprises to capital grants, soft loans, and advantageous financing of exports. It is quite likely, for example, that an analysis comparing the relative efficiency of steel making in the United States and in Western European countries (on a plant by plant basis) would demonstrate that any European competitive advantage is accounted for by government subsidies. The size of such subsidies could then form the basis for establishing countervailing duties or other policies.[10]

Recently, the idea of a reconstruction finance corporation has been proposed as a means for making capital available to revitalize declining industries.[11] The experience of the National Enterprise Board in the United Kingdom (and its predecessor, the Industrial Reconstruction Corporation) and of IRI in Italy should be studied to determine the applicability of such a strategy for the situation in the United States.

With the decline of some basic industries, certain regions will begin to decline as well, especially the Northeast and Midwest. Such a decline, which has already begun,[12] will inevitably lead to political pressures on the federal government to institute special economic programs to counteract this trend. Italy, France, Germany, and the United Kingdom have each experimented with different regional development strategies with varying degrees of success. Although it is not known whether regional decline will be temporary or permanent, the European experience could serve as valuable models for devising policy alternatives in the United States.

UNDERSTANDING THE SOE PHENOMENON

The heterogeneity of experience with the nationalization or the creation of an SOE suggests that there are many reasons for public ownership, some of them peculiar to a certain country. We have noted that state-owned enterprises are expected to direct their operations on the basis of two contradictory orientations. Being publicly owned, they are supposed to pursue various activities in the public interest. At the same time, they are expected to achieve strict economic goals and be profitable, or at least generate positive cash flows. They have to reconcile business requirements of financial and marketing flexibility with the need to assure public accountability and consistency with politically prescribed goals. While the state is expected to be an objective and neutral arbiter, its very ownership of enterprises implies that it has partners, competitors, and adversaries.

The increasing use of SOEs to implement a wide array of governmental policies, and the resulting clashes between these enterprises and private firms on the one hand and government on the other, is cause for increasing concern. Public committees in different countries and international organizations have been searching for a positive theory to guide them in handling the multitude of problems related to these enterprises. Theoretical models have made important contributions to the formalization of certain problems and the classification of the information needed to solve them. However, little is known about the operations of SOEs and their decision-making processes. Most researchers tend to deal with the formal structures and legal organizations of these enterprises rather than with management behavior and the decision process.[13]

Yet, SOEs constitute a large and important sector in a majority of countries today. As international importers, exporters, and investors, these enterprises are influencing the evolving structure of international trade and balance of payments relations in the 1980s. Their presence is often considered a threat to firms in the private sector. Their behavior is perceived as predatory (both within their national economies and in the international arena), and competition with them as difficult. Business Week quoted one U.S. airline manager as saying: "We're competing with other governments that have firm, consistent, and most protective aviation policies."[14]

In the coming decade, the competition policies of the EEC can be expected to provide further impetus for expanding the role of SOEs in member countries. This trend can already be discerned from the response of member countries to EEC rulings regarding fiscal monopolies (alcohol and cigarettes) and in the recent cases involving the "rationalization" of the shipbuilding and steel industries. As the role of SOEs expands, questions of social control and performance evaluation begin to emerge as central issues. A clearer understanding of the meaning and consequences of the proliferation of SOEs in the post–World War II period, and of their expansion into new fields, seems to be fundamental for developing both domestic and international economic policy.

NOTES

1. For a more complete listing of sources consulted for this chapter, see Arie Lewin, "Research on State Owned Enterprises," Management Science 27, no. 11 (November 1981):1520–25; and Arie Lewin and Kathryn Rauth, "Government in Business," working paper, Fuqua School of Business, Duke University, 1981. See also Raymond Vernon and Yair Aharoni, eds., State Owned Enterprises in Western Economies (London: Croom-Helm, 1981); and Renato Mazzolini, Government-Controlled Enterprises (London: Wiley, 1976).

2. The exact percentage partially depends on the definition employed for SOE. In the United Kingdom, for example, any wholly owned SOEs, such as those owned by the National Enterprise Board, are shown as a part of the private sector (see discussion under Definitions and Data).

3. Yair Aharoni, The No-Risk Society (Chatham, N.J.: Chatham House, 1981).

4. The Mitterrand government has since moved a long way toward implementing its nationalization plans.

5. One has only to think of the Concorde supersonic airliner, jointly built by the United Kingdom and France.

6. See Commission of the European Communities, Second Report on Competition Policy (Brussels and Luxembourg: EEC, April 1973).

7. The province of Saskatchewan's crown corporations are controlled by the Saskatchewan Crown Investment Corporation. See G. H. Beatty, "Bridling the Beasts: How Saskatchewan Combines Accountability and the Management Freedom in Its Crown Corporations," Policy Options 2, no. 2 (July/August 1981):35–38.

8. William G. Shepherd, "Public Enterprise in Western Europe and the United States," in The Structure of European Industry, ed. H. W. deJong (The Hague: Martinus Nijhoff, 1981), pp. 289-320.

9. One thoughtful attempt to do this in Canada is M. J. Trebilcock et al., The Choice of Governing Instrument (Ottawa: Economic Council of Canada, Minister of Supply and Services, 1982).

10. Most recently, the government of Margaret Thatcher has written off $7.8 billion of capital loans (excluding public dividend capital grants) that were previously advanced to British Steel Corp. as part of its development strategy. An equivalent capital grant to the 11 privately owned U.S. steel corporations would most likely have resulted in one of the most efficient steel industries in the world.

11. See, for example, Business Week, December 29, 1981, and June 1, 1981.

12. See Business Week, June 1, 1981.

13. Yair Aharoni, "Performance Evaluation of State Owned Enterprises: A Process Perspective," Management Science 27, no. 11 (November 1981):1340-47; Jeheil Zif, "Managerial Strategic Behavior in State-Owned Enterprises," Management Science 27, no. 11 (November 1981):1326-39.

14. Business Week, January 26, 1981.

3

OIL AND STATE ENTERPRISES:
ASSESSING PETRO-CANADA

Larry Pratt

INTRODUCTION

Blaming a "subterranean campaign of international groups joined with national groups" for his downfall, on August 24, 1954, Getulio Vargas, president of Brazil, confounded his enemies by committing suicide. Politically isolated and under an ultimatum from the Brazilian military to resign, Vargas took his life after writing an emotional and nationalistic appeal to the people of his country. His inflammatory testament, posthumously published, accused a conspiracy of "antinational" forces of subverting his plans for Brazil's development and of sabotaging Petrobrás, the recently established national oil company. "I wanted to create national freedom in realizing our national wealth through Petrobrás; hardly had it begun to function when the wave of agitation grew. They don't want the people to be free." Vargas's suicide note ended despairingly: "I offer my life in the holocaust. I choose this means to be with you always." By this final act, one historian has remarked, Vargas linked his name to petroleum in Brazil's national conscience and rendered Petrobrás immune from political attacks for years.[1]

Oil and nationalism have been inseparable in the political development of modern Brazil, indeed in the development of much of the South American continent. "O Petroleo e Nosso" (The Oil Is Ours) was the rallying cry of a broad coalition of nationalist groups who opposed the entry of American oil "trusts" into Brazil after the Second World War and advocated the creation of a national government monopoly over petroleum exploration and refining. Petrobrás emerged out of a domestic political struggle between nationalists and economic liberals and subsequently became the emblem of

Brazil's drive for industrialization and national independence.
Vargas's suicide rallied political support behind Petrobrás and—
despite its indifferent record in finding oil—helped it to develop into
Brazil's most powerful state enterprise, thereby strengthening one
of the three elements in the "triple alliance" of multinational, state,
and private national capital which, under the aegis of a repressive
military dictatorship, has spurred Brazil's growth. It was the state,
not private stimulus, that gave birth to Brazil's oil industry, and it
has been the state that has driven the domestic and overseas expansion of this industry.

It is not only in Brazil that oil has been organized along state
capitalist lines. It seems certain that, outside the borders of the
United States and a very few other countries, the international oil
industry of the 1980s and beyond will be increasingly controlled by
large state-owned petroleum companies.[2] The direction of change
in this vital industry is centrifugal—from multinational to national
oil; from a closely knit, highly integrated structure based on global
profit maximization to a loosely organized, decentralized system
based on the national interests of sovereign states. Ownership,
control, and management of petroleum resources are now in the
hands of national governments and state companies, not transnational
companies, in virtually every significant oil-exporting country, and
state oil companies are gradually assuming the responsibility for the
acquisition of offshore oil supplies in most importing countries as the
international oil market steadily disintegrates. National governments are using state oil companies as policy instruments to increase
their jurisdiction and control over energy resources and over the international oil industry. Once the proud advance guard of the era of
transnationalism, the major international oil companies still retain
significant market power through their control of technology and expertise and their access to finance, but in oil the age of transnationalism is almost finished and the majors are being jostled every-
where by the agents of economic nationalism and state capitalism.
Whether this movement from the multinational to the national oil
company is regarded as progressive or regressive is much less
relevant for the purposes of this chapter than the fact that it is happening. Why is it happening, and what implications follow?

This chapter explores the relationship between state and oil
industry by describing the expansion of national oil companies and
by examining the specific case of Petro-Canada—a company that
has experienced very rapid growth since its creation in the mid-
1970s. I shall attempt to show why state-owned companies are expanding their shares of trade and productive investment in oil, one
of the most dynamic and profitable centers of international capitalism, and how this is changing the balance of power between the

private and public sectors in countries such as Canada. For a number of reasons the state, which traditionally has acted as a <u>rentier</u> or tax collector in the international oil industry, is now behaving as an entrepreneur or capitalist in oil, and the principal vehicles for state entrepreneurship are government enterprises such as Japan's National Oil Company, France's Elf/Erap and Companie Francaise des Petroles, the British National Oil Corporation, Norway's Statoil, Petro-Canada, and more than a hundred others of widely varying size, functions, and competence. Nevertheless, these are oil companies with a difference. State oil companies may resemble their private counterparts in their corporate structure and, to a degree, in their behavior. For example, managers frequently profess their faith in "bottom-line" decision making. Fundamentally, however, these companies are instruments of <u>national</u> governments pursuing <u>national</u> objectives, including political goals, and governments seem determined to keep them from becoming otherwise. This constrains not merely their microprofitability, it also limits the capacity of such enterprises to act as surrogates for the integrated major oil companies that formerly controlled the world market.

The balance of this chapter is divided into two major sections. The first takes up the debate as to whether publicly owned oil companies are necessary and whether they can be as efficient as privately owned enterprises. It also examines several of the policy roles carried out by national oil companies on behalf of their government shareholders. The second part attempts to analyze Petro-Canada's objectives and corporate performance and to raise some critical questions about the federal government's new energy policies.

FROM MULTINATIONAL TO STATE OIL COMPANIES

The Case against State Oil Companies

Should governments go into the oil business? How efficiently do state-controlled petroleum companies use public resources? Can governments achieve their policy objectives through less costly means than through nationalization or the formation of their own oil companies? No simple answers can be given to these questions, but let me set out what I take to be the basic argument over state participation in the oil industry. In essence, of course, this is simply another version of the old market versus planning debate.

The right wing of political economy, represented by market-oriented oil economists,[3] has frequently argued that the case for direct state involvement in the petroleum industry is inherently weak. Governments have a range of licensing, fiscal, and regulatory policies available to achieve any reasonable economic objectives and to control the development of petroleum resources. Entry into the oil industry via nationalization or a state petroleum corporation is unnecessary and costly, as indeed are many other politically motivated government interventions in the energy sector. If a country lacks indigenous energy supplies and believes it is worthwhile promoting exploration for oil, it will be better off, given the substantial costs and risks of such activity, to rely upon private capital, with government confining its involvement to the issuing of licenses (preferably through competitive auction), regulation of the industry, and the collection of economic rent.

Neil H. Jacoby argues in his study <u>Multinational Oil</u> that the private international oil companies, motivated by profits, "are better adapted to accept the long risks and to allocate multinational investment economically than are governments." As experts in world oil logistics, the multinationals are able to balance production with consumption, adjust supplies from diverse sources in accordance with changes in relative costs, and compare prospective returns from many regions in allocating their investments.

> Private management, disciplined by competition, brings a greater flexibility of operations and adaptability to changing circumstances than would civil-servant management of socialized oil firms. Being prepared to invest in any country, the multinational oil company seeks the most profitable—which is normally the most efficient—way to meet petroleum demands. It takes a world view rather than a national view of consumers' requirements. Thus it promotes freedom of international trade and payments, and moderates the forces of extreme nationalism which tend to compartmentalize markets. [4]

By contrast, argue market economists, state oil companies inefficiently combine commercial and political objectives, raising final energy costs to consumers and lowering the overall performance of the economy. The goals of national oil companies are often vaguely defined, management lacks the incentive systems to operate efficiently and to take risks, and the norms of a government bureaucracy rather than that of the market govern the pattern of investments over the long run. Typically, a state-controlled oil company operates under political constraints that are bound to affect its commercial performance. For example, Petrobrás was required for many years to confine its exploration activities to Brazilian territory, in spite of mounting evidence that Brazil was not the vast storehouse of hydrocarbons that many nationalists held it to be. State companies such as Italy's ENI and Mexico's Pemex have often been directed by government to act as agencies of economic development and to carry out programs of regional subsidization or employment maintenance that a normal profit-maximizing oil company would not undertake.

Assuming private capital is available, there is little point in having a state oil company whose principal goal is to maximize profits; but if profitability is subordinated to economic development or political goals, it follows that the state firm will be less efficient than its private counterparts. As public resources are scarce, the question must then be asked whether society is obtaining the maximum social return via direct investment in the oil industry rather than by investing those resources in alternative uses, e.g., education. If not, are there less costly ways of pursuing the same objectives than by government entering the petroleum business?

Skeptics of state participation further argue that where national oil companies operate in a monopolistic environment and are not subject to competitive pressures, no yardstick will be available to compare costs, prices will be high, and the centralized government monopoly will probably become both inefficient and socially irresponsible. Where state oil companies operate in a competitive market but are given preferential rights by the government, then hidden subsidies and costs will make it extremely difficult to evaluate the commercial performance of the government-controlled enterprise. It is frequently added that governments cannot properly reconcile their role as regulator or umpire of the petroleum industry with entrepreneurial involvement within the same industry, and where they have attempted to do so they have often landed themselves in compromising conflicts of interest.

Do exhaustible natural resources such as petroleum constitute a special case for government ownership of an industry? Neoclassical political economists take the view that such resources "are basically no different from other factors of production,"[5] a presumption in favor of an allocation of resources through the market, not state planning. Stripped of technical complexity, the argument here is that while nonrenewable resources do present some special difficulties—e.g., the premature depletion of common property resources through unlimited access, the absence of futures markets or other mechanisms for coping with uncertainty, a tendency toward monopoly in the case of certain resources—none of these justifies nationalization or state participation. The petroleum industry is said to be reasonably competitive, and this means that government can collect any economic rent without moving into the industry—preferably by bidding away the rights to win resources through an auction system. There are, according to neoclassical theorists, extensive possibilities for substitution between nonrenewable resources and other factors. In an open market with prices operating freely and technology improving, further substitutions and new resources will become available as the process of growth "generates antidotes to a general increase in resource scarcity," according to a famous study of natural resource economics. [6]

The exhaustible nature of petroleum resources does present a special set of problems for market-oriented writers in that there is a strong possibility of divergence between the socially optimal rate of depletion and the rate of use preferred by a private individual or firm. It is often argued that private interest rates are likely to be higher than an appropriate social rate of discount, and this may encourage resources to be depleted too quickly. While admitting this possibility, neoclassical economists reply that this is at best an argument for depletion controls, not state investment. Some go on to argue that governments with an eye on the next election may use an even higher discount rate than that used in the private sector (i.e., politicians may encourage a faster exploitation of resources in order to distribute benefits to the electorate today rather than in the future). [7]

Generally, such writers are skeptical of all arguments for government planning and participation in the oil industry. Although markets may well be imperfect, they argue, there is little reason to presume that a government bureaucracy or a state-owned enterprise will be any better equipped to forecast an uncertain future or that their decisions will be more enlightened in the long run than those of private managers. Colin Robinson and Jon Morgan concluded in their critique of British policies in the North Sea that

> better results are likely to flow from a system of
> diffused power which channels personal self-interest
> in desirable directions rather than from a system of
> central direction which concentrates power in the
> hands of a few people who can plead pursuit of the
> "national interest" for any of their actions. [8]

Summarizing the case against government participation in the U.S. petroleum industry, James M. Griffin and Henry B. Steele concluded that "national oil companies are grossly inefficient as judged by standard tests of business performance, such as the ratio of employees to oil production." Although all oil-exporting countries have national oil companies, only in Mexico and Algeria have these state firms found "significant" new reserves of oil. Despite the advantages that accrue to them as native operators competing with foreigners, the Middle East national oil companies "have been unable to establish a record for discoveries per unit of exploration input which is in any way comparable with that of the private companies." Why? Griffin and Steele offer the following explanation:

> First and foremost, exploration in new and potentially highly productive areas is very risky, and public companies by their very nature do not hold out large rewards to risk taking. Neither the president of the national oil company nor the minister of petroleum will be able legally to achieve any financial benefits from success in facing high exploratory risks with long lead times, but they will certainly be subject to political criticism if they fail. The optimal strategy for remaining in control of the national oil company is to minimize investment in true exploration and focus on tactics such as more intensive field development in order to keep capacity up in the short run. . . . political criticism is sure to find a vulnerable target in the person of a national oil company president who has "wasted" tens or hundreds of millions of dollars in drilling dry holes. But to avoid dry holes one must avoid exploration, thus avoiding new discoveries and ultimately depleting oil supplies prematurely. [9]

The Case for State Oil Companies

In the aftermath of two serious international oil supply crises in only half a decade, these arguments have a distinctly scholastic ring about them. No national government could seriously entertain the proposition in today's world that petroleum is merely another commodity. Given the preponderant place of oil in world energy consumption and its central role in virtually every important economic sector (including national defense industries), petroleum supply has for many governments—as one European strategist argues—begun to assume the characteristics of a public good that is too essential to be entrusted to the swings of a highly politicized market. [10] In the absence of supranational accord between oil producers and consumers, all of the industrialized capitalist states have attempted to protect themselves from the worst effects of instability in the world oil system and to ensure that their respective national society has access to scarce petroleum supplies—even if others do not. To be sure, not all such states have established national oil companies—the United States, West Germany, and

Australia have not, for example. Yet all have intervened in the market in order to protect their lines of supply, to accelerate the development of indigenous energy resources, to raise revenues from oil producers and consumers, and so on. Even the United States, a country which is home base for five of the seven major international oil companies, enacted legislation in the late 1970s creating a government-owned Synthetic Fuels Corporation with a mandate to capitalize the development of a domestic oil industry based on coal and shale. Economists may quarrel with such interventions on efficiency grounds. Yet this largely misses the point that governments confronted with instability and uncertainty react defensively by protecting their own national interests.

State oil companies are almost by definition instruments of national interest and jurisdiction operating in an international industry. They are oil companies that in some cases operate with a fair measure of commercial autonomy, but are also state enterprises accountable in the final analysis to their government shareholders. How the balance between commercial and policy drives is handled in practice varies greatly from company to company, but at a minimum it can be said that governments create national oil companies as policy instruments, not to maximize profits. Rationales vary once again with circumstances but, speaking broadly, there appear to be four general objectives that governments expect to serve by going into the oil business:[11] first, to secure energy supplies, either by arranging for oil imports or by advancing the development of indigenous oil resources or substitutes; second, to enhance the state's knowledge of and control over the oil industry and oil developments; third, to maximize the state's share of total economic benefits; and fourth, to promote the interests of domestic capital owners by arranging for their participation in the direct and indirect benefits flowing from new energy developments. Each of these needs some brief elaboration.

To Secure Energy Supplies

First, the state is moving into the oil industry in order to secure national energy supplies. This may involve using a state corporation to arrange purchases of imported oil on a government-to-government basis; or it may involve using a state enterprise to accelerate the development of domestic energy stocks. Since 1913 when First Lord of the Admiralty Winston Churchill convinced his British cabinet colleagues to invest government funds in the Anglo-Persian Co. (today British Petroleum), national governments have had recourse to publicly funded corporations as a way of obtaining access to foreign oil supplies. Anglo-Persian was not, by modern standards, a national oil company. Indeed, a later British government established the British National Oil Corporation in part because it lacked influence over British Petroleum. But Churchill's motivation was to give the Royal Navy an independent source of fuel and to prevent the Admiralty from becoming dependent on "a universal oil monopoly"—that is, on the Shell and Rockefeller interests. Similarly, the French, Italian, and Spanish state petroleum companies were all set up to acquire secure supplies of foreign oil and, not incidentally, to reduce their country's reliance on the Anglo-American majors. Japan's National Oil Company was a late arrival to the world of state oil companies. The Japanese have attempted throughout the postwar period to promote the development of stable overseas oil supplies and to avoid becoming excessively dependent on a single supplier or on the commercial instincts of the private companies. The Arab embargo of the United States and the Netherlands in 1973, and the inability of the majors to guarantee third-party sales during the Iranian crisis of 1979, forced the Japanese to rely on their own private and public enterprises to guarantee the security of their imported oil. West Germany has no national oil company, but in the late 1960s a German "national champion" called Deminex was created out of the larger units in the German industry primarily to explore for oil and to acquire reserves of petroleum outside of Germany. Despite the laissez-faire economic philosophy of the German government, Deminex has received substantial subsidies from the state. Albeit with many reservations, governments are increasingly moving into the acquisition of foreign oil, and a growing proportion of internationally traded oil now moves on a state-to-state basis.

To Secure Knowledge and Control

A second purpose of state participation concerns control and learning. Governments are moving into the oil industry to obtain a more direct control over petroleum activities and to learn what actually happens in the petroleum sector and why. Many governments have found the international oil industry exceedingly difficult to control, and even today the largest multinational firms continue to hold a number of advantages that translate into impressive bargaining power. The majors have historically been horizontally concentrated (each controls a substantial market share of the industry) and vertically integrated (the same entity controls successive phases of the industry). These features derive, in turn, from the high-risk and capital-intensive nature of the oil industry and from the large barriers to entry in all of its stages. Characterized by above-average levels of profitability and controlling vital know-how and technology, the international oil companies have been surprisingly adaptable and resistant to external interference. Spreading out from their American and European home bases, the majors organized their operations on a transnational basis and at one time dominated the world petroleum market through an informal but highly effective network of joint producing companies, pooling arrangements, and production-sharing agreements. [12]

Paul Frankel remarks that the multinational oil companies "represented a system of global optimization which might have been perfectly justified in itself, yet might conceivably have been deleterious to some individual country or other. No one will accept being optimized out of the system." [13] No single government could hope to regulate more than a national segment of these global firms' operations: regulation stopped at the water's edge. Not even the governments of the most powerful industrialized countries—the United States, France, Italy, Great Britain, Japan—have felt competent to exercise effective control over the international majors. (One reason why the British government created the British National Oil Corporation in 1975 was that it had been unable to control British Petroleum—a company partially owned by the British state since 1913—during the Arab embargo of 1973.) In developing nations the concerns over a loss of sovereignty have of course been accentuated by the fact that the oil companies have been seen as instruments of Anglo-American imperialism.

Licensing and taxation provide one set of methods for a government to evolve a system of "national optimization" in dealing with the petroleum industry. Many countries have gone beyond this to move directly into the industry in order to obtain greater knowledge of and control over such matters as the timing of exploration and production, the regional distribution of capital investment, and the impact of large new developments in sensitive areas. A national oil company may be viewed by its government shareholder as an entreprise témoin—a company that can be a day-to-day witness to what goes on in the complex oil business.

Canada, as will be seen later, created Petro-Canada in 1975 in order to gain a greater measure of control over the timing of frontier exploration and production and to establish a "window" on a foreign-controlled industry. In 1972 Norway established its state oil company, Statoil, not only to optimize its control over the international oil industry, but also to acquire the operating skills and insight necessary to plan and control the pace of development of its North Sea resources. Given the magnitude of the anticipated offshore developments and their large potential impact on the Norwegian society and economy, a state oil company was deemed necessary as a policy instrument to back up the government's macroeconomic planning. A Norwegian government official later explained why his government had opted for active state involvement in the North Sea:

> That was due to a very, very firm belief and due to what we have seen historically in other parts of the world; namely, that there is a very great difference between having control over the formal decision-making process and over the real decision-making process, and the real decision-making process is probably the only way of implementing the national ideas in the business. We felt that only through direct engagement, a fingertip feeling for what this business is about, only through that way of handling things could we achieve a national supervision and control over the business and build our competence. . . . [14]

To Secure the Largest Economic Benefit

A third purpose of state participation is to maximize the host country's share of the total economic benefits generated by the petroleum industry. Here we must distinguish the formal concept of state participation, which may be a strictly passive device for acquiring oil revenues, from the more ambitious idea of a state oil company capable of carrying on its own exploratory and development activities within a highly complex industry. The former is used as a supplement to rentals, royalties, and taxes and is merely one of a number of different instruments available to the state's tax collectors to capture the economic rent from resources licensed to the oil industry: the state's interest is purely financial and need not be represented in the day-to-day decision making. The latter involves the creation of an entrepreneurial presence within the oil industry that can be called upon by the state to act as a policy instrument. Whether state participation agreements negotiated with the oil industry are an efficient way of collecting rent is a question on which opinions differ, but probably they are at best no more efficient than a well-designed licensing system, and at worst they may be much less efficient. [15]

Most governments, however, appear to take a broader view of economic benefits than this. In the first place, the available economic surplus from today's oil developments is much larger than the rents that can be taxed away at the production stage. It includes the capture of a variety of employment and related spin-offs from exploration and development, the mitigation of severe inflationary effects and other negative impacts, the promotion of new industries linked to the primary resource sector, and the manner in which the public sector invests its oil rents. All of these involve much more than simply collecting the rent. In devising its economic plans and in bargaining with the multinational firm over the distribution of the economic surplus, the state may find it a considerable advantage to control a public company with the capability of operating independently at all levels of the industry. Without such an instrument, the state lacks the bargaining leverage necessary to neutralize the power of the oil companies by playing producers off against one another.

Although market-oriented economists tend to emphasize the rent-extraction function of state participation, in practice governments seldom enter into participation contracts for purely financial reasons. Norway undoubtedly spoke for many other oil-producing states when its government noted in the early 1970s that

> as "landowner" the Government is not interested in the income alone, but is also interested in the manner in which the country's natural resources are utilized. Operations of such magnitude as these will naturally have effects upon the community, effects far beyond the direct results of actual exploration and exploitation. [16]

Raising revenue is undoubtedly important, but the state's interest in the development of a vital resource such as petroleum is necessarily broader and more complex than maximizing its share of the rent. Control, learning, and planning seem to be at least as important as the financial drives. Oystein Noreng, whose views are heavily influenced by North Sea experience, has argued that state participation is essentially a mechanism to satisfy the many political considerations that superimpose themselves on the government's oil policy. A state oil company, being government owned, can be required to operate according to political criteria, though not of course without affecting its commercial performance. [17]

To Secure Opportunities for Domestic Capital

Finally, if we examine national oil companies on the level of class analysis, it seems clear that these state enterprises are increasingly performing certain functions for different categories of capital as well as mediating alliances between local and international business. Generalization is risky, but one or two broad trends can be discerned. The Conference Board noted at the close of the 1970s that 100 percent equity ownership in overseas multinational sub-

sidiaries "is rapidly becoming a thing of the past," and went on to
show how multinationals are of necessity adapting to pressures from
virtually all developing countries for joint ventures and local equity
ownership. Such pressures for "indigenization" frequently involve
the linking of government incentives to an agreement by the multinational to offer partnerships to local state and private capital.[18]
The catalyst here is frequently the developing country's public corporations. In Brazil, for example, giant state companies such as
Petrobrás have played an aggressive role in bringing about three-
way alliances among multinational, state, and private Brazilian
capital, and have thereby fostered the growth of new industries such
as petrochemicals.

These arrangements have their analogues in developed oil-
producing states such as Canada and Norway, where national oil
companies are being used to compensate for the weakness of the
local bourgeoisie and to ensure that domestic business interests are
able to participate in profitable new resources ventures. Cui bono?
Dependency theorists would probably argue that these are alliances
of unequals and that the principal beneficiaries of such arrangements
are the multinational oil companies. In some instances this is almost certainly true. In Brazil and Norway (and in Canada since the
1980 National Energy Program)[19] the multinationals have attacked
the growth of state capitalism by arguing that the national oil company has been expanding much faster than either the local private
sector or the multinational subsidiaries.

Who Bears the Risk?

Who bears the risk of investing in costly new energy sources
and of testing new energy-related technologies? This may be the
critical issue in the international oil industry in this decade and beyond as national governments attempt to reduce their dependence on
insecure OPEC-controlled oil and the major petroleum companies
emphasize the search for new sources of crude supply. Despite
much initial enthusiasm for diversification, several of the majors
have run into serious financial difficulties in their haste to blossom
overnight into mature energy companies. For the remainder of the
century and well into the next, the international oil companies will
in all likelihood be concentrating the bulk of their capital expenditures on the job they do best: finding and exploiting new reserves
of conventional oil and gas, especially in non-OPEC petroliferous
regions such as offshore Australia, the North Sea, Alaska, the Gulf
Coast, the Beaufort Sea and Canadian Arctic Islands, and along the
continental shelf off the east coast of Canada and the United States.

(Some of the more far-sighted national oil companies, such as Italy's ENI, are promoting the concept of a "second cycle" of foreign exploration in the established producing areas of OPEC, but in the absence of long-term supply and pricing agreements the prospects of this seem remote.)

Although the geological outlook for finding new oil and gas is bright in many non-OPEC reas, the costs, lead times, and risks of failure are very large—so large that many projects cannot be undertaken under normal commercial practices. It is here that national oil companies, backed by their government shareholders, will increasingly be required: to mobilize public capital, shoulder risks, operate on the technological frontier, and to act as intermediaries between multinational companies and government ministries. Unlike its private sector counterparts, a state oil company can afford to invest a disproportionate share of its capital budget as "patient money" in high-risk projects, and on policy grounds it can afford to be more concerned with proving out national stocks of oil and gas reserves rather than with moving quickly into commercial production. (Whether such investment promotes the optimal use of public lands and resources is a question to which we return below.) The costs of such a policy mandate are significant, however. It involves the expenditure of hundreds of millions or even billions of dollars a year in long-term investments with little prospect of early cash flow, and to be an effective player a state oil company must also be sufficiently large and competent to operate alongside the multinationals in some of the world's most hostile physical environments. It is partly for these reasons that some state oil companies, once established, tend to expand very rapidly, prompting their critics and even their supporters to fret over the specter of rampant state capitalism. Once inside the oil business, does the state know when to quit?

Balancing Objectives

The preceding paragraphs have stressed the policy or national interest objectives of state oil companies: security of supply; learning, control, and planning; raising revenue; and so on, none of which is to deny that these same companies operate in a commercial environment or that public managers sometimes put their "bottom line" before the government's policy objectives. As is the case in most state-owned enterprises, the investment criteria employed in national oil companies include both public policy goals and commercial tests. There is a constant need to balance the government's view of the national interest and the pursuit of earnings. State enterprise managers frequently strive for a healthy bottom line as a way of putting distance between themselves and governments. Paul Frankel remarks in his biography of Enrico Mattei, founder and empire builder of ENI, that

> Generally speaking, the managers of such enter-
> prises will have the tendency to make them stand on
> their own feet as quickly as they possibly can; the
> less they depend on support out of the public purse—
> the idea of being subsidized out of "the taxpayers'
> money" is a distasteful one—the more independent
> and powerful they become. The feudal barons were
> strong as long as they were sustained by their own
> local wealth and not dependent on favours bestowed
> upon them by the king. [20]

Where a government itself is weak or unable to define the policy objectives it wants the state company to pursue, then the "feudal barons" of modern-day public enterprise will be free to set their own priorities and to pursue their own corporate ambitions without the distraction of worrying about the public interest. Some of the older state oil companies in Western Europe, notably the French and Italian, have frequently allied themselves with the international majors against their own governments and are only nominally under a system of political control and accountability.

Nevertheless, it remains true that national oil companies have been created by governments as policy instruments. While some may be gravitating in the direction of state capitalism, there appear to be very few that are permitted to operate wholly unfettered by political constraints. For example, many governments restrict the overseas investments of their national companies, limit their ability to raise capital in private markets, control the disposal of their profits, and so on—all of which act as barriers to accumulation and qualify the tendency of state oil corporations to act as private units of capital.

These facts have a major bearing on the evaluation of state oil companies. If such enterprises had originally been established to operate on a purely commercial basis, there would be little problem in assessing their results and little doubt as to the outcome of such an assessment. Judged by the normal criteria of financial performance, national oil companies probably have been a good deal less efficient or profitable than privately owned oil companies. (It is difficult to be categorical because of a paucity of reliable comparative data and also because a few national oil companies, such as Statoil, have been judged efficient by economists.)

Notwithstanding the prejudices of Griffin and Steele and other economists, however, it is not the lack of risk-taking incentives or the fear of political criticism that accounts for this. State oil companies are probably less risk-averse and conservative than many private oil corporations, and some—Petro-Canada being the outstanding example—devote a far larger share of their capital expenditures to high-risk investments than do their private-sector counterparts. The appropriate criticism of these state enterprises is that far from being excessively cautious and oriented to immediate returns, they are unduly absorbing private risks and perhaps also prematurely hastening the development of higher-cost energy resources.

If state oil companies are inefficient, the explanation lies in the blending of the policy directives and commercial drives that shape their corporate behavior. Governments, unlike many economists, seldom have a single-minded fixation with economic efficiency, and, as we have seen, most expect and require their national oil companies to perform tasks that a profit-maximizing firm would not choose to do without subsidy.

This means, of course, that a state oil corporation should not be evaluated using criteria employed in the private sector. To put the same point differently, if a public enterprise operating in the oil and gas sector does not take into account the external economic and social effects of its actions, but confines its attention to its own microprofitability, then what conceivable rationale can there be for public ownership in the first instance?

We expect (or ought to expect) state enterprise to internalize externalities: literally to take the public interest "into account." It follows that we cannot assess the performance of a state-owned oil company in isolation from its social purposes. What is the social rate of return on the investments of a national oil company? What has been the state corporation's wider impact on the economy as a whole? What have been the benefits and costs of direct public investment, and what might have happened in the absence of such investment? Could the state's policy objectives have been pursued with less costly methods of intervention? Such questions do not easily lend themselves to sweeping generalizations about the performance of national oil companies in general, and for the remainder of the chapter I intend to turn to an analysis of a single case—Petro-Canada's purpose and its record of performance.

PETRO-CANADA: PURPOSES AND PERFORMANCE

Purposes

Canada's national oil company, Petro-Canada, was created by a special act of Parliament on July 30, 1975, some 18 months after the Trudeau government made the decision to establish such an enterprise. It has been operating from its Calgary, Alberta, head office since January 1976. Under the terms of the Financial Administration Act, the legislation that governs the administration of Canadian federal public corporations, Petro-Canada is designated a "Schedule D" or proprietary crown corporation. That is, it is a public enterprise that is expected to operate in a commercial environment and ultimately to be self-financing. Pursuant to its act of incorporation, Petro-Canada is an "agent of Her Majesty" and reports to Parliament through the Minister of Energy, Mines and Resources. The federal crown is Petro-Canada's sole shareholder. It is important to note that although the company has an important advisory role, it does not have regulatory or policymaking powers and responsibilities.

Although the issue had been under consideration by the federal government since 1971, the decision to establish a Canadian national oil company was made in late 1973 during the Arab oil embargo and at a moment when the then-minority Liberal government of Pierre Trudeau was under considerable political pressure on energy matters. The decision was based on a number of factors, [21] including:

A desire to promote exploration for oil and gas resources in Canada at a rate and in high-risk areas that could not be expected of the private sector; public investment was deemed necessary if the government hoped to enhance the known stocks of Canadian petroleum reserves without committing itself to early commercial production and export;

A related interest in promoting a more rapid pace of oil sands research and development as a potential backup supply for Canada;

A desire to improve the government's knowledge of Canadian energy stocks and of costs, markets, technology, and so forth, and thus to assist it in its regulatory and policymaking functions. In the idiom of the day, a national oil company would serve as a "window on the industry";

An urgent interest in improving the security of supply of foreign crude—an area where Canada was under pressure from OPEC producers such as Venezuela to move into state-to-state trading and where the government felt particularly dependent on the subsidiaries of the several international firms that controlled foreign production and supply;

A wish to increase Canadian control of and participation in an industry overwhelmingly dominated by foreign multinational firms;

A desire to increase the financial return to Canadians of the development of Canadian resources—while the national oil company was not to be used principally as a rent collector, indirectly it would be used to improve the government's very shaky performance in this area.

Of these various objectives, the first three were undoubtedly the most significant and have had the most lasting effects on Petro-Canada's corporate planning. The company was not originally intended to be a rent collector, nor was its principal objective that of "Canadianizing" the oil industry[22] or of making that industry more competitive and efficient. The government's overriding aim in creating a state petroleum company was to promote Canadian energy self-sufficiency by accelerating the timing of high-risk exploratory and development work. By entering into joint ventures with private capital and supplementing the market-generated rates of frontier exploration and oil sands development, the national oil company would play a catalytic role within the petroleum industry. Once the company became a significant player, it would strengthen the national government's capacity to control the major oil companies and to manage Canadian energy resources, and notably give it leverage to influence the pace and extent of large energy investments.

The Minister of Energy, Mines and Resources proposed an ambitious agenda for the new "agency of government" in his memorandum to the federal cabinet in late October 1973:

> It would explore in Canada's frontier areas for various energy resources; research the problems of tar sands and heavy oil development and perhaps into further uses of petroleum; acquire existing production capacity that comes available; seek to establish reliable import supply links; and potentially enter the downstream activities of refining and distribution. In doing this it would enhance the degree of governmental control over the rate and pattern of the development of Canadian energy resources; back up the revision of other policies such as land tenure and rent collection by giving the government the operating capacity to fill any undesirable gaps. . . .[23]

Accordingly, the 1975 Petro-Canada Act established a new crown corporation with broad powers and a mandate strongly oriented to the development of energy supply:

> The purpose of this Act is to establish within the energy industries in Canada a Crown owned firm with authority to explore for hydrocarbon deposits, to negotiate for and acquire petroleum and petroleum products from abroad to assure a continuity of supply for the needs of Canada, to develop and exploit deposits of hydrocarbons within and without Canada

in the interests of Canada, to carry out research and
development projects in relation to hydrocarbons and
other fuels, and to engage in exploration for, and the
production, distribution, refining and marketing of,
fuels. [24]

The incorporating legislation gives Petro-Canada's board of directors and officers an open-ended mandate and sweeping powers, but
this is balanced to some extent by provisions intended to keep the
company accountable to the public authorities. For instance, the
federal government must give its prior approval to Petro-Canada's
annual capital budget before it receives the authority to spend
monies, it appoints the company's board and approves the appointments of the chairman and president, and it can also direct the corporation as an agent of the crown to undertake activities that it
might otherwise choose not to do, say, on commercial grounds.
These provisions were carefully drafted as part of the incorporating legislation and reflect the government's perspective that Petro-
Canada is not merely an oil company but, first and foremost, is an
important instrument of national policy and development. This is
perhaps even more firmly the view of the Canadian government today than it was in the mid-1970s.

How has the National Energy Program (NEP), announced in
October 1980, modified Petro-Canada's original purposes? This
is not the place for a comprehensive analysis of the NEP, but we
should remind ourselves that the Liberal Party returned with a
majority in the House of Commons in February 1980, after having
fought the plans of the short-lived Conservative minority government to "privatize" Petro-Canada in conjunction with a more market-
oriented approach to energy policy. (In the final analysis, when it
was much too late to make a difference, the Conservatives decided
to sell only some of Petro-Canada's shares and to retain controlling
interest in the corporation.) During the election campaign the Liberals pledged to keep Petro-Canada in the public sector and to expand its activities. They also committed themselves to the Canadianization of the petroleum industry and to strengthening the national government vis-à-vis the oil-producing provinces. This ambitious and interventionist agenda is reflected in the NEP and in
accompanying legislation, the principal features of which are: an
expanded public sector via the acquisition of a number of foreign-
owned oil and gas companies; new taxes and energy prices that re-
direct a much greater share of the total energy revenues to Ottawa;
a comprehensive management program for the federally owned
"Canada Lands" in the north and offshore; and a system of new incentive exploration grants designed to promote the rapid exploitation

of the frontiers by Canadian-owned and controlled oil companies and, implicitly, to shift future Canadian production from provincial to federal lands. [25]

While the federal government has not explicitly revised Petro-Canada's purposes, the original developmental objectives of the company have now been supplemented and blurred somewhat by the redistributive nature of the NEP policies. Thus, for example, the NEP places at least as much emphasis, and perhaps more, on the Canadianization of the oil industry as it does on the exploration for and development of new energy supplies. Not only has Petro-Canada's strategy of rapidly exploiting the frontiers been reinforced (by an increase in government equity capital and the introduction of the new incentive grants for exploration), but in addition the state company is evidently expected to be an important agent of Canadianization, a rent collector, [26] and perhaps an instrument of regional economic development as well. There have been indications that the federal government also would like to use Petro-Canada to increase competition in the oil industry. There is little evidence that either the government or Petro-Canada has thought through the difficulties of reconciling these competing goals or the likely impact of such a reconciliation on the company's long-term performance.

Performance

Economic Measures

Since commencing operations in 1976, Petro-Canada has gone through six years of very rapid growth. The central elements in this expansion have been the acquisitions of several foreign-controlled properties: the purchase in 1976 of Atlantic Richfield Canada Ltd. for $342 million, of Pacific Petroleums Ltd. for $1.5 billion in 1978-79, and of Petrofina Canada Inc. for $1.5 billion in 1981. [27] As a result of these acquisitions, the transfer to Petro-Canada of the government's prior interests in Panarctic Oils Ltd. and Syncrude Canada Ltd., and the infusion of close to $1.5 billion in government equity capital in the period 1976 to 1980, Petro-Canada's assets are now conservatively estimated at between $4 and $5 billion. [28] The state company is Canada's fifth largest oil and gas producer and is now in the process of becoming integrated on a coast-to-coast basis.

Petro-Canada's corporate strategy has closely matched its initial mandate of accelerating the development of new Canadian energy stocks. The company's cumulative capital expenditures in the six-year period 1976-81 (excluding property acquisitions and asset transfers) have amounted to some $2.24 billion, with annual capital spending rising to an estimated $902 million in 1981. These spending requirements for capital projects have been met by 48 percent equity funds from government and 52 percent from internally generated earnings. The distribution of Petro-Canada's cumulative capital expenditures between 1976 and 1981 is shown in Table 3.1.

TABLE 3.1

Petro-Canada's Capital Expenditures, 1976-81

Expenditure	Percentage
Western Canada exploration and development	34
Frontier exploration	30
Syncrude plus other oil sands	16
Manufacturing and marketing	7
International exploration and development	3
Other (Arctic Pilot Project, R & D, and so on)	10
Total	100

Source: Petro-Canada.

Table 3.2 illustrates the relationship between Petro-Canada's capital spending and its use of funds provided from operations in the current 1981 capital budget (before the purchase of Petrofina).

Tables 3.1 and 3.2 demonstrate that Canada's state oil company has been devoting a disproportionate share of its capital expenditures to longer-term, high-risk investments, and particularly to northern and offshore exploration activity and the oil sands. It has been drawing heavily on the cash flow provided by Western Canadian oil and gas production, Syncrude, and the sale of products to finance this strategy. Only the direct backing of the federal government permits the corporation to invest its earnings this way. No private-sector oil company, large or small, could afford to commit 30 percent of its total capital spending and fully 60 percent of its exploratory funds to investments of a highly risky and uncertain nature with no prospect of early returns. Petro-Canada participated in 72 of the 130 frontier wells drilled by industry between 1976 and 1980. The East Coast offshore wells accounted for close to 40 percent of its Canadian exploration funds. By contrast, in the same period, the petroleum industry as a whole committed less than 20 percent of its Canadian exploration funds to the frontiers and under 10 percent of its total upstream (including development) expenditures went to the frontiers in the late 1970s. [29]

TABLE 3.2

Petro-Canada's 1981 Capital Budget

	Capital Spending		Cash from Operations[a]	
	$ million	%	$ million	%
Exploration & development				
Frontiers	315	35	—[b]	—
Western Canada	282	31	314	56
International	42	5	16	3
Oil sands				
Syncrude	20	2	47	8
Other	42	5	—	—
Petroleum products	92	10	145	26
Other (Canertech, R & D, and so on)	110	12	38	7
Total	903		560	

[a]Net of operating expenses and PGRT.
[b]Nil.
Source: Petro-Canada.

The balance of Petro-Canada exploration expenditures from 1976 to 1981 was distributed between the conventional basins of Western Canada (30 percent) and international activity (10 percent). Investments in Western Canada exploration are designed to maximize the economic benefits of the land position obtained through acquisitions, to generate near-term cash flow that can be used to support frontier exploration and heavy oil projects, and to acquire expertise, organizational strength, and technology. Overseas exploration has been undertaken in jurisdictions such as the Norwegian sector of the North Sea where participation by Petro-Canada might give Canada access to foreign equity crude.

Similarly, Petro-Canada's development expenditures have emphasized the so-called "technological frontier": development of synthetic oil from the Alberta oil sands, the upgrading of heavy oil, in situ recovery techniques, and a number of energy pilot projects and feasibility studies. As with the emphasis on frontier exploration, the state company's development expenditures have been concentrated in the higher-risk "exotic" areas and are designed to stimulate private-sector interest and participation.

Social Measures

What are the social benefits and costs of this pattern of direct public investment? The answer rests in large part on one's view of an autarkic energy strategy—that is, on whether it is rational to invest public resources in self-sufficiency in petroleum or substitutes. The federal government and Petro-Canada justify the company's strong emphasis on the frontiers on the grounds: that the market-determined rate of exploration in the northern and offshore areas and the pace of oil sands and heavy oil research and development have been much too slow, given the steep decline in Canada's existing stocks of conventional oil supplies and the insecurity and cost of foreign energy; and that the government has a "need to know" the extent and cost of developing frontier oil and gas reserves so that it can make rational energy decisions. Although the federal government has underwritten some 90 percent of all exploration costs in the frontiers, the pace of exploratory drilling in the Northwest Territories, Arctic Islands, and eastern offshore has declined sharply since 1973. After the early 1970s, most of the large oil companies holding frontier acreage began to shift their attention back to the Western Canada producing region. Higher oil and gas prices, attractive provincial incentives and stiffer provincial work obligations, the prospect of early returns on investment, and significant new natural gas discoveries made in Alberta and British Columbia increased the attractions of Western Canada. On the other hand, the ability of the northern and offshore areas to compete for exploration capital was hampered by a disappointing exploration record, the absence of tough work obligations, uncertainty over land regulations and offshore jurisdiction, and, of course, the much less attractive environment and economics. Pretax drilling costs per exploratory well in the late 1970s averaged between $250,000 and $490,000 in Western Canada and from $20 million to $40 million in the north and offshore areas. Furthermore, these figures are insignificant when compared to frontier development and transportation costs. The forbidding economics of the frontiers go a long way in explaining the growing role of the state in the Canadian oil and gas industries.

Petro-Canada's frontier drilling program, launched in 1976 shortly after the company started operations, was designed to attract private capital back to the frontier areas. Through joint ventures with the companies holding the best land positions, it was to determine whether significant quantities of hydrocarbons could be developed in any of the major sedimentary basins of the north and offshore areas at prevailing international prices. In selecting prospective areas for drilling, Petro-Canada has given particular attention to those basins that might not be immediately attractive to a profit-maximizing firm, but that still had merit from a public policy standpoint (e.g., the Scotian Shelf, which was contiguous to the energy-insecure Atlantic Provinces). Those areas already being explored by private oil companies—e.g., Dome Petroleum's Beaufort Sea drilling program—would receive less attention from Petro-Canada.

The intelligence gathered through Petro-Canada's seven-to-eight-year frontier drilling program would enable the Canadian government to make a decision in the early 1980s whether or not to abandon the frontier areas and commit massive public resources to full-scale exploitation of the Alberta oil sands and heavy oil—two secure but exceedingly costly sources of supply. Success in the frontier areas, it was hoped, might offer Canada larger volumes of energy at lower unit costs than would nonconventional alternatives such as the oil sands.[30] The basic purpose of Petro-Canada's frontier exploration program, together with its feasibility studies, pilot projects, research and development, and so forth, was to provide the federal government with a continuing evaluation of the relative economics of various supply alternatives open to Canada.

Frontier Exploration

How successful has Petro-Canada's frontier drilling program been? It is important to note here that after 1976 the oil industry as a whole showed very little interest in either the eastern offshore or in backing Panarctic's exploration ventures in the Arctic Islands. These have been the two regions where Petro-Canada has invested most of its effort and exploratory funds. The state company argues, not disinterestedly but also not without justification, that without its presence in eastern waters and its backing of 80 percent of Panarctic's program, several of the most promising frontier oil and gas discoveries might not have been made at all, and certainly would not have been made as soon as they were. These include the major Venture gas discovery on the Scotian Shelf, gas discoveries off the Labrador coast (where Petro-Canada is now operator for a multidrillship program), the 1979 Hibernia P-15 discovery well, the Char and Whitefish gas discoveries in the Arctic Islands, and others. These successes, combined with Dome Petroleum and Imperial Oil's discoveries of commercially recoverable oil fields in the Beaufort Sea, tend to confirm the government's view that the Canada Lands contain large recoverable reserves of oil and gas. Petro-Canada, in fact, argues that Canada may well be exporting oil from the frontiers in the early 1990s.[31]

Undoubtedly there are advantages accruing to decision makers from the knowledge that the frontier sedimentary basins do contain commercially recoverable deposits of hydrocarbons. It could be argued that if such knowledge permits the national government to postpone or avoid altogether a massive and costly program of oil sands development or large public investments in nuclear power, then the limited funds allocated to frontier exploration via Petro-Canada, tax deferrals, and other incentives will have been well invested. However, we still must ask whether Canadian energy policies are not now excessively biased in favor of early frontier development and whether these policies do not favor the exploitation of high-cost resources relative to lower-cost alternatives, including any remaining undiscovered reserves of Western Canadian conventional oil. It appears that the combined effect of Petro-Canada's budgetary allocations, the low conventional oil and gas prices and higher taxes contained in the National Energy Program, and the new system of exploration incentive grants is to tilt energy investment away from the conventional basins of Western Canada toward the Canada Lands (where the federal government as sole landowner is in a position to capture economic rents and control the pace of development). Why frontier oil and gas resources and developers should receive such exceptional subsidies, relative to the treatment given other energy sources, is not clear. To the extent that government commitments to support exploration implicitly involve subsequent commitments to support early production, the policy may involve considerable costs.

The Timing of New Supplies

The question of the timing of new resource developments is important from the perspective of energy efficiency. Energy policy has a dynamic dimension since it involves choosing among competing investment alternatives over time. There is an optimal time—that time at which its net present value is maximized—for bringing each new unit of a resource, say petroleum, into production. The social objective should be to find the optimal time for bringing new resources onstream, and to avoid bringing higher-cost resources into production any sooner than absolutely necessary. Had high-

cost Arctic Gas been developed in the mid-1970s, for instance, as
the proponents of the Mackenzie Valley gas pipeline advocated, then
gas consumers would have paid higher prices and the marketing of
lower-cost Western Canadian gas reserves would have become that
much more difficult.

If the exploitation of high-cost frontier oil is induced prematurely by government policies, including Petro-Canada's investments, then far from being socially beneficial, these policies could
involve a significant misallocation of scarce resources—the cost of
which would have to be borne by taxpayers and energy users (not to
mention western provincial governments and producers owning Western Canadian reserves, the value of which is depressed by federal
energy policies). In a prescient overview and critique of Canadian
energy policy, John Helliwell has noted that federal oil supply measures

> have all been undertaken on the basis of conventional
> oil supply forecasts that are almost bound to be severe
> underestimates of the eventual production of conven-
> tional oil from primary, secondary, and tertiary re-
> covery from oil deposits in the western provinces. By
> directly and indirectly subsidizing the development of
> frontier deposits and oil sands oil, relative to conven-
> tional crude oil, the federal policies raise the average
> cost of Canadian crude oil production, and lower the
> average net benefit from Canadian oil resources. The
> economic costs of this strategy are increased by the
> use of oil demand forecasts that almost surely over-
> state the rate of increase in the Canadian demand for
> crude oil at world prices. This in turn means that
> there will be greater amounts of shut-in conventional
> capacity and hence even greater discrimination in
> favor of the higher cost synthetic and frontier de-
> posits.[32]

Some evidence that Petro-Canada may be interested in an
overly rapid rate of development of the frontiers, and not merely in
accelerating exploration, may be deduced from the company's strenu-
ous lobbying on behalf of the Arctic Pilot Project (APP). It was conceived by Petro-Canada and a group of Canadian gas and shipping
interests as a way of bringing liquefied natural gas in tankers from
the Arctic Islands to eastern (and by displacement) foreign markets.
Since Canada clearly does not need Arctic gas today, and is not
likely to require it in the foreseeable future, the question arises as
to why scarce public resources should be invested in an energy

export project, especially one involving considerable environmental, economic, and technical hazards. Petro-Canada and its private-sector partners justify the APP on the grounds that it will open up the Arctic to full-scale mineral development, encourage additional oil and gas exploration by providing cash flow to Panarctic (45 percent owned by Petro-Canada), and place Canada in the forefront of Arctic marine technology.

However, since most of the tangible economic and technological benefits of the project will flow to Petro-Canada and its partners, there is some risk of confusing the state company's own commercial interests with the public interest. Petro-Canada's vigorous lobbying on behalf of early exports of Arctic gas is more than a little ironic, considering its good standing with Canadian nationalists and the fact that it was established, in part, to break the so-called "nexus" between exploration and early production and exports. The moral of the APP—which has still to be approved by the National Energy Board and the Cabinet—is clear. State companies, like their private counterparts, develop vested interests of their own and favor policies that will promote their growth and independence, improve their cash flow, and give them a healthy bottom line.

Overall Assessment of Performance

Having raised some questions about Petro-Canada's strategy, let me conclude by putting the criticisms in perspective. First, in accelerating the pace of frontier exploration and development the Canadian government is making its policies in the context of uncertainty about the future price of energy and the availability of supplies. The prognosis, under pre-NEP policies, was pessimistic: a worsening of Canada's oil supply-demand balance, with an increasing dependence on imports. Oil demand was expected to continue rising, while supply capacity declined, over most of this decade. The government's promise to strengthen Petro-Canada's role as a catalyst in frontier exploration is only one aspect of an ambitious program to increase Canadian oil supply capacity while dramatically reducing oil demand. As with all insurance policies, we will not know whether the costs of the premium paid are excessive until much later.

Second, the federal government now intends to use Petro-Canada to back up its new policy of Canadianizing the oil industry and to ensure that an increasing percentage of the direct and spin-off benefits from new energy developments are captured by Canadians. Thus the company is being used as an agent to acquire foreign-controlled oil companies. This is to be financed, in part, from a new Canadian ownership levy on oil and gas consumption. Moreover, Petro-Canada will be given a central role in the government's strategy of managing developments on the Canada Lands. While the petroleum industry and the federal Conservative Party have strongly attacked these features of the National Energy Program, most Canadians appear to agree with the government's view that it would be inappropriate to raise domestic oil and gas prices toward world levels without ensuring that the economic rents and other benefits accrue to Canadians, not to the shareholders of the large foreign-owned petroleum companies. The latter should not be encouraged to expand their control into other sectors of the Canadian economy as part of the price of greater energy efficiency. Undoubtedly the Canadianization program also involves costs, but it is not clear that these exceed those that would have been incurred by raising prices without attempting to restructure the petroleum industry. Inertia carries its own opportunity cost.

Critics of the National Energy Program have argued that the Canadian Ownership Account, which is a new levy on oil consumption to finance an increase in public ownership in the energy sector, encourages inefficiency in the public sector since it allows crown corporations to acquire new properties without drawing on their own resources or increasing their burden of debt. They charge that Petro-Canada's purchase of Petrofina Canada Inc. in early 1981— for $120 per share—permitted the Belgian shareholders of Petrofina to capitalize future economic rents, thus vitiating the entire aim of the Canadianization program. Petro-Canada and the government have sidestepped this claim, arguing that the price paid for Petrofina Canada was reasonable and not at all out of line with some of the premiums recently paid by private-sector Canadian firms for foreign-controlled assets.[33] It is exceedingly difficult to say whether the price paid for Petrofina was unreasonably inflated, but it is clear that the Canadian ownership levy does give Petro-Canada an opportunity to expand its share of ownership of Canadian petroleum industry assets without significantly increasing its already large debt/equity ratio. Since the federal government apparently does not wish to contemplate the alternative of nationalization and insists on using Petro-Canada as its vehicle for acquiring foreign-owned properties, it seems reasonable for the government itself to pay for the program. To insist that Petro-Canada do so would only cripple the state company with debt and make it impossible for it to carry out its policy mandate. On the other hand, the critics of the NEP are probably right to argue that this method of increasing public ownership contains few incentives for the efficient expenditure of scarce public resources, and it is not surprising that private-sector oil companies are displeased with the concept.

Third, notwithstanding the opinions of many oil industry spokesmen, Petro-Canada's record of finding new oil and gas re-

serves appears to be strong when compared with the industry's overall performance. Aside from its participation in several of the major
frontier discoveries, noted earlier, the state company maintains a
fairly large program of exploratory and development drilling in
Western Canada to augment its earnings. Its investment criteria
are little different here than that of the industry in general. In 1980
Petro-Canada's success ratio in exploratory drilling was the same
as that for the oil and gas industries—about 65 percent. The state
company spent $320 million in Western Canada in 1980, or less than
4 percent of total industry expenditures for exploration, capital
projects, and operating costs, and produced 22.5 million barrels
of oil and natural gas liquids and 122 billion cubic feet of natural
gas, while adding 11.6 million barrels of new proven oil reserves
and 391 billion cubic feet of new proven gas reserves. The state
company's proven oil reserves declined less than the industry's as
a whole and its record of adding new gas reserves was somewhat
better than that of the industry.[34]

Finally, although it is inherently difficult to assess Petro-
Canada's value to the government as a "window on the industry," it
can be plausibly argued that the company's operational experience
has given Ottawa a stronger capacity to bargain with the producing
provinces and the major oil companies and has diminished the ability of the companies to impose their terms by reallocating their investments. And while there certainly are grounds for questioning
some aspects of federal energy policy, there can be little doubt that
the national government is much more competent today in the area
of energy analysis than it was, say, in early 1975 when the hurried
decision was made to rescue the Syncrude project.[35] Again it
seems not unreasonable to attribute some of the growth in competence and expertise to the insights acquired from Petro-Canada's
activities.

There is much more to be said on these subjects and about
Petro-Canada's future growth and role in the Canadian oil and gas
industries. Enough however has been said here to make it clear
that, in my view, Canada is better off on balance for having established its own national oil company. The levels of public ownership and state participation envisaged in the National Energy Program remain modest by international standards. They are modest
enough that fears about runaway state capitalism in the Canadian oil
industry seem premature, to say the least.

NOTES

1. P. S. Smith, Oil and Politics in Modern Brazil (Toronto:
Macmillan, 1976), p. 101.

2. In this chapter, "state oil companies" and "national oil companies" are used interchangeably. There are state oil companies (e.g., Quebec's Soquip or Saskatchewan's Saskoil) that are owned by subnational governments, but here we are only dealing with those operating at the national level.

3. For example, see Kenneth Dam, Oil Resources: Who Gets What How? (Chicago: University of Chicago Press, 1976); Colin Robinson and Jon Morgan, North Sea Oil in the Future (London: Macmillan, 1978); Neil H. Jacoby, Multinational Oil (New York: Macmillan, 1974); James M. Griffin and Henry B. Steele, Energy Economics and Policy (New York: Academic Press, 1980).

4. Jacoby, Multinational Oil, p. 282.

5. J. E. Stiglitz, "A Neoclassical Analysis of the Economics of Natural Resources," in Scarcity and Growth Reconsidered, ed. V. Kerry Smith (Baltimore: Johns Hopkins University Press, 1979), p. 64.

6. H. J. Barnett and C. Morse, Scarcity and Growth: The Economics of Natural Resource Availability (Baltimore: Johns Hopkins University Press, 1963), p. 240.

7. Robinson and Morgan, North Sea Oil in the Future, pp. 43-44.

8. Ibid., p. 200.

9. Griffin and Steele, Energy Economics and Policy, pp. 284-86.

10. Ian Smart, "Energy and the Public Good," International Journal 36 (Spring 1981):225-72.

11. For a useful discussion, see Oystein Noreng, The Oil Industry and Government Strategy in the North Sea (Boulder, Colo.: International Research Center for Energy and Economic Development, 1980). See also L. E. Grayson, National Oil Companies (New York: Wiley, 1981), for a good comparative overview of Western Europe's national oil companies.

12. See, for example, Anthony Sampson, The Seven Sisters: The Great Oil Companies and the World They Made (London: Hodder and Stoughton, 1975).

13. P. H. Frankel, "The Rationale of National Oil Companies," in State Petroleum Enterprises in Developing Countries, U.N. Center for Natural Resources, Energy and Transport (New York: Praeger, 1980), p. 5.

14. Canada, House of Commons, Standing Committee on Natural Resources and Public Works, Minutes of Proceedings (Ottawa: Minister of Supply and Services Canada, 1981).

15. The two systems are discussed at length in Dam, Oil Resources.

16. Norway, Report No. 30 to the Norwegian Storting (1973-74), p. 44: "Operations of such magnitude as these will naturally have effects upon the community, effects far beyond the direct results of actual exploration and exploitation. Active participation creates insight and through that a better basis for exercising influence upon events connected with activities on the continental shelf."

17. Noreng, The Oil Industry and Government Strategy in the North Sea, pp. 120-24.

18. J. La Palombara and S. Blank, Multinational Corporations and Developing Countries, Report No. 767 (New York: The Conference Board, 1980).

19. Department of Energy, Mines and Resources, The National Energy Program, 1980 (Ottawa: EMR, 1980).

20. P. H. Frankel, Mattei: Oil and Power Politics (New York: Praeger, 1966), p. 167.

21. This material is taken from L. Pratt, "Petro-Canada," in Public Corporations and Public Policy in Canada, ed. Allan Tupper and G. Bruce Doern (Montreal: The Institute for Research on Public Policy, 1981).

22. This was done largely by the National Energy Program announced in October 1980. See note 19.

23. Hon. D. S. Macdonald, "A National Energy Company," Memorandum to Cabinet, October 31, 1973, p. 34. See also Pratt, "Petro-Canada."

24. Petro-Canada Act (1975), Canada Gazette 1, no. 11, see pt. III, chap. 61, clause 7(1).

25. See note 19. A conservative critique of the NEP is contained in C. Watkins and M. Walker, eds., Reaction: The National Energy Program (Vancouver: The Fraser Institute, 1981).

26. The Canada Oil and Gas Act reserves to the federal crown a 25 percent carried interest in every right on Canada Lands. These interests will probably be held by Petro-Canada.

27. Petrofina is to be paid for over a period of years.

28. These figures and the ones that follow are in Canadian dollars. During most of 1981 the Canadian dollar traded at U.S. 80¢ to 85¢.

29. See Pratt, "Petro-Canada," for the relevant tables.

30. In 1981 the capital cost of adding 140,000 barrels per day of synthetic oil from a new oil sands mining project is estimated at $13 billion. This is close to $80,000 of capital investment per daily barrel, about twice the current estimated unit costs of developing offshore oil finds in the Beaufort Sea or the Newfoundland Grand Banks!

31. These forecasts are contained in Petro-Canada's analyses of Canadian oil supply and demand and in speeches by the company's

exploration executives. The government itself appears to view these forecasts skeptically.

32. John Helliwell, "Canadian Energy Policy," Annual Review of Energy, 1979, p. 210.

33. Editors' note: On February 2, 1981, Petro-Canada offered $120 per share for Petrofina Canada. In August 1980 the stock had been selling for about $56 and in November it was about $73 per share. A major investment dealer, Wood Gundry Ltd., estimated Petrofina's net asset value at $82 per share. The Minister of Energy, Mines and Resources in a letter to the editor defended the deal; see Vancouver Sun, February 25, 1981, p. A5.

34. The most detailed analysis of Petro-Canada's performance concludes that the company has effectively accelerated the development of energy resources in high-cost, high-risk areas and that it has served the Canadian government as a useful "window" on the petroleum industry. It also argues that "Petro-Canada operates as efficiently as the private sector, neither producing substantially less than private companies nor providing an increase in conventional oil and gas production beyond what private companies could have supplied." There was, the study concludes, insufficient evidence to determine whether Petro-Canada is a more or less effective oil importer than private firms or whether state-to-state transactions will enhance security of supply. U.S. General Accounting Office, Petro-Canada: The National Oil Company as a Tool of Canadian Energy Policy (Washington, D.C.: U.S. Government Printing Office, 1981). See also data from Petro-Canada sources and from Oilweek's annual review of the industry.

35. See Larry Pratt, Tar Sands (Edmonton: Hurtig, 1976).

4

SELLING PUBLIC ENTERPRISES TO THE TAXPAYERS: THE CASE OF THE BRITISH COLUMBIA RESOURCES INVESTMENT CORPORATION

T. M. Ohashi

INTRODUCTION

The British Columbia Resources Investment Corporation (BRIC) story is a real life example of privatization, that is, the opposite of nationalization. If nationalization is taking control of something from the private sector to the public sector, then privatization is taking control of something from the public sector to the private sector. Because privatization is a less frequent occurrence, BRIC has attracted considerable attention.

BRIC was spawned in the political arena. The province of British Columbia has been governed by the Social Credit Party (SOCRED) 26 of the past 29 years.[1] But it is not the 26 years that are of as much interest as those three scant years in which the New Democratic Party (NDP) was in power.[2] The New Democratic Party between 1972 and 1975 nationalized a number of assets in British Columbia. It took over Columbia Cellulose, Plateau Mills, Kootenay Forest Products, and 10 percent of Westcoast Transmission.[3] The NDP entered the housing field, coal mining, purchased a bus line, and an alfalfa plant. In addition, it provided a grant for a fish canning cooperative, planned a poultry corporation, and monopolized automobile insurance. The widely read and influential Barron's Magazine at the time called British Columbia the "Chile of the North."

The platforms for the December 1975 provincial election were set. The self-acknowledged Socialist NDP promised more nationalization while the self-appointed free enterprise SOCREDs promised, in effect, some privatization. When the smoke cleared and the SOCREDs were back in power they discovered their promise was easier said than done. These were the horns of their dilemma. If they took the assets and sold them back to the public and they subsequently fell in value, it would be the "big bad business-backed government" dumping assets on the "poor helpless public." If they took the assets and sold them back to the public and they rose in value, it would be a case of the big bad business-backed government making a poor judgment about the future of the fine investments made by the former NDP government. In game theory, this is called "lose-lose." In real life, it is called "no win." In politics, it is called suicide.

So it fell to the financial community to defy the laws of nature and make a "lose-lose" into a "win-win." I will not go into the details of how their proposals developed but I will say that we shed some new light on the term "complex."[4] It was not until 1977 that the B.C. Resources Investment Corporation Act was given first reading.

THE BRIC LEGISLATION

These were some of the key points in the legislation establishing BRIC:

The lieutenant-governor in council (cabinet) is empowered to appoint five people to incorporate a new company. Those persons can establish the articles and memorandum of the company.

If the government holds 10 percent or more of the shares, it can appoint: one director if the total is four or less; two directors if the total is five to eight; three directors if the total is more than eight.

In any offering of shares, preference will be given to residents of British Columbia.

Shareholdings are restricted to 1 percent for individuals and 3 percent for institutions.

Associated members are precluded. Associated members are ". . . Parties to an agreement or arrangement a purpose of which, in the opinion of the board, is to require the members to act in concert with respect to their interests in the company." If you are deemed to be an associated member, you can be required to sell your shares within 60 days, or have your share redeemed (read expropriated) at the lesser of the issue price or the market price.

The company is not a crown agent.

The BRIC Act came into law on September 1, 1977, but it was a case of the cart before the horse. While the political process was creating law, the financial alchemists were still wrestling with the formula to transform "lose-lose" to a "win-win" situation. The problem was not lost on the leader of the opposition, David Barrett, who said: "The people of this province are now being given the opportunity to sell off something to themselves that they already own. . . . We own these assets and we are going to sell them to ourselves for the second time . . . what we are dealing with is the opportunity to sell to ourselves something we have already paid for once."[5]

Of course, the argument does not stand up under the scrutiny of cold clear logic. However, logic often takes a back seat to other forces when it comes to British Columbia's resources.

FINANCIAL AND POLITICAL ALCHEMY

As of late 1978, the company had a board of directors comprised of five top businessmen in Vancouver and a president ahd chief executive officer. There was still, however, no resolution to the essential problem of how the issue was going to be done. In order to gain some insight into the final answer, you need to know a little bit about where the financial proposals had led.

From the perspective of the financial people, the assets under question were rich in value and poor in earnings. In addition, the analysts had their own unique perspective on the same problem: if the government transferred the assets to the new company too cheaply, the company might succeed but the government would fail; if the government transferred the assets to the new company too dearly, the company would fail and bring down the government with it. Within these parameters, a new security was needed that could pay a dividend, despite a shortage of income, and that could create a higher value despite the need to transfer assets at close to prevailing market worth. The answers the financial community was coming up with amounted to saving what income there was to pay to the public shareholders while giving the government nonincome-bearing paper with a nominal value close to market and a real value far below it.

The solution to this problem proved to be rather simple. Instead of selling the shares to the public they should be given to the public. Prior to this time, it had always been assumed that the government would sell its assets to the new company and the company would, in turn, sell its shares to the public. Now, however, a plan was conceived whereby the government would transfer assets to the new corporation in return for common shares and the government would then give those common shares to the public. It all seemed to be neat, clean, and simple.

So where did this solution come from? Out of the several possibilities I uncovered, three stand out as most likely. I mention
them in chronological order.

In December 1976, Milton Friedman stated in Newsweek,
"The supposed argument is that the people of Great Britain own the
steel industry: It is the property of all the citizens. Well, then,
why not give each citizen his piece." It is quite possible that the
words of the well-regarded and influential Friedman found their way
into the minds of the planners of B.C. Resources.

In August 1977, Gordon Gibson, leader of the Provincial Liberal Party, proposed a giveaway during a second reading of the
BRIC Act. His concept was to transfer assets to the new company
and have the government buy shares from the new company, thus
putting some funds into the corporate coffers. Then the government
would give away shares to the public. Because so many participants
were directly aware of Gibson's plan, it is most likely that this was
the source of the giveaway approach.

In December 1978, Bill Bennett, premier of British Columbia,
upon hearing a proposal that the government receive noninterest-
bearing securities in return for its assets, is reputed to have said,
in effect, "If that's all you're going to pay us for these assets, we
might as well give them away." Again, because it is the view of
many of the participants that the idea filtered down from above, it
is possible that it was the premier's idea born of a little frustration.

The giveaway plan resolved the key stumbling blocks. The
first was the "lose-lose" outcome: Because the shares were to be
given away, the "lose-lose" became a "win-win." If the shares
came out, began trading, and then dropped in value, it mattered
less because the shareholder cost was zero. If the price were $10,
$6, or $4 it mattered little. It was still more than the public paid
for them—nothing. If the shares rose in value it also mattered
little. Since the government was, in effect, a conduit in the transaction it was merely passing along the assets acquired by the former
administration in a different form. The political objectives were
met. Above all, each person (read voter) would be given securities
with a value of $25 to $50.

Second, the financial adviser's problem was overcome as
well. The privatizing process was accomplished by the share giveaway. Dividends were less important. Immediate appreciation was
less important. Again, it was now a no-lose situation.

The third stumbling block involved separation of privatizing
and financing. As long as shares were to be sold, the privatizing
process and the financing process were as one. With privatization
as a giveaway, the sale of shares was not encumbered by the act of
privatization. The giveaway almost ensured the success of the

privatization process. As long as privatization depended on investors putting up money to buy shares, it could fail. With the giveaway,
a successful subscription was almost a certainty.

A fourth stumbling block was the "sell out to the rich" perception. As long as privatization were to proceed by a share sale, the
sell out to the rich concept existed. That is because a wealthy person can more easily afford to buy the shares or, if possible, buy
more. Under the giveaway, everyone gets the same number of
shares.

Once this solution had been found, the issue gained renewed
momentum.[6] The BRIC issue was two issues in one. First, there
was the giveaway portion. The company had issued some 15 million
common shares to the government in return for $151.5 million in
assets. The government, in turn, would privatize British Columbia
resources by giving their shares to the residents of British Columbia at the rate of five per person. At the same time, BRIC was
offering to sell additional common shares at a price of $6 each to a
maximum of 5,000 shares per resident.

The results for both issues were astounding. First, 2,072,807
persons applied for their free shares. This was an estimated response rate of 86 percent. By all accounts, this was an exception-
ally high rate and well in excess of the 70 percent expected.[7]

Second, some 170,000 residents purchased additional shares
of B.C. Resources Investment Corporation: 128,211 individuals
bought 100 or more shares, 40,000 purchased less than 100 shares,
and 4,969 purchased the maximum 5,000 shares—an investment of
$30,000 each. In total, the issue raised $487.5 million, the third
largest common share underwriting in North American financial
history up to that time.

Who sold the shares? There were four major groups of
issuers: chartered banks, investment dealers, credit unions, and
trust companies. The chartered banks sold over one-half the
shares, the investment dealers over one-fourth, the credit unions
around 10 percent, and the trust companies approximately 5 percent.

Finally, how much did it all cost? I have estimated that the
total cost of the exercise was around $40 million. That is an all-
inclusive cost figure that includes printing of promotional material
and prospectuses, data processing, all fees and commissions, and
so on. That works out to a per capita cost of almost $17. It is
high when you consider that over 90 percent of individuals simply
applied for five free shares worth about $30. If you consider that
the normal gross underwriting commission averages around 4.5
percent of gross proceeds, then we can say that the underwriting
costs were roughly $18 million. Therefore, the giveaway was the
rest, or between $5.50 and $7.50 per person.

The issue was completed in June 1979 so we have seen the company operate for around two full years. It has been a boisterous period—full of controversy, turmoil, and experience. In that time, the shares have traded from an issue price of $6.00 to a high of $9.25 to a low of around $4.00.[8] In the next section I would like to look back and offer an assessment of the privatization process based on my experience with B.C. Resources. Then, in the last section I will take a brief look ahead at BRIC's prospects.

ASSESSING THE BRIC EXPERIENCE

In looking back, I have found that none of the original observations published in the fall of 1979[9] has changed much. Subsequent events, however, have affirmed the importance of some of the conclusions made at the time.

First, the sample of the British Columbia Resources Investment Corporation can be used as a model for other privatizations. Milton Friedman was probably just thinking out loud when he said ". . . give each citizen his piece," but B.C. Resources took that idea and made it happen. The pendulum has been swinging toward nationalization for some time but there is evidence of a new mood in North America. If the momentum shifts, who knows what changes might occur. Petro-Canada is certainly a candidate for privatization.[10] I would rather own my common shares of the Canada Development Corporation directly, thank you.[11] And, I can certainly see many benefits from having the president of the Canada Post Corporation, motivated by profits, delivering the mail to his shareholders and having his performance judged by the stock market every day.[12]

A second conclusion made at the time has gained particular importance with the benefit of hindsight. We have seen that the privatization and the financing processes were separate and distinct. I argued at the time that the privatization and financing in the case of BRIC were too closely related and that it would have been better to isolate the two. The problem currently faced is that a highly successful privatization has been clouded by a less successful common stock underwriting. One can only speculate what would have happened if the government had taken the original 15 million shares and purchased another 15 million shares for $100 million cash from B.C. Resources and given away 10 free shares per person. I suspect there would be far less dissatisfaction than there seems to be at present.

A third observation is that the desire to own shares is alive and well in our society. Part of this idea is derived from the statistics of the BRIC share sale—2 million shareholders; 170,000 purchasers buying extra shares. But the post-BRIC effect has also been significant. The inquiries, the articles on the stock market, the radio and television news reports all seem to suggest that having broken the ice by purchasing BRIC shares, many people went on to consider further investments. All of this is hard to measure, of course, and even harder to isolate as a BRIC effect but on a subjective basis, the BRIC issue certainly seemed to promote investment in the province.

The point I made about associated members remains valid, in my view. However, I believe that privatized companies should be the same as other companies and the associated members legislation seems unnecessary. In the spring of 1981, when there was a fair amount of public criticism directed toward the company, dissident shareholders were only able to gain the support of around one million shares or 10 percent of the total. To say that you need the associated members legislation to prevent shareholders from unnecessarily disrupting corporate operations is like saying you should use chemotherapy to combat the common cold.

Finally, I have a new observation based on the events of the past two years. A privatized company, at least in the early going, is much like a sports franchise. It makes its decisions in a goldfish bowl and it will be subjected to criticism, much of it ill-founded or misinformed. Let me give you two examples.

First, at the 1981 annual meeting BRIC intended to seek an increase in its authorized capital from 100 million to 200 million common shares and to authorize 100 million preferred shares. In the case of common shares, the company had issued 96.2 million of its 100 million authorized. In the case of preferred shares, it represented creation of a new class of security. This proposal relative to changing the authorized shares outstanding caused so much confusion, management withdrew the motion. Shareholders felt increasing the authorized shares outstanding would dilute their interests. They wanted to know why management wanted to issue more shares. In other words, due to a complete misunderstanding of the facts, management had to withdraw a normal and sensible corporate amendment.

Second, an article appearing in the Vancouver Sun during BRIC's attempt to acquire MacMillan Bloedel Ltd. was headlined "BRIC hasn't the money to raise its bid."[13] This headline was based upon analysis such as the following. Obviously ignorant of the fact that net earnings are calculated after interest payments are already deducted, one writer claimed that ". . . net earnings for the fourth quarter alone were only $4.1 million while its interest payments for the fourth quarter are estimated at about $18.1 million for a shortfall of $14 million." And another writer overlooked the fact that when you purchase shares, you are entitled to the earnings on those shares as well as expenses, stating ". . . and if BRIC manages to get MB at $46 a share, its annual net earnings would have to increase a whopping 148 percent, again just to cover the interest payments."

The power of the press is substantial and if that power is used irresponsibly as it was against BRIC the damage can be almost irreparable. The lesson here seems to be that a privatized company must be cognizant of its unique shareholders base and ensure that it communicates directly and through the press with the characteristics of its shareholders in mind.

THE FUTURE OF BRIC

I can see BRIC as a soundly based, resource-oriented company offering values that should be more highly regarded by investors across Canada. The company has a major interest through B.C. Coal (formerly Kaiser Resources Ltd.) in the largest, most modern, and most efficient coal operator in Canada.[14] The company has established production capacity in metallurgical coal, additional capacity due to come on-stream in late 1983, and an almost untapped potential in thermal coal production. In forest products, the company's operations under B.C. timber rank as the eleventh largest lumber producer in North America, which is significant if you consider the other participants. In addition, the company has two pulp mills capable of producing 520,000 tonnes of bleached kraft pulp annually.

In addition to B.C. coal and B.C. timber, BRIC has sizable interests in oil and gas exploration. The company has 929,000 net hectares of land in British Columbia and Alberta and 83,000 net hectares in the United States. It will participate in 59 wells in the current year and if it can successfully acquire an established oil and gas company, B.C. resources oil and gas exploration activities could be self-financing in short order.

When you add everything up, the company has a net asset value of around $10 per share compared with a market value of around $4.50 per share.[15] I believe the market value is depressed because of some misunderstandings: the thought that BRIC paid too much for their interest in Kaiser resources, the idea that management past and present has done a poor job, the notion that the company will not be able to withstand the current slump in demand for resources. In other words, the price of the shares is depressed by factors that will change over the next year. In my view, a year from now, shareholders in this privatized public enterprise will have been rewarded well in excess of the straight return on holding cash.

NOTES

1. For a general history, see Martin Robin, The Company Province (Toronto: McClelland and Stewart, 1972), 2 vols.

2. See Lorne Kavic and Gary Nixon, The 1200 Days: A Shattered Dream (Coquitlam, B.C.: Kaen, 1978).

3. Columbia Cellulose, renamed Canadian Cellulose, produces lumber and pulp. Westcoast Transmission operates a natural gas pipeline from northeastern British Columbia to Vancouver.

4. Editors' note: As senior vice-president of a major investment firm, T. M. Ohashi personally participated in this process. See T. M. Ohashi, "Privatization in Practice: The Story of the British Columbia Resources Investment Corporation," in Privatization: Theory and Practice, ed. T. M. Ohashi and T. P. Roth (Vancouver: The Fraser Institute, 1980), pp. 3-107.

5. British Columbia Hansard, August 31, 1977. Barrett is the leader of the New Democratic Party and was premier of British Columbia between 1975 and 1978.

6. A number of details have been omitted. See Ohashi, "Privatization in Practice."

7. Some 2,200 persons were so enthusiastic they applied for the five free shares more than once.

8. Editors' note: In December 1981 BRIC shares fell to $3.15.

9. See note 4.

10. Editors' note: Larry Pratt, the author of Chapter 3 on Petro-Canada, would probably disagree.

11. Editors' note: Presently the federal government owns 49 percent of the common shares of the Canada Development Corporation (CDC). CDC is not a crown corporation, although when it was created in 1971 its purpose was to "create, develop or acquire corporate ventures of benefit to Canada while simultaneously extending opportunities for Canadians to participate in their country's development." While the government contributed the entire equity ($250 million) in 1971, CDC has grown by selling its debt and equity to the private sector. Today CDC ranks in the top dozen corporations in Canada. At the end of 1980 its total revenues exceeded $2.5 billion and its assets $3.5 billion. Net income was $189 million—a 24.1 percent rate of return on equity. With the acquisition of Acquitane Canada Ltd., an oil company, and all of the Canadian assets of Texasgulf Sulphur in 1981, CDC's assets will exceed $6 billion.

More generally, see F. W. Sellars, "The Canada Development Corporation: What Happens When the Government Owns 49%?," paper presented to the Institute for Research on Public Policy/UCLA Conference on Managing Public Enterprises, Vancouver, B.C., August 13-14, 1981. See also Chapter 9 in this volume.

12. Editors' note: In November 1981 the Canadian Post Office was transformed into a federal crown corporation, the Canada Post Corporation. See R. Michael Warren, President Designate, Canada Post Corporation, "The Canadian Post Office: Will Making it a Crown Corporation Make Any Difference?," paper presented to the Institute for Research on Public Policy/UCLA Conference on Managing Public Enterprises, Vancouver, B.C., August 13-14, 1981.

13. Editors' Note: MacMillan Bloedel Ltd. is the largest forest products company in Canada. Its headquarters are in Vancouver. On April 6, 1981, Noranda Mines Ltd. offered $62 per share for 49.8 percent of MacMillan Bloedel Ltd. The total value of the offer, which was successful, was $625 million. BRIC had originally bid $46 per share for up to 49 percent of MacMillan Bloedel.

14. On September 3, 1980, BRIC offered $55 per share for control of Kaiser Resources Ltd. (KRL). The day before KRL shares were trading for $32 to $33. BRIC eventually obtained 66 percent of Kaiser's shares at a total cost of $655 million. In 1979 KRL's revenues were $597 million.

15. See note 8.

II
THE PERFORMANCE OF PUBLIC ENTERPRISES

5

ECONOMIC PERFORMANCE OF U.S. AND CANADIAN RAILROADS: THE SIGNIFICANCE OF OWNERSHIP AND THE REGULATORY ENVIRONMENT

Douglas W. Caves, Laurits R. Christensen,
Joseph A. Swanson, and Michael W. Tretheway

INTRODUCTION

Assessing the economic performance of firms under varying forms of industrial organization is a major concern of economists. Two aspects of organization that are of particular interest are the type of ownership (private versus public) and the degree to which economic regulation prevents (or shields) firms from freely competing in their product markets. Regulation may include or exclude freedom to enter or exit from specific markets and freedom to set prices on goods and services.

Many discussions of the effects of ownership and regulation do not address the possibility of significant interactions between these two aspects of organization. In particular, it is often not recognized that publicly owned firms are not necessarily given monopoly status and shielded from competition. Some writers have recognized this possibility, and have generally conjectured that publicly owned firms would exhibit better economic performance if they were subject to competition. For example, Sam Peltzman suggests: "The differences between government monopolies and government firms with private competitors might be greater than the differences between government firms and private firms in competition with one another."[1] A similar opinion is expressed by Spann: "One would expect competition to exert some market pressure on government enterprises to hold down costs . . . and to eliminate some of the opportunities for discretionary behavior on the part of bureaucracies."[2]

Sorting out the effects of ownership and regulation is not an easy task, but an opportunity to gain some insight on this issue is provided by the North American railroad industry. In this industry we have examples of all possible combinations of ownership and regulation. Until very recently U.S. railroads have been heavily regulated while Canadian railroads were relatively unfettered in their commercial pursuits. In Canada two railroads dwarf the remaining few. These two railroads are roughly equal in size, and have been direct competitors throughout most of Canada since the 1920s. The most interesting aspect of this competition is that one of the railroads is privately owned—the Canadian Pacific (CP)—and the other is public owned—the Canadian National (CN). In the United States, railroads have been almost exclusively privately owned and operated, but the formation of Conrail in 1976 provides an interesting counterpoint.

Our objective in this chapter is to document the economic performance of U.S. and Canadian railroads in the postwar period and to draw whatever inferences are possible with respect to the issues of differential ownership and regulation. The measure of economic performance that we employ is total factor productivity (TFP), which is widely regarded as the best single measure of productive efficiency. TFP reflects real output per unit of real resources expended.[3]

This chapter presents estimates of relative levels of productivity for U.S. and Canadian railroads, in addition to the more commonly reported rates of growth of productivity.

PUBLIC POLICY TOWARD THE U.S. AND CANADIAN RAILROAD INDUSTRIES

The purpose of this section is to provide background information that is relevant to the comparison of economic performance among U.S. and Canadian railroads.

The Canadian Pacific became a transcontinental railroad in 1885, largely as the result of massive aid from the Canadian government. The major impetus was a desire to tie British Columbia to the other provinces and to facilitate development of all of Canada's western provinces.[4] During the last half of the nineteenth century numerous other railroads were established, also with generous amounts of government construction, financing, subsidies, and land grants. By World War I it was clear that the Canadian rail network was severely overexpanded.

After the war the federal government took over three large privately owned rail systems that were near bankruptcy, and amalgamated them with the existing Canadian Government Railways to form the Canadian National Railway. Thus the CN had an inauspicious beginning as a government-owned firm with massive amounts of debt and extensive overlapping facilities.[5] However, the structure of the Canadian railroad industry was clearly established in the 1920s, a structure that has persisted to this day.

The beginnings of the U.S. railroad industry were similar to those of Canada with numerous railroads commencing operations in the nineteenth century. Contrary to Canada, however, U.S. public policy proscribed rather than encouraged the development of any transcontinental railroads. As a result, the structure of the industry evolved more slowly than in Canada. Many U.S. railroads fell on hard times in the twentieth century, but the U.S. federal government did not assume ownership of any railroads. Although reorganizations gradually reduced the number of U.S. railroads, there were still more than 60 Class I U.S. railroads in 1955. They varied tremendously in size, but all were privately owned.

Not until the 1970s did the U.S. government become actively involved in the running of railroads. In 1971 the government formed Amtrak, which took over the bulk of long-haul passenger service from U.S. railroads.[6] Then in 1976 Conrail was formed after the Penn Central bankruptcy. These developments have both been sufficiently recent that they do not provide us with data on the performance of government-run U.S. railroads. Thus, for the time period covered in this chapter we treat the entire U.S. railroad industry as privately owned.

Thus far we have noted two ways in which Canadian policy toward the railroad industry differed from that of the United States. Canada fostered the development of large transcontinental railroads as well as creating the largest railroad in the country as a public enterprise. These differences were far from the only ones, however, and the rest of this section describes the evolution of regulatory policies in the two countries.

In the early decades of their existence the railroads of both the United States and Canada were viewed as having substantial monopoly power. Consequently, they faced substantial government regulation. But in the 1930s railroads began to face significant competition from trucks and water carriers. These modes were not regulated by the Canadian government. In the United States, however, Interstate Commerce Commission (ICC) regulation was extended to trucking in 1935 and to water carriage in 1940, largely as an attempt to protect the railroads. In spite of such regulation, there were incursions into the railroads' market share in the United States as well as Canada. During World War II railroad freight traffic in both countries more than doubled, but in the postwar period intermodal competition, aided by government investment in highways and waterways, resulted in sharply declining market shares for the railroads. In the United States, the railroads' share of freight ton-miles supplied by rail, truck, and water fell from 78 percent in 1945 to 60 percent in 1955. The share in Canada fell from 73 percent in 1944 to 61 percent in 1956.[7]

Low earnings of the railroads in the postwar period led to the establishment of government committees in the United States and Canada to study their problems. In Canada, W. F. A. Turgeon headed the Royal Commissions on Transportation in 1948 and 1954. In the United States, President Eisenhower appointed a Presidential Advisory Committee on Transport Policy and Organization, which was chaired by Secretary of Commerce Sinclair Weeks. The Weeks committee and the Turgeon commission issued reports in 1955 that were remarkably similar in tone. Both recommended that competition be allowed to play a greater role in the evolution of the transportation system.

The scope of the Weeks committee report was very broad, declaring that the U.S. national transportation policy should ". . . encourage and promote full competition between modes of transportation . . ." and ". . . reduce economic regulation of transportation to the minimum consistent with the public interest. . . ." The report was favorably received by many transportation economists, but opposition from truck and water interests and from the ICC was strong. Although a Transportation Act was passed in 1958, by the mid-1960s a number of ICC and court decisions made it clear that the Weeks committee and the act had failed to produce any significant changes in U.S. regulatory practice.

The scope of the Turgeon commission report was narrower than its U.S. counterpart, but it had an immediate effect on Canadian transportation policy. The principal result was that the railroads acquired substantial freedom to negotiate "agreed charges" with individual shippers in lieu of published rates.[8] Agreed charges were first permitted by the Canadian Transport Act of 1938, but they were little used until it was modified on the recommendation of the Turgeon commission. Thereafter, the use of agreed charges increased rapidly; the number of agreements nearly doubled in each year from 1956 to 1959 and grew at an annual rate of 14 percent from 1959 to 1966.[9]

Not only did the Turgeon commission have an immediate impact on transportation policy, it also provided momentum for further change. In 1959 another Royal Commission on Transportation (the MacPherson Commission) was appointed that made broad recommendations in 1961 similar to those of the Weeks committee. Contrary to the U.S. experience, most of these recommendations were adopted in the National Transportation Act of 1967. This legislation was important not so much in terms of providing new opportunities for selective rate making by the railroads, but rather in removing much of the government's power to countermand such actions. For example, the 1967 act repealed the power of the Board of Transport Commissioners to postpone the effective date of a rate or suspend any rate pending investigation.[10]

Deregulation of the Canadian railroad industry was a gradual process. Furthermore, the opportunities that were thereby afforded to the railroads were only gradually exploited. Not until the late 1950s did the Canadian railroads perceive their environment as being substantially less regulated than the United States. By 1960 both Canadian railroads had set up new Traffic Research Departments. These departments were expected to ". . . study ways and means to facilitate competition with other transport modes," mainly trucking, by differential competitive pricing techniques and by improved services.[11] During this period the proportion of revenues realized from class rates and noncompetitive commodity rates declined substantially while the proportion of revenue realized from agreed charges and competitive commodity rates rose greatly.[12] Information in trade journals also points to the late-1950s as a watershed. For example, according to a current high official of the CN: "Thus, from 1957 onwards, there was decreasing interference from regulatory agencies in the rate action taken by the railways."[13]

In sharp contrast to developments in Canada, U.S. railroads continued to operate in an environment with substantially less pricing freedom. Attempts at selective rate making were generally thwarted by an anachronistic regulatory tradition that encouraged protection of potentially "injured" competitors. Regulatory proceedings during this era contain numerous examples of the frustrations experienced by U.S. railroads.[14]

Although Canadian railroads enjoy substantial commercial freedom, this freedom is not complete. Canadian railroads have limited discretion to withdraw from markets. They are also required to haul some commodities at fixed rates. For example, Canadian railroads are required by law to haul grain and flour destined for export at the rates that prevailed in 1897.[15] They incur large deficits hauling these commodities, which account for more ton-miles than any other—27 percent of combined CN and CP ton-miles in 1973.[16] The burden that this imposes on the CN and CP is that they must cover these losses from other revenues. This makes it more difficult for them to be competitive with other transport modes.

The CN and CP have thousands of miles of lightly used and unprofitable branch lines, some of which is a consequence of having to haul grain and flour at very low rates. Although the 1967 National Transportation Act ended rate regulation, it protected unprofitable branch lines from abandonment. As a result, there has been no decline in miles of railroad operated by the CN and CP. Thus the regulatory policy toward railroad abandonment in Canada has been similar to that in the United States, where until recently only limited abandonment was permitted.

In summary, for at least the last two decades, Canadian railroads have operated in a much less regulated environment than U.S. railroads. Thus we have the somewhat paradoxical situation of a large government enterprise, the CN railway, operating in a situation with much more commercial freedom than the privately owned railroads in the United States. This provides us with two interesting comparisons: first, between the public and privately owned railroads in an unregulated environment; and second, between regulated and unregulated railroad industries.

TECHNOLOGY AND OPERATING CONDITIONS FOR U.S. AND CANADIAN RAILROADS

Railroads in the United States and Canada have historically had similar access to improvements in technology. We are aware of only one major dissimilarity in the diffusion of new technology in U.S. and Canadian railroads. With few exceptions, U.S. railroads had effectively replaced steam locomotives with diesels by 1956. On the other hand, the transition to diesel locomotives by the CN and CP was not completed until 1960.

Labor practices have been very similar in U.S. and Canadian railroads, in large part due to substantial overlap in the unions that represent U.S. and Canadian railroad employees. While restrictive work rules have been cited as impediments to U.S. railroad efficiency, there appears to be little difference in such practices between the United States and Canada. In the late 1950s and early 1960s the CP was more successful than the CN or U.S. railroads in reducing the employment of firemen. By 1974, however, there was no readily discernible difference in labor practices between U.S. and Canadian railroads.

The climate in Canada is less hospitable to railroad operations than in the United States. The longer and more severe winters in Canada impose major costs on the CN and CP. Few, if any, U.S. carriers must bear these costs to such an extent. In extremely cold weather, train sizes must be reduced to counter losses in air brake efficiency, and train speeds must be lowered to cope with frost damage to roadbeds. Locomotive failures also increase at very low temperatures. Snow impedes both train operations and classification yard activity as well as imposing significant costs of removal. In 1974 the combined CN and CP snow removal expenditures were nearly as large as those of the entire U.S. Class I railroad industry. Both cold weather and snow inhibit track maintenance and repair for much longer periods in Canada than in the United States.

METHODOLOGY FOR MEASUREMENT OF TOTAL FACTOR PRODUCTIVITY

Laurits R. Christensen and Dale W. Jorgenson proposed the following index of total factor productivity:[17]

$$
\ln (TFP_k/TFP_l) = \sum_i \left(\frac{R_{ik} + R_{il}}{2} \right) \ln (Y_{ik}/Y_{il}) \tag{1}
$$
$$
- \sum_i \left(\frac{S_{ik} + S_{il}}{2} \right) \ln (X_{ik}/X_{il}),
$$

where k and l are adjacent time periods, the Ys are output indexes, the Xs are input indexes, the Rs are output revenue shares, the Ss are input cost shares, and the i subscripts denote the individual outputs or inputs. W. E. Diewert has shown equation 1 to be the exact index procedure that corresponds to a homogeneous translog production or transformation function.[18] Douglas W. Caves, Christensen, and Diewert have further shown that no restrictions of separability or neutral technological change are implicit in equation 1.[19]

Caves, Christensen, and Swanson (CCS) have noted that it is not justifiable to use equation 1 to measure TFP in the railroad industry.[20] The problem is that the revenue shares in equation 1 are used as estimates of the elasticities of total cost with respect to the individual outputs. This procedure is satisfactory only if the price of each output is equal to its marginal cost of production. It is widely accepted that prices for railroad services do not reflect marginal costs of production. Thus CCS proposed that railroad TFP measurements make use of estimated output cost elasticities in place of revenue shares:

$$
\ln(TFP_k/TFP_l) = \sum_i \left[\frac{1}{2} \left(\frac{\partial \ln C}{\partial \ln Y_i} \right)_k + \frac{1}{2} \left(\frac{\partial \ln C}{\partial \ln Y_i} \right)_l \right] \ln(Y_{ik}/Y_{il})
$$
$$
- \sum_i \left(\frac{S_{ik} + S_{il}}{2} \right) \ln(X_{ik}/X_{il}). \tag{2}
$$

We follow CCS in using equation 2 to compute TFP for the CN and CP in the next section. As pointed out by Jorgenson and Meiko Nishimizu, formulas such as equations 1 and 2 can be used to make both time-series and cross-sectional comparisons of TFP.[21] In the case of cross-sectional comparisons, the indexes k and l are interpreted as different firms rather than different time periods. We follow Jorgenson and Nishimizu in choosing a base year (1963) to carry out a comparison of the levels of CN and CP productivity. The growth rates of CN and CP productivity are used to extend the level comparison to earlier and later years.

In the later section on total factor productivity growth for Class I U.S. railroads, we require a procedure for making a multilateral comparison of TFP for 19 railroads over a 20-year period. Caves, Christensen, and Diewert have proposed the following procedure for such a comparison:[22]

$$ln\ (TFP_k/TFP_l) = \tfrac{1}{2}\sum_i (R_i^k + \bar{R}_i)(ln\ Y_i^k - \overline{ln\ Y_i}) \tag{3}$$

$$- \tfrac{1}{2}\sum_i (R_i^l + \bar{R}_i)(ln\ Y_i^l - \overline{ln\ Y_i})$$

$$- \tfrac{1}{2}\sum_n (S_n^k + \bar{S}_n)(ln\ X_n^k - \overline{ln\ X_n})$$

$$+ \tfrac{1}{2}\sum_n (S_n^l + \bar{S}_n)(ln\ X_n^l - \overline{ln\ X_n}),$$

where $\bar{R}$ is the revenue share for output i averaged over all firms and time periods, $\bar{S}_n$ is the average cost share for input n, $\overline{ln\ Y_i}$ is the average of the log of output i, and $\overline{ln\ X_n}$ is the average of the log of input n. All bilateral comparisons based on equation 3 are both base-firm and base-year invariant; they are also transitive as well as having a high degree of characteristicity (as defined by L. Dreschler.[23] In addition, equation 3 reduces to equation 1 if there are only two firms in the sample. For use with railroad data, equation 3 must be modified by substituting cost elasticities for the revenue shares, as in equation 2.

A further modification of equation 2 is required because not all of the railroads to be compared in the later section on total factor productivity growth have passenger operations. Equation 3 does not permit zero values for any output or input levels. Thus we are faced with the choice of eliminating the firms with zero output levels or employing a different procedure for the multilateral comparison. This same problem was confronted in the context of econometric estimation by Caves, Christensen, and M. W. Tretheway.[24] They developed a new functional form, the generalized translog, that permitted zero levels of passenger output. We have derived the multilateral index number formula from a generalized translog transformation function. Making this formula as well as substituting cost elasticities for revenue shares yields the index number procedure that we employ later:

$$\ln(TFP_k/TFP_l) = \frac{1}{2} \sum_i (W_i^k + \overline{W}_i)(Z_i^k - \overline{Z}_i) \qquad (4)$$

$$- \frac{1}{2} \sum_i (W_i^l + \overline{W}_i)(Z_i^l - \overline{Z}_i)$$

$$- \frac{1}{2} \sum_n (S_n^k + \overline{S}_n)(\ln X_n^k - \overline{\ln X_n})$$

$$+ \frac{1}{2} \sum_n (S_n^l + \overline{S}_n)(\ln X_n^l - \overline{\ln X_n}),$$

where $W_i = (\partial \ln C / \partial \ln Y_i)(Y_i^{-\lambda})$, $Z_i = (Y_i^{\lambda} - 1)/$, and λ is the Box-Cox parameter.

BILATERAL COMPARISON OF CANADIAN NATIONAL AND CANADIAN PACIFIC TOTAL FACTOR PRODUCTIVITY

In this section we make use of data for the CN and CP to perform a binary productivity comparison. A detailed description of the sources and methods used to develop our data base is contained in Caves and Christensen.[25] We have relied heavily on the annual reports of the CN and CP filed with the Canadian Transport Commission (CTC). The CTC provided us with access to these reports and made available supplementary data that were essential for completion of the study. The annual reports follow the Uniform System of Accounts instituted in 1956. Accounting procedures and reporting practices before 1956 were significantly different from those instituted in 1956. Thus, our study is limited to the period from 1956 to 1979, the most recent year for which annual reports were available. The major task in the data development involved the estimation of capital input for structures and equipment. The procedures that we have used are very similar to those suggested by Christensen and Jorgenson.[26]

We use equation 2 for the bilateral comparison, which requires data on individual inputs and outputs and their corresponding
cost shares and cost elasticities. We proceed to discuss the individual series used in the comparison.

In principle, it would be desirable to treat as distinct outputs
all railroad services that have different cost elasticities. In practice, however, it is not possible to distinguish more than a few
relatively homogeneous output categories. The most important
distinction is between freight and passenger services. It would
also be desirable to allow for different cost levels associated with
hauling different commodities. Unfortunately, it is not possible to
do so with any assurance on the basis of available data.[27] Thus,
we limit our output categories to freight and passenger services.

In measuring output, rail analysts have long recognized that
freight service has both weight and distance components. These
are reflected in the number of tons loaded and the distance over
which the tons are hauled. Passenger service can be broken into
two analogous components, the number of passengers boarded and
the length of the trip. Traditionally, measures of freight and passenger service have been formed by multiplying the weight and
distance components, resulting in ton-miles and passenger-miles.
A less restrictive procedure is to maintain the distinction between
weight and distance and to use four output indexes: tons of freight,
average length of freight haul, number of passengers, and average
length of passenger trip. These indexes can be combined in various
ways as long as weight and distance are both indicated. Our procedure is to use the following four indexes: ton-miles of freight,
average length of freight haul, passenger-miles, and average length
of passenger trip. The advantage of this procedure is that the traditional output measures appear explicitly, and therefore comparisons between the two approaches are facilitated. One can interpret our specification either as utilizing the two traditional
output measures and controlling for length of haul, or as utilizing
four distinct output indexes. The results are, of course, invariant
to the interpretation one prefers. In Table 5.1 we present the
ratios of the four output indexes for the CN relative to the CP.

The CN and CP experienced declines in both freight and passenger output in the late 1950s. After 1960, however, freight output grew steadily for both carriers. Passenger output continued to
fall except for the mid-1960s. Over the full period CN and CP
freight ton-miles grew at very similar rates, but CP passenger-
miles declined much more than those of the CN. In 1979 the CN
had 1.34 times as many ton-miles as the CP and nearly five times
as many passenger-miles. The CN's average length of freight haul
was only slightly longer than the CP, but its average passenger trip
was more than three times as long.

TABLE 5.1

Ratios of CN to CP Output Indexes

Year	Ton-Miles	Average Haul	Passenger- Miles	Average Trip
1956	1.235	0.948	1.055	0.647
1957	1.211	0.906	1.040	0.665
1958	1.187	0.920	1.019	0.679
1959	1.241	0.999	1.060	0.706
1960	1.200	1.002	1.105	0.708
1961	1.199	1.043	1.195	0.668
1962	1.241	1.033	1.245	0.690
1963	1.260	1.007	1.329	0.703
1964	1.205	0.967	1.504	0.710
1965	1.249	0.953	1.907	0.781
1966	1.199	0.943	3.466	1.282
1967	1.263	0.976	3.881	1.352
1968	1.313	0.982	4.008	1.522
1969	1.312	0.963	3.658	1.418
1970	1.237	1.019	3.948	1.627
1971	1.254	1.031	4.400	1.777
1972	1.255	0.993	4.548	1.982
1973	1.195	0.954	4.810	2.181
1974	1.284	0.991	3.812	1.648
1975	1.290	1.095	4.625	2.115
1976	1.373	1.060	5.555	2.613
1977	1.345	1.086	5.466	2.213
1978	1.315	1.024	5.077	1.973
1979	1.339	1.060	4.930	3.133

Average Growth Rates

Year	Ton-Miles	Average Haul	Passenger- Miles	Average Trip
1956-60	-0.7	1.4	1.2	2.3
1960-65	0.8	-1.0	10.9	2.0
1965-70	-0.2	1.3	14.6	14.7
1970-75	0.8	1.4	3.2	5.2
1975-79	0.9	-0.8	1.6	9.8
1956-79	0.4	0.5	6.7	6.9

Source: Compiled by the authors.

Cost elasticities with respect to output levels are not directly observable. They must be estimated in order to implement our approach to productivity measurement. The most attractive approach to obtaining cost elasticities is the estimation of a multi-product cost function using cross-section data. There are not enough Canadian railroads to provide data for such estimation; however, Caves, Christensen, and J. A. Swanson have used cross-section data from the U.S. railroad industry to estimate the structure of rail costs.[28] We have taken the approach of using their estimated equations to infer Canadian cost elasticities. The CCS estimates were developed from cross-section data for 1955, 1963, and 1974.[29] We use their estimated coefficients along with data on CN and CP output levels and input prices to estimate the cost elasticities for ton-miles and passenger-miles for the CN and CP in 1956, 1963, and 1974.[30] The cost elasticities are then interpolated between the cross-section years and extrapolated to 1979 in order to provide annual weights for the productivity indexes. The cost elasticities are quite stable over the full period. For both railroads 1 percent increases in each output index give rise to approximately the following increases in total costs: ton-miles 0.8 percent, passenger-miles 0.2 percent, average freight haul -0.1 percent, average passenger trip -0.02 percent.

We use five categories of inputs for the CN and CP in equation 2: labor, structures (including right of way), equipment (including rolling stock), fuel, and materials. Labor input is measured by an index of hours worked. Structures and equipment input are measured by perpetual inventory capital stock estimates. Fuel is measured by the British thermal unit (Btu) content of the various fuels used. Materials is a catchall category that includes deflated expenditures for all other inputs. In Table 5.2 we present the ratios of the five input indexes for the CN relative to the CP.

Labor input fell almost continuously for the CN and CP after 1956. The decline averaged 2.6 percent per year for the CN and 3.4 percent per year for the CP. Fuel input fell even more for both railroads, due principally to the switchover from coal to diesel fuel. Structures and equipment input increased for both railroads, but the increases were less than 1 percent per year except for CN equipment, which rose at an average rate of 3.3 percent per year. The large increase in CN equipment shows up most dramatically in Table 5.2: the ratio of CN to CP equipment grew from 1.2 in 1956 to 2.1 in 1979. The other input ratios grew much less, and the materials ratio actually declined. The cost shares for the CN and CP are quite similar. The largest difference is that the CN labor share is roughly 6 percentage points higher than that of the CP.

TABLE 5.2

Ratios of CN to CP Input Indexes

Year	Labor	Structures	Equipment	Fuel	Materials
1956	1.327	1.363	1.187	1.347	1.381
1957	1.368	1.436	1.150	1.464	1.505
1958	1.321	1.478	1.193	1.446	1.681
1959	1.339	1.593	1.299	1.360	1.529
1960	1.324	1.668	1.300	1.363	1.620
1961	1.378	1.756	1.334	1.437	1.649
1962	1.374	1.776	1.297	1.469	1.561
1963	1.344	1.796	1.314	1.467	1.507
1964	1.382	1.827	1.359	1.481	1.562
1965	1.443	1.838	1.408	1.476	1.429
1966	1.439	1.808	1.394	1.457	1.616
1967	1.479	1.786	1.377	1.525	1.536
1968	1.457	1.758	1.359	1.523	1.456
1969	1.469	1.742	1.433	1.527	1.434
1970	1.494	1.772	1.389	1.437	1.199
1971	1.506	1.777	1.429	1.467	1.251
1972	1.647	1.779	1.712	1.440	1.168
1973	1.633	1.763	1.749	1.297	1.211
1974	1.660	1.771	1.809	1.324	1.379
1975	1.723	1.761	2.025	1.328	1.491
1976	1.652	1.751	2.117	1.289	1.442
1977	1.613	1.687	2.180	1.306	1.278
1978	1.585	1.624	2.290	1.357	1.336
1979	1.590	1.602	2.139	1.398	1.270
Average Ratios					
1956–79	0.8	0.7	2.6	0.2	−0.4

Source: Compiled by the authors.

We have presented all the figures required to obtain productivity estimates from equation 2. We present the productivity estimates themselves in Table 5.3. The first two columns of Table 5.3 contain the annual percentage growth rates of TFP for the CN and the CP. The third column of Table 5.3 contains the level of CN productivity relative to that of the CP. We also present in Table 5.3 the growth rates of aggregate output and input for the CN and CP. Neither the CN nor CP had a strong productivity performance in the late 1950s, but the situation changed dramatically in the 1960s. From 1960 to 1970 the CN and CP averaged 5.8 percent and 3.2 percent TFP growth per year respectively. This strong performance continued in the 1970s, such that over the full 1956-79 period they averaged 3.0 percent and 2.2 percent TFP growth per year respectively. The CN TFP level was only 0.88 that of the CP in 1956, but the CN surpassed the level of CP TFP in 1967 and has remained higher except for 1973-75. The relative TFP levels of the CN and CP are presented graphically in Figure 5.1. Columns 4 and 5 of Table 5.3 show that there is a substantial degree of association between TFP growth and output growth for the CN and CP.

FIGURE 5.1

CN and CP TFP Levels

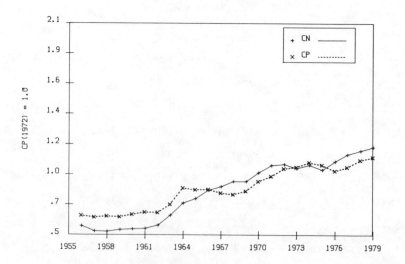

TABLE 5.3

Productivity Growth and Level Comparison for the CN and the CP
and Growth Rates of Aggregate Output and Input

	TFP		CN Relative to CP	Output		Input	
	CN	CP		CN	CP	CN	CP
1956	—*	—	0.879	—	—	—	—
1957	-7.6	-2.7	0.837	-9.8	-8.2	-2.2	-5.5
1958	-0.7	0.8	0.825	-7.2	-5.0	-6.5	-5.8
1959	3.3	-0.0	0.853	1.0	-2.6	-2.3	-2.6
1960	0.8	3.1	0.834	-4.6	-3.0	-5.5	-6.0
1961	0.5	2.5	0.818	-0.5	-1.9	-1.1	-4.4
1962	4.5	-0.3	0.858	2.7	-1.0	-1.8	-0.7
1963	12.0	8.3	0.890	10.8	8.0	-1.2	-0.3
1964	12.7	15.7	0.864	15.5	15.5	2.8	-0.1
1965	4.8	-1.5	0.921	4.7	-3.1	-0.1	-1.6
1966	8.1	0.5	0.993	8.6	0.0	0.5	-0.5
1967	3.5	-3.3	1.062	3.5	-3.2	0.0	0.1
1968	4.4	-1.3	1.124	-3.4	-6.2	-7.8	-4.9
1969	-0.3	2.4	1.094	0.7	2.7	1.0	0.3
1970	7.4	9.3	1.074	5.6	9.9	-1.8	0.6
1971	5.3	3.9	1.089	6.7	4.1	1.4	0.2
1972	0.8	6.0	1.034	4.4	4.3	3.6	-1.7
1973	-2.7	1.3	0.993	-6.1	-1.7	-3.4	-3.0
1974	2.3	3.4	0.981	10.4	7.5	8.1	4.1
1975	-3.8	-2.0	0.964	-3.0	-5.2	0.8	-3.2
1976	6.6	-4.4	1.075	3.6	-4.3	-3.0	0.1
1977	4.4	2.4	1.098	2.7	4.7	-1.7	2.3
1978	1.6	4.5	1.066	3.4	5.8	1.8	1.2
1979	2.0	1.6	1.071	1.3	2.5	-0.7	0.9
			Average Growth Rates				
1956-60	-1.0	0.3	-1.3	-5.2	-4.7	-4.1	-5.0
1960-65	6.9	4.9	2.0	6.6	3.5	-0.3	-1.4
1965-70	4.6	1.5	3.1	3.0	0.7	-1.6	-0.9
1970-75	0.4	2.5	-2.2	2.5	1.8	2.1	-0.7
1975-79	3.7	1.0	2.6	2.8	2.2	-0.9	1.1
1956-79	3.0	2.2	0.9	2.2	0.9	-0.8	-1.3

*Data not available.
Source: Compiled by the authors.

TOTAL FACTOR PRODUCTIVITY GROWTH
FOR CLASS I U.S. RAILROADS

Since the CN and CP are the only two Class I railroads in
Canada, the previous section documents productivity growth for the
full set of Class I Canadian railroads. There are approximately 50
Class I U.S. railroads, so the task of documenting the productivity
performance of all of them would be enormous. The situation is
further complicated by the fact that there have been many mergers,
consolidations, and reorganizations of individual railroads. As a
consequence of these difficulties, we begin our analysis of U.S.
railroads by using the index number approach to estimate productivity growth for all Class I U.S. railroads combined. There are
some important shortcomings to this approach but it has the great
advantage of yielding a direct comparison of U.S. and Canadian
railroad productivity growth.

Caves, Christensen, and Swanson have provided estimates of
productivity growth rates for Class I U.S. railroads for 1951-74.[31]
We have updated, and revised where necessary, their estimates.
Thus we proceed to present the updated results—using the 1956-79
period for direct comparability with the Canadian results in the
previous section.

Our principal data source is Transport Statistics of the United
States, published annually by the U.S. Interstate Commerce Commission. This source provides most of the data necessary to follow
the procedures described above for the CN-CP comparison. The
cross-section regression estimates in CCS are used to estimate the
cost elasticities for the four output indexes.

In Table 5.4 we present the growth rates of productivity, aggregate output, and aggregate input of Class I U.S. railroads. Note
that freight output declined in the late 1950s and again in the early
1970s, but over the full 1956-79 period, growth in ton-miles averaged 1.5 percent per year. Freight hauls steadily increased in
length, especially in the later 1970s. Passenger output fell continuously until 1973, after which there was substantial growth. The time
paths of the individual input are similar to those of the Canadian railroads. The cyclical pattern of TFP growth in U.S. railroads is similar to those of the CN and CP, but the growth rates are, on average,
considerably lower. As with the Canadian railroads, the association
between TFP growth and output growth is apparent for U.S. railroads.

The patterns of growth rates for the CN, CP, and U.S. Class I
railroads are presented in Figures 5.2 and 5.3. Figure 5.2 shows
that U.S. and Canadian railroads performed in a very similar manner until the early 1960s. Thereafter input growth rates were very
similar, but output and TFP (Figure 5.3) performance for U.S. and
Canadian railroads diverged widely.

TABLE 5.4

Growth Rates of Productivity, Aggregate Output,
and Aggregate Input for Class I U.S. Railroads

Year	TFP	Output	Input
1956	—*	—	—
1957	-1.0	-5.3	-4.3
1958	-2.0	-11.1	-9.2
1959	2.6	2.0	-0.6
1960	1.3	-1.3	-2.6
1961	2.3	-2.3	-4.6
1962	4.6	3.4	-1.2
1963	2.9	2.3	-0.6
1964	3.4	4.3	0.8
1965	4.4	3.2	-1.2
1966	3.4	4.0	0.6
1967	-2.3	-3.9	-1.6
1968	0.1	0.1	0.1
1969	0.9	1.3	0.4
1970	-3.6	-2.4	1.2
1971	-3.6	-5.8	-2.2
1972	6.3	3.2	-3.1
1973	4.6	8.3	3.7
1974	1.3	1.4	0.1
1975	-1.3	-10.0	-8.7
1976	2.0	4.3	2.3
1977	-0.3	3.0	3.3
1978	2.4	4.3	1.9
1979	7.6	5.4	-2.1
Average Growth Rates			
1956-60	0.2	--3.9	-4.2
1960-65	3.5	2.2	-1.3
1965-70	-0.3	-0.2	0.1
1970-75	1.5	-0.6	-2.1
1975-79	2.9	4.3	1.3
1956-79	1.6	0.4	-1.2

*Data not available.

Source: Compiled by the authors.

FIGURE 5.2

Comparison of U.S., CN, and CP Railroad Output Growth

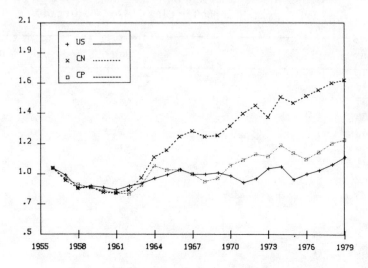

FIGURE 5.3

Comparison of U.S., CN, and CP Railroad TFP Growth

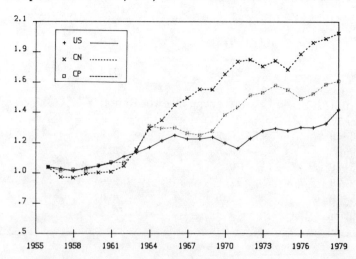

MULTILATERAL COMPARISON OF CANADIAN
NATIONAL, CANADIAN PACIFIC, AND
INDIVIDUAL U.S. RAILROADS

The comparison of productivity growth for the CN, CP, and
the aggregation of Class I U.S. railroads in the previous section is
less than completely satisfactory because there are so many details
hidden in the U.S. aggregate. For many purposes we would be more
interested in the comparison of the CN and CP with individual U.S.
railroads. For several years we have been developing a data set
that is suitable for this purpose. To date we have completed development of data for 17 U.S. railroads from 1951 through 1975. These
railroads are:

>Clinchfield (CLN)
>Chicago & Eastern Illinois (CEI)
>Boston & Maine (BM)
>Denver, Rio Grande & Western (DRGW)
>Atchison, Topeka & Santa Fe (ATSF)
>Southern Pacific (SP)
>Texas & Pacific (TP)
>Florida East Coast (FEC)
>Milwaukee Road (MILW)
>Missouri Pacific (MOP)
>Union Pacific (UP)
>Louisville & Nashville (LN)
>Baltimore & Ohio (BO)
>Chicago, Rock Island & Pacific (ROCK)
>Reading (RDG)
>Delaware & Hudson (DH)
>Chesapeake & Ohio (CO)

We have used these 17 railroads and the CN and CP to perform a
multilateral comparison of output, input, and productivity. The
procedure used for this comparison is equation 4 in the last section.

In Table 5.5 we present the growth rates of productivity for
the full 1956-75 period, followed by the growth rates for the sub-
periods. The growth rates reported for the CN and CP are somewhat different from those presented in Table 5.3 because the basis
of comparison is different. Table 5.3 growth rates are based on
equation 2 for bilateral comparisons. In Tables 5.5 and 5.6 the
comparisons are all made via a representative firm that reflects
the characteristics of all 19 railroads. The railroads are ranked
in Table 5.5 by their 1956-79 TFP growth rates.

TABLE 5.5

Growth in Total Factor Productivity for Individual Railroads
(percent per year)

Firm	1956-75	1956-60	1960-65	1965-70	1970-75
CN	2.9	-0.9	6.9	4.5	0.4
CP	2.6	1.1	4.7	2.0	2.1
CLN	1.7	-1.2	5.8	1.6	0.1
CEI	1.7	0.6	2.4	-2.6	6.3
BM	1.7	1.3	3.5	-0.2	2.0
DRGW	1.6	1.9	2.8	-0.7	2.5
ATSF	1.4	1.1	3.1	-1.0	2.4
SP	1.3	3.1	2.6	-1.2	1.1
TP	1.2	1.0	3.4	-3.8	4.3
FEC	1.1	1.6	-1.0	-0.5	4.4
MILW	1.0	0.1	2.9	0.0	0.7
MOP	0.2	1.3	2.7	-3.6	0.6
UP	0.2	1.8	3.0	-1.2	-2.5
LN	0.2	-3.1	4.1	-3.5	2.4
BO	0.1	1.1	4.2	-4.4	-0.4
ROCK	0.0	0.1	2.1	-0.8	-1.3
RDG	-0.2	-0.2	5.0	-3.4	-2.0
DH	-0.9	-2.6	4.4	-3.6	-2.2
CO	-1.1	-3.3	2.6	-2.7	-1.3

Source: Compiled by the authors.

The CN and CP dominate all of the U.S. railroads in terms of
1956-75 TFP growth rates, with annual average growth rates of 2.9
percent and 2.6 percent, respectively. The highest TFP growth by
a U.S. railroad is the Clinchfield with a 1.7 percent rate. Several
of the U.S. railroads show negative TFP growth over the full period,
the lowest being the Chesapeake & Ohio with a -1.1 percent average
growth rate.

There is a clear correlation between output growth and TFP
growth. The CN is the highest in both measures and the three railroads with negative TFP growth are the three railroads with the
most negative rates of output growth. Furthermore, of the nine
best railroads in TFP growth only three had declines in output;
whereas, all but one of the ten worst railroads in TFP growth had
declines rather than growth of output.

TABLE 5.6

Relative Levels of Total Factor Productivity
for Individual Railroads

Firm	1956	1960	1965	1970	1975
CN	0.652	0.630	0.892	1.120	1.141
CP	0.739	0.773	0.980	1.083	1.205
CLN	1.388	1.325	1.771	1.921	1.930
CEI	1.098	1.124	1.265	1.108	1.518
BM	0.657	0.693	0.823	0.816	0.900
DRGW	1.151	1.241	1.425	1.373	1.554
ATSF	0.899	0.940	1.097	1.045	1.178
SP	0.867	0.983	1.120	1.055	1.113
TP	0.874	0.909	1.076	0.890	1.104
FEC	0.813	0.866	0.824	0.805	1.003
MILW	0.850	0.855	0.986	0.988	1.026
MOP	0.904	0.953	1.090	0.912	0.941
UP	0.912	0.980	1.136	1.068	0.942
LN	1.021	0.903	1.110	0.933	1.054
BO	0.788	0.825	1.017	0.814	0.800
ROCK	1.028	1.034	1.147	1.103	1.035
RDG	0.873	0.864	1.109	0.934	0.847
DH	1.177	1.062	1.322	1.103	0.987
CO	1.090	0.957	1.091	0.952	0.893

Source: Compiled by the authors.

With only one exception, the railroads had lower levels of
total input in 1975 than they had in 1956. The exception is the
Louisville & Nashville, which had input growth of 1.5 percent per
year. The largest decline in input was the Boston & Maine, at 4.0
percent per year, but several other railroads had input declines in
excess of 3 percent per year.

In Table 5.6 we present the relative levels of TFP in 1956,
1960, 1965, 1970, and 1975 resulting from the multilateral comparison. In 1956 the CN had a lower level of TFP than all the other
railroads. Similarly, the CP had a lower level of TFP than all but
one U.S. railroad. This situation changed dramatically over the
following 20 years due to the large disparity in TFP growth rates.
By 1975 the Canadian railroads had achieved productivity levels

equal to or exceeding that of the U.S. railroads. Only three of the U.S. railroads in our sample had productivity levels exceeding that of the CN. All three of these were many times smaller than the CN. The CP fell below the CN's level of productivity, with the Santa Fe falling between the two Canadian railroads.

The relative levels of aggregate output and input resulting from the multilateral comparison provide good indications of the relative sizes of the railroads that we have studied. For the U.S. railroads there appears to be little relationship between size and productivity performance.

More detailed information on the growth of outputs and inputs for the railroads over the full 20-year period indicates that every railroad experienced a decline in passenger output, while all but five railroads had increases in freight output. The input data portray a substantial substitution of equipment for labor, structures, and fuel inputs for most of the railroads in the sample.

ANALYSIS OF DIFFERENCES IN PRODUCTIVITY

Numerous factors, including regulatory policies and ownership, might account for the substantial differences we have found for level and growth rates of TFP among the U.S. and Canadian firms we have analyzed. It is beyond the scope of this chapter to conduct a full study of the structure of railroad costs; however, we believe it is worthwhile to carry out some preliminary analysis.

Our point of departure is the fact that many studies have concluded that excess capacity—i.e., excess stock of way and structures—is a pervasive problem among North American railroads.[32] The TFP results reported above are based upon an aggregate input measure that assumes the railroads' way and structures stocks are optimally utilized. If utilization is suboptimal then we would expect TFP differences to be partially explained by differences over time and among firms in capacity utilization. We observed above that TFP growth for individual firms is related to output growth. While this observation is consistent with the effect of excess capacity, no conclusive statement can be made without an analysis of the joint relationship between TFP and both output and the stock of way and structures. We now turn to a formal analysis of this relationship.[33]

We have used the multilateral TFP results in Table 5.6 to estimate the equation:

$$ln\,\mathrm{TFP}_{it} = \alpha + \beta \ ln\,\mathrm{Y}_{it} + \gamma \ ln\,\mathrm{S}_{it} \qquad (5)$$

where TFP_{it}, Y_{it}, and S_{it} are respectively the multilateral TFP level, aggregate output, and the stock of way and structures for firm i in period t. The coefficient γ indicates whether capacity utilization is important as a factor in explaining TFP differences. A negative estimate of γ indicates excess capacity, a positive estimate indicates a capacity shortage, and $\gamma = O$ implies that capacity utilization is optimal. The interpretation of β is not as straightforward: it reflects both the effects of capacity utilization and returns to scale.

In Table 5.7, column 1, we report estimates of equation 5. Both β and γ are very significant. The negative estimate of indicates excess capacity in the industry; thus, we can expect change in capacity utilization to play a role in explaining TFP growth.

TABLE 5.7

The Effect of Output and Structures on
Total Factor Productivity

	Equation 5	Equation 7
α	0.010	−0.073
	(0.008)	(0.075)
β	0.514	0.380
	(0.032)	(0.024)
γ	−0.593	−0.273
	(0.033)	(0.041)

Note: Standard errors in parentheses.
Source: Compiled by the authors.

The regression equation 5 does not recognize systematic differences among firms or time periods. Thus we cannot use the results in column 1 to determine how our estimates of TFP might be altered by controlling for capacity utilization. In addition it has long been recognized that failure to control for systematic differences may actually create a bias in the coefficients (see J. Mundlak[34]). To correct these problems we can expand equation 5 by adding terms to control for systematic differences among years and firms. The resulting model is:

$$ln\,\text{TFP}_{it} = \alpha + \underset{t\neq72}{\Sigma}\ \delta_t + \underset{i\neq CN}{\Sigma}\ \rho_i + \beta\ ln\ Y_{it} + \gamma\ ln S_{it}. \qquad (6)$$

The δ_t are the effects associated with years other than 1972, and the ρ_i are the effects associated with firms other than the CN. Although equation 6 is considerably more general than 5, it still does not allow for systematic differences in the growth rate of TFP between the United States and Canada. Therefore, we permit the δ_t terms to differ for the United States and Canada:

$$ln\ \text{TFP}_{it} = \alpha + \underset{t\neq72}{\Sigma}\ \delta_t + \underset{t\neq72}{\Sigma}\ \delta_{ct} + \underset{i\neq CN}{\Sigma}\ \rho_i + \beta\ ln, Y_{it} + \gamma\ ln S_{it}, \qquad (7)$$

where δ_t and δ_{ct} are respectively the terms associated with the United States and Canada for year t.

In the second column of Table 5.7, we present estimates α, β, and γ for equation 7. Controlling for systematic effects due to years and firms causes both the β and γ coefficients to decline in absolute value relative to equation 5. However, the structures coefficient, γ, is still significantly negative and the output coefficient, β, is still significantly positive. Thus controlling for effects of firms and time periods does not alter the conclusion that excess capacity is an important factor in the industry.

The ρ coefficients indicate the difference in level of productivity between the individual firms and the CN in 1972. The δ coefficients give the systematic effects due to time periods. To calculate the average annual growth rate in TFP, not accounted for by changes in utilization and output, we computed $(\delta_{75} - \delta_{56})/19$. For Canada this value is 2.45 percent per year. This compares to the average of the CN and CP values of 2.75 percent per year from Table 5.5. For the United States, the average growth rate not accounted for by changes in utilization and output is 0.97 percent per year. This compares to an average of 0.67 for the U.S. firms in Table 5.5. Controlling for changes in utilization reduces Canadian TFP 30 percent per year and increases U.S. TFP by about the same amount. Thus, approximately 30 percent of the difference (0.60/2.08) in TFP growth between Canadian and U.S. railroads is explained by different patterns of utilization and output.

SUMMARY AND CONCLUSIONS

We find that the degree of economic regulation has a strong influence on the economic performance of North American railroads. We also conclude that when one controls for the influence of regulation, there is little indication that ownership form influences performance. These conclusions are reached in the following manner. First, we observe no substantial differences in productivity growth rates between the government-owned Canadian National and the privately held Canadian Pacific. If anything, we find a slightly superior record for CN. Second, when the productivity growth rates for CN and CP are compared with similar rates for all U.S. railroads, we note a distinctly better performance for the substantially less regulated Canadian carriers. Third, when we examine company-by-company productivity levels and growth rates, the two Canadian railroads reveal not only greater growth rates, but also levels exceeded by only three small U.S. railroads.

We are willing to make a strong case for the influence of regulation on economic performance because our analysis has taken into account those factors that we believe might also have a bearing on measured efficiency progress. For example, we have examined the influence of operating practices, and have found that these would tend to impart a downward bias to Canadian efficiency statistics. In making pairwise comparisons of Canadian and U.S. railroads, we have formally controlled for the influence of excess capacity in U.S. railroads (even though we would argue that such excess capacity is a regulation-induced phenomenon). And, our techniques for measuring productivity levels and growth rates control for the influence of differences in output composition and input prices.

It might have been more convenient if the results of the section on the analysis of differences in productivity had indicated that, allowing for differences in capacity utilization, the differences in productivity growth between Canadian and U.S. railroads were negligible. We could have then argued that the relatively poor productivity record of U.S. carriers is simply due to lack of flexibility in pricing of services. The implication would be that the removal of rate regulation as practiced in the United States should quickly produce a dramatic increase in efficiency. However, we are unable to reach such a conclusion.

The specific explanation for the superior economic performance of the two Canadian railroads must ultimately lie in the area of organizational design and control. More specifically, regulation in general, and direct price regulation in particular, has a strong bearing on how production is organized. For example, we have noted that as the Canadian railroads were deregulated the marketing organizations of those companies were radically altered. Pioneering work by Trevor D. Heaver and James C. Nelson suggests that such change has resulted in price and service offerings by the Canadian railroads that are without U.S. counterpart. Canadian control procedures also appear quite different. While we have not

had the opportunity to make extensive comparisons of such procedures, we are aware that the Canadian railroads have much more
elaborate "costing" systems than those of their U.S. counterparts.
There is also the indication that computer-based systems for operating and financial management are better integrated.

These findings serve to confirm the conjectures of a number
of our predecessors. They have suggested that perhaps the greatest
costs associated with transportation regulation are not those associated simply with misallocation of traffic between modes (due to
regulations that cause disparities between rates and marginal costs)
or expenses incurred in maintaining services that would not be
provided in a competitive setting, but those associated with a lack
of innovation. This chapter provides dramatic evidence of just that.

The Staggers Rail Act of 1980 provides U.S. railroads with
new pricing freedoms and abandonment opportunities; however,
there are still considerable uncertainties and debate on the implementation of the act. For those concerned with implementation, the
Canadian experience with rail deregulation provides a highly useful
lesson—actions that bring the U.S. regulatory climate more in line
with that in Canada have the potential for substantially improving
the performance of the U.S. railroad industry.

NOTES

1. Sam Peltzman, "Pricing in Public and Private Enterprises:
Electric Utilities in the United States," Journal of Law and Economics 14 (April 1971):147.

2. Robert M. Spann, "Public vs. Private Provision of Gov-
ernment Services," in Budgets and Bureaucrats: The Sources of
Government Growth, ed. Thomas E. Borcherding (Durham, N.C.:
Duke University Press, 1977).

3. For a general discussion of productivity measurement, see
Solomon Fabricant, "Perspective on Productivity Research,"
Review of Income and Wealth 20 (September 1974):235-49.

4. For a popular account, see Pierre Berton, The National
Dream: The Great Railway, 1871-1881 (Toronto: McClelland &
Stewart, 1970).

5. Editors' note: See Chapter 11 in this volume.

6. Editors' note: See Chapter 8 in this volume.

7. The U.S. data are from the Statistical Abstract of the
United States, and the Canadian data are from H. L. Purdy, Transport Competition and Public Policy in Canada (Vancouver: University of British Columbia Press, 1972), pp. 58-59. The Canadian
railroad share stabilized at 53 percent in 1962 and rose to 55 percent

in 1968, the most recent year for which such figures have been published. The U.S. rail share has declined continually, reaching 52 percent in 1968 and 48 percent in 1976.

8. An agreed charge is a rate negotiated by a carrier and a shipper, which generally applies for a period of a year for a specified percentage of the shipper's traffic.

9. See Trevor D. Heaver and James C. Nelson, Railway Pricing Under Commercial Freedom: The Canadian Experience (Vancouver: University of British Columbia, Centre for Transportation Studies, 1977) for further data and discussion.

10. Ibid., p. 85.

11. Ibid., p. 65.

12. Ibid., p. 33. According to Heaver and Nelson, class and non-competitive commodity rates accounted for 75 percent of total freight revenue in 1951 and 37 percent in 1963. Competitive and commodity rates and agreed charges accounted for 13 percent of freight revenue in 1951 and 51 percent in 1963.

13. R. R. Latimer, "The Challenge of Rate Freedom," Railway Age, May 28, 1979, pp. 50-53.

14. See A. F. Friedlaender, The Dilemma of Freight Transport Regulation (Washington, D.C.: The Brookings Institution, 1969); and P. W. MacAvoy and J. Sloss, Regulation of Transport Innovation (New York: Random House, 1967).

15. See D. F. Harvey, Christmas Turkey or Prairie Vulture? An Economic Analysis of the Crow's Nest Pass Grain Rates (Montreal: The Institute for Research on Public Policy, 1980).

16. This figure is provided by Shedd, who also indicates that in 1973 the rate level for hauling grain in Canada was less than one-quarter of the equivalent U.S. rate. See T. Shedd, "The Canadian Connection," Modern Railroads 30 (September 1975):66-68.

17. Laurits R. Christensen and Dale W. Jorgenson, "U.S. Real Product and Real Factor Input, 1929-1967," Review of Income and Wealth 16 (March 1970):19-50.

18. W. E. Diewert, "Exact and Superlative Index Numbers," Journal of Econometrics 4 (May 1976):115-45.

19. Douglas W. Caves, Laurits R. Christensen, and W. E. Diewert, "Multilateral Comparisons of Output, Input, and Productivity Using Superlative Index Numbers," Discussion Paper #8002, Social Systems Research Institute, University of Wisconsin-Madison, November 1980, Economic Journal, in press.

20. Douglas W. Caves, Laurits R. Christensen, and J. A. Swanson, "Productivity in U.S. Railroads, 1951-1974," Bell Journal of Economics 9 (Spring 1980):166-81.

21. Dale W. Jorgenson and Meiko Nishimizu, "U.S. and Japanese Economic Growth, 1952-1973: An International Comparison," Economic Journal 88 (December 1978):707-26.

22. See note 19.

23. L. Dreschler, "Weighting of Index Numbers in Multi-lateral International Comparisons," Review of Income and Wealth 19 (1973):17-34.

24. Douglas W. Caves, Laurits R. Christensen, and M. W. Tretheway, "Flexible Cost Functions for Multiproduct Firms," Review of Economics and Statistics 62 (August 1980):477-81.

25. Douglas W. Caves and Laurits R. Christensen, "Productivity in Canadian Railroads, 1956-1975," Discussion Paper no. 7825, University of Wisconsin-Madison, Social Systems Research Institute, October 1978 (also available as Research Report 1078-16 from the Canadian Transport Commission, Research Branch).

26. Laurits R. Christensen and Dale W. Jorgenson, "The Measurement of U.S. Real Capital Input, 1929-1967," Review of Income and Wealth 15 (December 1969):293-320.

27. In a previous version of this analysis, we explored the importance of using waybill data to distinguish different commodities. There are serious reliability problems with waybill data, but, in any case, the qualitative conclusions of the study were not affected. Thus, we have not pursued that line of research further. See Douglas W. Caves and Laurits R. Christensen, "The Relative Efficiency of Public and Private Firms in a Competitive Environment: The Case of Canadian Railroads," Journal of Political Economy 88 (October 1980):958-76.

28. Douglas W. Caves, Laurits R. Christensen, and J. A. Swanson, "Productivity Growth, Scale Economies, and Capacity Utilization in U.S. Railroads, 1955-1974," American Economic Review 71, no. 5 (December 1981):994-1002.

29. The number of firms included in the samples for these years were 58, 56, and 40, respectively. They employed the generalized translog multiproduct cost function, proposed by Caves, Christensen, and Tretheway (note 24) to obtain the estimated cost elasticities. This cost function has the same form as the translog multiproduct cost function, except for output levels, where the Box-Cox metric is substituted for the natural log metric. This generalization permits the inclusion of firms with zero output levels for some products. In railroad applications, it permits the inclusion in the sample of firms with no passenger output. (David F. Burgess, "A Cost Minimization Approach to Import Demand Equations," Review of Economics and Statistics 56 (May 1974):225-34; and Randall S. Brown, Douglas W. Caves, and Laurits R. Christensen, "Modeling the Structure of Cost and Production for Multiproduct Firms," Southern Economic Journal 46 (July 1970): 256-73.

30. Although CCS did not compile U.S. cross-section data for 1956, their analysis showed that the formula for the cost elasticity as a function of output and input prices was independent of time. Therefore, to estimate 1956 cost elasticities for the CN and CP we have inserted 1956 output levels and input prices for the CN and CP into the estimated 1955 cost-elasticity equation.

31. See note 20.

32. For analysis of this issue see Caves, Christensen, and Swanson, note 20.

33. For discussion of TFP regressions of the type presented below, see Douglas W. Caves, Laurits R. Christensen, and M. W. Tretheway, "U.S. Trunk Air Carriers, 1972-1977: A Multilateral Comparison of Total Factor Productivity," Productivity Measurement in Regulated Industries, ed. T. Cowing and R. Stevenson (New York: Academic Press, 1981).

34. J. Mundlak, "Empirical Production Functions Free of Management Bias," Journal of Farm Economics 43 (February 1961): 44-56.

6

PUBLIC ENTERPRISE UNDER COMPETITION: A COMMENT ON CANADIAN RAILWAYS

T. D. Heaver and W. G. Waters II

Douglas W. Caves, Laurits R. Christensen, J. A. Swanson, and M. W. Tretheway (CCST) present a number of interesting findings. We think that the sophistication of the techniques and the care in developing their data are such that their results are likely to be quite robust in the face of whatever technical nitpicking we might raise. Further, their results are not surprising to those who have monitored and studied the performance of rail transportation in the United States and Canada. [1]

Our comments are in four parts. Our major objective is to elaborate on some lessons that can be learned from the workings of the essentially deregulated rail industry in Canada. But prior to that we clarify several points about the evolution and status of Canadian transport regulation and railway markets, raise a few questions about specific parts of CCST's findings, and comment on the economics that underlies railway pricing in Canada and its implications for managerial incentives and performance.

THE EVOLUTION AND STATUS OF CANADIAN RAIL REGULATION

CCST provide a capsule summary of important legislative developments affecting rail regulation in Canada. We wish, however, to clarify a couple of points. First, CCST are correct to convey the impression that the rise of intermodal competition to railways in Canada has tended to be met by reductions in the regulatory restrictions on railways. However, Canada's policy was not a steady drift toward deregulation. For example, one of the important re-

152

sults of the 1951 Turgeon Royal Commission (there were two commissions headed by him) was the so-called "one and one-third rule" limiting rates to intermediate points of a long haul to 1.333 times the long-haul rate. This was a policy to combat long-haul/short-haul discrimination, a traditional equity concern in railway pricing. The point is railways were freed to meet intermodal competition where it arose but faced specific limitations in other rates. In the 1950s, there were a number of across-the-board rate increases that were disallowed in whole or in part. This "hot potato" was one of the major reasons for the formation of the MacPherson Royal Commission in 1959.

The MacPherson Commission report in 1961 and subsequent National Transportation Act (NTA) of 1967 represent a major shift in regulatory policy. The NTA both facilitated rail rate making in the face of intermodal competition and removed the antidiscrimination constraints on rail pricing and service. Canada thereby embraced fully (apart from statutory grain rates) the principle enunciated by the MacPherson Commission that "public policy must recognize that railway rates and services cannot now be determined and cannot now be controlled by considerations other than those set by commercial and competitive necessity."[2] It does not appear that U.S. policy has gone that far. This change, along with the inability of the Canadian Transport Commission (CTC) to delay implementation of rate changes for investigation (the traditional tactic of regulators and opposing shippers to block changes in rail rates in the United States), was vital in the exercise of freedom for the design and pricing of railway services. It enabled the railways to practice selective service design and pricing, a concept that we wish to emphasize.

Before concluding this section on the Canadian regulatory environment, we also wish to comment on the status of trucking regulation. Interprovincial trucking was affirmed as a federal responsibility in 1954. Nonetheless, the specific regulation of interprovincial trucking regulation has always been exercised by the provinces.[3] The provinces vary immensely in their regulations of both entry and rates.[4] The result is a patchwork of regulations facing both intra-provincial and interprovincial trucking. As implied by CCST, generally less stringent regulation has applied to trucking in Canada than in the United States. However, the mixed pattern of trucking regulations means we have much greater difficulty in establishing consistency in the regulation of railways and trucking.

COMMENTS ON AND POSSIBLE EXPLANATIONS
FOR SOME CCST RESULTS

Several findings might merit further comment and investigation. We shall briefly suggest a couple of other factors that might help explain the observed differences in productivity between the United States and Canada.

Variability and Timing of TFP Gains

We were struck by the year-to-year variation in measures of total factor productivity (TFP) for CN and CP (Table 5.3). There are significant variations, in the growth rate of TFP (-7.6 percent to 12.7 percent for CN; -4.4 percent to 15.7 percent for CP; -3.6 percent to 7.6 percent for U.S. railroads, Table 5.4). Do the authors attach any significance to these high variations or are they simply manifestations of an old railway problem, namely that the time period when inputs are acquired does not necessarily correspond to when outputs are produced?

Another interesting point: the years of highest annual growth of TFP are 1963 and 1964, before the passage of the NTA. This makes us a little uneasy in assuming the significance of a changed regulatory environment as the sole factor explaining the high performance of Canadian railways.

Capacity Utilization and TFP

CCST have extended their previous work in this area in Chapter 5 of this volume. One extension is their recognition and analysis of the possibility that increased utilization of the excess capacity that characterizes the North American rail industry could be a partial explanation of the increased TFP in both the United States and Canada. They find this is statistically significant but not a major factor in explaining the TFP increases. We do not disagree with their analysis, but we are uneasy about just what kind of "excess capacity" is represented by their capital stock estimates. Railways possess low density lines and yards as well as more heavily used main-line facilities. If traffic increases take place on low density portions of their system, or via favorable route or backhaul developments, then utilization of excess capacity could be an important factor explaining high output increases with relatively low input increases. Conversely, traffic increases in "bottleneck" regions

may require significant increases in inputs. Therefore, we are
uneasy about the amount of aggregation implicit in their capital
stock estimates. Further analysis of the type of traffic increases
and where it occurs on a rail system may yet be an important explanation of TFP increases.

Changes in Traffic Composition

It is possible that a part of the relative improvement in Canadian railway productivity is the result of a shift in commodity composition and associated transport technology not controlled for in
the tonnage and ton-mile data of CCST. For example, in the early
1960s, grain traffic declined from 39.1 percent of railway ton-
miles in 1961 to 31.6 percent in 1965. In Canada over the last two
decades, there has been a substantial increase in the movement of
bulk commodities amenable to unit train and multiple car movements. We have not been able to ascertain whether this development has been more significant in Canada than in the United States
as we suspect. If the cost elasticity with respect to these kinds of
ton-miles is less than that for traditional rail traffic, then there
could be a systematic difference between the United States and
Canada that is hidden in the CCST aggregated data. The productivity increases shown for Canadian railways could be partly due to
shifts in traffic composition that have not been explicitly incorporated.

We note that there is also an identification problem here. To
what extent is the growth in bulk traffic handled in less costly multiple car shipments merely a fortuitous event in Canada, or is it
partly in response to Canadian rail management's ability to solicit
or at least respond favorably to shipper initiatives in this area and,
at the same time, to discourage or eliminate unprofitable traffic
such as less than carload (LCL) shipments? In short, even if there
is an underlying bias in the data due to favorable shifts of traffic
composition in Canada, it may still be relevant to observe that rail
management has been able to take advantage of and exploit these
profitable opportunities in the deregulated Canadian environment.

The Effects of Railway Size and Extent

The Canadian railways have been successful in improving
significantly the output levels achieved with existing resources.
For example, significant improvements have been achieved in car
utilization. The magnitude of these improvements has been aided
by deregulation but the Canadian railways have also enjoyed the

benefits of a high proportion of traffic being local to one carrier. Many U.S. railways must rely on cooperating carriers between the origin and destination, and there is all the paperwork and adminis- trative hassle of negotiating revenue divisions, keeping track of cars, and per diem charges among railways. In brief, there may be some economies in controlling the movement of cars from the origin to the destination. These might be correlated with rail size and thus show up as economies of scale estimates but the correla- tion is not likely to be perfect.

THE ECONOMICS OF RAILWAY RATES, OR THE REJUVENATION OF VALUE-OF-SERVICE PRICING

There are important economic implications that grow out of railway pricing freedom. For the most part, the Canadian railways are free to negotiate a price with individual shippers, and the rail- ways very definitely practice value-of-service pricing (VOSP). That is, railways approximate the economics textbook model of a discriminating multiproduct monopolist. However, the presence of intermodal competition and/or market competition greatly limit the ability of railways to take advantage of their apparent monopoly position.

It is important to note that modern VOSP is different from what was practiced years ago and which is often criticized in eco- nomics texts. The basic idea has not changed: setting prices that are influenced by the ability of the shipper to pay. In its origin, VOSP was basically a revenue-maximizing tactic: costs were ig- noted (more likely they simply were unknown) and treated as a com- mon burden to be borne by all traffic on an ability-to-pay basis. The lack of knowledge or attention paid to some costs meant the re- sulting cross-subsidization was common, with the resulting resource misallocation. Another interpretation of VOSP refers to a simplis- tic formula approach to pricing that links prices according to the value of a commodity. That is, recognizing that product value can be proxy for ability to pay, a railway might try to set prices in pro- portion to product value and ignore the presence of competition. This causes the carrier to lose traffic because some prices will be too high. It is common for transportation economics texts to con- trast VOSP mechanisms with cost-based pricing and to demonstrate the economic inefficiency inherent in prices not based on costs.

The foregoing value-of-service pricing frameworks are straw men now. Modern VOSP is a cost-based pricing scheme. The identifiable costs of serving the traffic provide the minimum basis for setting a rate. But costs are jointly incurred on behalf of mul-

tiple markets. Optimal pricing under these conditions results in
rates that reflect value of service considerations, i.e., the relative
abilities to pay of jointly supplied traffics.

Many rail costs cannot be traced to specific variations in
traffic; there are overheads or "constant costs" to be covered by
overall operations. The directly identifiable costs of serving the
traffic provide a minimum basis for rate making but the rate will
be set somewhere above this imprecise measure of incremental
costs with the markup reflecting the shipper's ability to pay. To
the carrier concerned, this is profit-maximizing behavior. There
are further economic implications.

There has long been concern that application of the economists'
ideal of marginal cost pricing to the railway industry would render
it bankrupt because marginal costs lie below average costs when
there are economies of scale (CCST results suggest constant returns or very slight scale economies) or excess capacity due to
lumpy inputs. If as a matter of policy we wish the railway system
to be financially viable, i.e., self-sustaining without public subsidy, then the economically optimal pricing policy on efficiency
grounds is VOSP until the overall rates of return exceed competitive alternatives. This is known as Ramsey or Boiteux pricing in
the economics literature.[5] In brief, there is an economic efficiency
argument for VOSP up until the point where monopoly returns result.

This brings us to the lessons that we wish to emphasize as
growing out of the Canadian experience with rail deregulation.

LESSONS FROM THE CANADIAN EXPERIENCE

Pricing Freedom and Rates of Return

Strictly speaking, deregulation itself does not produce more
efficient railway (or other) services. Improved performance comes
about through the improved effectiveness of management encouraged
by their full accountability for corporate profits.[6] The commercial
freedom given to Canadian railways was intended to encourage them
to pursue true commercial viability. The railways have learned to
use the new freedom, albeit slowly. They are now acknowledged to
be efficient and aggressive firms free to discriminate in dealing
with shippers. But on average, we get a better return than they do
by putting our money in the bank. They make attractive returns at
the margin, but there is little indication that they are conspicuously
larger than marginal rates of return in other industries. In short,
the Canadian experience reveals that we are very fortunate: it appears that there is sufficient competition and/or inability to pay by

shippers that the traditionally feared potential monopolists are not able to earn monopoly rates of return. We do not need to regulate the railways because of fears of them exploiting a monopoly position overall.

The Concern for Captive Shippers

One concern about the working of commercial freedom is the plight of the "captive shippers" dealing with a "rapacious railway." The Canadian experience suggests that efficiency is improved by maintaining only limited regulation to constrain railway monopoly power in dealings with particular shippers. In practice, the constraint in Canada has been to ensure that the railways respond to competitive conditions (i.e., behave efficiently) not to constrain railway profits on particular traffic (i.e., not to determine rates on some "equitable" basis). Since 1967 no rates in Canada have been regulated on the basis of their relationship with costs. There have been no maximum rate cases. In the limited number of cases based on the public interest section of the NTA, Section 23, argument has dealt primarily with the appropriateness of rates in the light of conditions, especially market competition, not on the equity of railway profits on particular traffic.[7] It is not clear that the United States has adopted this policy but it is an important part of railway pricing freedom.

The Importance of Service As Well
As Rate Freedom

The freedom to control service type and levels as well as freight rates has important ramifications. First, it allows the railways to allocate scarce rolling stock in profitable ways. For example, during the spring when covered hopper cars are in great demand, priority has been deliberately and explicitly given to customers whose business is the more profitable, whether it is because they have a year-round demand, have higher rates, a better car cycle time, or other factors. Second, the railways have been free to make service arrangements with particular shippers that may be reflected in rate concessions or even rate penalties. For example, volume and car utilization commitments may bring rate concessions; some solid train tariffs include heavy rate penalties for shipper-induced delays in a train cycle. Appreciation of the extent of this freedom enjoyed by the railways has led to a reduction in the use of agreed changes. In effect, any commodity rate can be associated with terms appropriate to the traffic in question.

Through rate concessions and, in some cases, penalty charges, the railways have induced shippers to use railway services in more efficient ways to the overall advantage of the railways and shippers. The net impact of these services in the economy must be considered in the context of total physical distribution costs. In some cases, improved railway services may have allowed shippers to realize further benefits in other parts of their distribution systems. In other cases, the benefits of more efficient railway service may have been partially offset by higher shipper costs. For example, railway tariffs designed to pass on the benefits of even traffic flow may raise shipper storage costs if demand is seasonal.

The Value Attached by Shippers to
Rate and Service Flexibility

Value-of-service pricing as practiced in Canada means that the railways have considerable latitude in negotiating particular rate and service arrangements to meet the needs of particular traffic. The resulting flexibility in rate and service conditions means that some traffic that might not otherwise move has been handled profitably. This flexibility is particularly important to shippers dependent on this service.

Summary: The Importance of Deregulation

Deregulation has been important to the improvement of the efficiency and profitability of the railways in Canada because it has given management the freedom to practice selective service design and pricing. The railways early recognized that this process requires a knowledge of the variability of specific costs, specific by commodity volume, route, and direction. The demands placed on railway and shipper management are greater than in earlier periods when an average or across-the-board approach could be taken. The rewards, however, are evident in the findings of CCST. Their findings are strong evidence of the long-term effects of deregulation on economic performance. But it is important to recognize that deregulation in Canada applied to both pricing and service decisions, i.e., the Canadian railways are able to discriminate among shippers in prices and services supplied. The United States is moving to relax restrictions on pricing freedom of U.S. railroads. It is not yet evident that U.S. policy recognizes the importance of relaxing restrictions on service levels and discrimination. But the latter may be even more important in facilitating the survival and revival of the U.S. railroad industry.

NOTES

1. See, for example, T. D. Heaver and James C. Nelson, Railway Pricing Under Commercial Freedom: The Canadian Experience (Vancouver: University of British Columbia Centre for Transportation Studies, 1977).
2. Report of the Royal Commission on Transportation (Ottawa: Queen's Printer, 1967), vol. 2, p. 144.
3. See Richard J. Schultz, Federalism, Bureaucracy and Public Policy: The Politics of Highway Transport (Montreal: McGill-Queen's University Press for the Institute of Public Administration of Canada, 1980).
4. See F. P. Nix et al., "Motor Carrier Regulation: Institutions and Practices," Economic Council of Canada and Institute for Research on Public Policy Working Paper no. E/I 1, August 1980.
5. The original argument was formulated by Ramsey, but independently formulated and in a more general way by Boiteux. See F. P. Ramsey, "A Contribution to the Theory of Taxation," Economic Journal (March 1927):47-61; and M. Boiteux, "Sur la question des Monopoles Publiques astreints à l'equilibre budgetaire," Econometrica (January 1956):22-40, translated by W. J. Baumol and D. F. Bradford as "On the Management of Public Monopolies Subject to Budgetary Constraints," Journal of Economic Theory (September 1971):219-40. See W. J. Baumol and D. F. Bradford, "Optimal Departures from Marginal Cost Pricing," American Economic Review (June 1970):265-83 for a review of the subject.
6. See the discussion by Gratwick in Chapter 11 of this volume.
7. See Martin Westmacott, "The Canadian Transport Commission, Freight Rates and the Public Interest," in Transportation Policy: Regulation, Competition, and the Public Interest, ed. K. R. Ruppenthal and W. T. Stanbury (Vancouver: University of British Columbia Centre for Transportation Studies, 1976), pp. 49-91.

7

PERFORMANCE OF NORTH AMERICAN AND AUSTRALIAN AIRLINES: REGULATION AND PUBLIC ENTERPRISE

William A. Jordan

INTRODUCTION

This chapter investigates the effects on airline performance of two forms of government activity—direct economic regulation by an independent commission and government ownership. Reflecting this dual purpose, the chapter first provides evidence regarding some effects of direct economic regulation by the respective federal commissions of Canada and the United States. Then, with these effects of regulation identified, the second part seeks to determine what additional effects, if any, government ownership has on the performance of regulated airlines in North America.[1] Finally, in order to determine whether or not the North American experience regarding government ownership is unique, it will be compared with David G. Davies' findings regarding the effects of government ownership on the regulated Australian domestic airlines.[2] Overall, it

---

This chapter summarizes the relevant findings of a study undertaken during 1979-81 for Consumer and Corporate Affairs Canada, with major financial assistance from the Economic Council of Canada in collaboration with Transport Canada. Additional information from the study is found in William A. Jordan, Performance of Regulated Canadian Airlines in Domestic and Transborder Operations (Ottawa-Hull: Ministry of Consumer and Corporate Affairs, 1982). Of course, the conclusions of this chapter and the underlying study are those of the author and do not necessarily reflect the views of any unit of the Canadian government.

will be demonstrated that, while major differences in airline performance have been associated with direct economic regulation, government ownership appears to have had little or no additional effect on airline performance in both North America and Australia. This latter finding is contrary to Davies' conclusion, but the apparent inconsistency is resolved by broadening Davies' analysis through the use of more detailed information that apparently was not available when he wrote his first article.

METHODOLOGY

The methodology used to obtain evidence on these matters consists of comparing the performance of airlines operating in different regulatory environments and under different categories of owners. First, the performance of airlines operating in regulatory monopolies with closed entry will be compared with that of airlines operating in regulatory duopolies in which the entry of new airlines has been allowed. Second, within regulatory monopolies, the performance of airlines that are government owned will be compared with those that are privately owned.

Regulatory monopolies have characterized federal regulation in both Canada and the United States since 1938. In Canada, the Air Transport Committee of the Canadian Transport Commission [CTC(A)] has regulated all commercial air activities from the largest airline to the smallest flying club. In the United States, until the introduction of deregulation in late 1978, the Civil Aeronautics Board (CAB) exercised similar regulation over all airlines providing interstate air transportation with large aircraft.[3]

In contrast to these regulatory monopolies, regulatory duopolies existed within California, Florida, and Texas because the CAB's jurisdiction did not extend to airlines operating wholly within a single state and the regulatory commissions in those states permitted the entry of new intrastate carriers. These new intrastate carriers operated in parallel with the CAB-regulated airlines between local city pairs in each state and intense rivalry developed between these two groups of airlines. Furthermore, because the state commissions were sympathetic to requests for fare reductions, this rivalry could be expressed both through fare reductions and through differentiations in service quality. This was in contrast to the situation in the regulatory monopolies in Canada and in the remainder of the United States where reductions in general fares from commission-approved fare formulas were rarely allowed so that rivalry among carriers serving the same city pairs was limited primarily to innovations in service quality.

The federally regulated airlines to be studied consist of the two Canadian mainline carriers (Air Canada and CP Air), the five Canadian regional carriers (Eastern Provincial, Nordair, Pacific Western, Quebecair, and Transair), three selected U.S. trunk carriers (Delta, Northwest, and Trans World), and four selected U.S. local service carriers (Allegheny, Frontier, North Central, and Southern). All the U.S. carriers, except Delta and Southern, were selected because their systemwide geographic operating areas were the most similar to those of the Canadian carriers.[4] Delta and Southern, in contrast, were selected because their operating areas were largely in the southern United States and both were headquartered in Atlanta, Georgia. Thus, if adverse weather has a significant impact on operations, their performance should be superior to that of the Canadian and the more northern U.S. carriers. These 14 airlines operating under regulatory monopolies are compared with the four major intrastate carriers—Air California and PSA in California, Air Florida located in Florida, and Southwest in Texas—operating under state regulation in competition with CAB-regulated airlines.

All of the U.S. airlines are privately owned, but in Canada there are presently three government-owned airlines as well as three privately owned airlines. Air Canada has been a crown corporation owned indirectly or directly by the federal government since 1937,[5] Pacific Western was purchased by the province of Alberta in 1974,[6] and Air Canada purchased 86.4 percent of Nordair's issued shares in January 1979.[7] Unfortunately, not all of these three government-owned carriers can be compared with the privately owned airlines in the United States because the adoption of the Airline Deregulation Act (ADA) on October 24, 1978 (92 Stat. 1705) makes it inappropriate to extend the comparison with regulated U.S. airlines beyond that year. This eliminates Nordair from consideration. It also makes Pacific Western's inclusion questionable since its relatively recent change in ownership means that the full effects of government ownership may not have had time to occur. This is especially true since Alberta's acquisition was challenged by the federal government and did not receive final approval from the Supreme Court of Canada until February 1977. Therefore, the comparison used in this chapter to investigate the effects of government ownership will be limited to Air Canada in relation to similar large, privately owned Canadian and U.S. airlines.

The time period covered by these comparisons of North American airlines is from 1975 to 1978. The selection of 1978 was dictated by the adoption of the ADA in the United States, while 1975 was chosen to provide a four-year period designed to eliminate the effects of unusual events that could make information for just one year misleading. In some cases, however, data for shorter time periods will be used when it is clear that they are representative of the matter being analyzed and are not influenced by unusual events.

EFFECTS OF REGULATORY MONOPOLIES

The hypothesis underlying this section is that similar regulatory environments should yield similar performance. This implies that the performance of the Canadian mainline and regional carriers should be similar to that of the CAB-regulated trunk and local service carriers since both groups operated under regulatory monopolies through 1978. In contrast, there should be significant differences between their performance and that of the intrastate carriers operating under regulatory duopolies. These similarities and differences should be apparent in a number of areas, including fares, operating expenses, and profits.

Fares

Figure 7.1 depicts the fares per mile as of December 31, 1978, for the Canadian mainline, U.S. trunk, and U.S. intrastate carriers. The curved lines represent the fares per mile derived from the fare formulas from which all U.S. trunk coach fares and all Canadian mainline economy fares (except those for a few short-haul city pairs) were calculated at that time. Since explicit fare formulas were not used by the U.S. intrastate carriers, their fares per mile for representative city pairs are plotted in the lower left-hand corner of Figure 7.1, with straight lines connecting each carrier's points.

It should be recognized that the fares per mile in Figure 7.1 are given in the currency of each carrier's country; that is, Canadian fares per mile are in Canadian cents while U.S. fares per mile are expressed in U.S. cents. To give some perspective regarding the range of possible effects of exchange rates, the U.S. trunk carriers' fares per mile were converted into Canadian cents using the average exchange rate in effect during December 1978.[8] These adjusted fares per mile appear as the broken line lying above the Canadian fares per mile. It can be seen from this that the Canadian fares per mile lie between the U.S. fares per mile expressed first in U.S. cents and then in Canadian cents (the higher U.S. line). Given that some intermediate position depicts the true effects of exchange rate differences (since we are comparing domestic prices for domestic goods in the two countries rather than domestic prices

FIGURE 7.1

Fares per Mile for Canadian Mainline, U.S. Trunk, and U.S. Intrastate Carriers, December 31, 1978

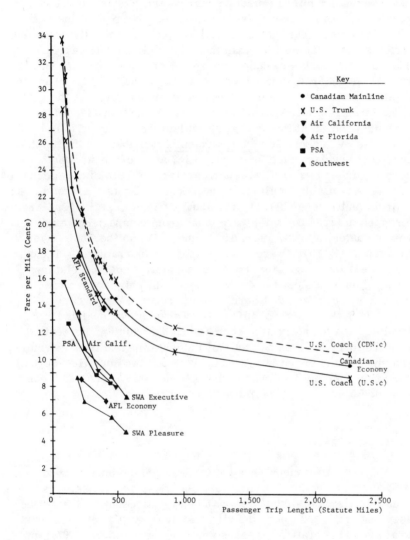

Source: William A. Jordan, Performance of Regulated Canadian Airlines in Domestic and Transborder Operations (Ottawa-Hull: Ministry of Consumer and Corporate Affairs, 1982), p. 6.

for imported goods), it is clear that the fares per mile of the regulated Canadian mainline carriers were remarkably close to those of the regulated U.S. trunk carriers, both in terms of fare level (the heights of the curves) and fare structure (the steep taper showing lower fares per mile as distance increases).[9] This, of course, is consistent with the underlying hypothesis of this part of the study.

It is also clear that the fare levels of the federally regulated airlines were much higher than those of the intrastate carriers operating in regulatory duopolies (except for Air Florida's standard fares). In general, detailed comparisons of the U.S. trunk and intrastate carriers' fares per mile (and remembering that the U.S. trunk fares per mile approximated those of the Canadian mainline carriers) show that the federally regulated fares per mile in both countries were about 50 to 100 percent higher than the intrastate carriers' regular coach fares per mile, and were from 100 to 180 percent higher than the intrastate carriers' off-peak fares per mile that were available on all night and weekend flights operated by Air Florida (until December 14, 1978) and by Southwest.[10] Similar differences in fares per mile were found from comparisons made for various dates in 1966, 1971, 1975, and 1977, so the findings for December 31, 1978, were not a temporary aberration.[11] It can be concluded, therefore, that the fares per mile under regulatory monopolies with closed entry have been much higher than under regulatory duopolies that permitted the entry of new airlines.

Since the fares per mile of the Canadian regional and U.S. local service carriers have been as much as 30 to 40 percent higher than the formula fares per mile of the mainline and trunk carriers, and since the transborder fares between the two countries were almost the same as the formula fares,[12] the above conclusion can be extended to all city pairs in North America.

Operating Expenses

Major differences also existed between the operating costs of the federally regulated airlines and the low-fare intrastate carriers once the effects of distance were taken into account. This can be seen in Figure 7.2 where the weighted average of each carrier's total system operating expenses per revenue ton-mile (RTM) for the four years from 1975 through 1978 are plotted against its average system trip length for combined scheduled and charter passengers.[13] Also depicted is the trend line giving the best fit for the federally regulated airlines' data from among six mathematical relationships.[14]

FIGURE 7.2

Total Operating Expenses per RTM in Relation to System Trip Lengths, 1975–78 Average Values

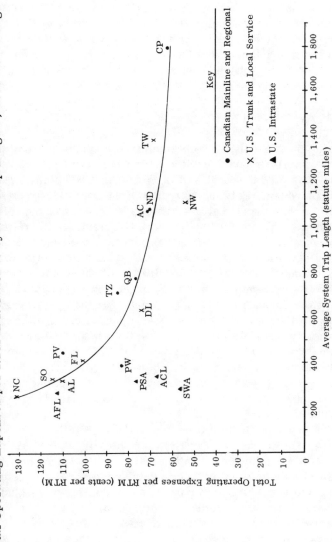

Source: William A. Jordan, _Performance of Regulated Canadian Airlines in Domestic and Transborder Operations_ (Ottawa–Hull: Ministry of Consumer and Corporate Affairs, 1982), p. 26.

167

The close association between distance and operating expenses per RTM for the federally regulated airlines is indicated by the high, and statistically significant, R^2 of 0.866.[15] At the same time, the appreciably lower operating expenses per RTM of the three largest U.S. intrastate carriers (excluding Air Florida) are clearly evident from Figure 7.2. PSA was -31.8 percent below the federally regulated airlines' trend line, while Air California was -38.0 and Southwest was -52.8 percent below that line.[16] These large differences are similar to the differences in fare levels found in the previous section and they indicate that the intrastate carriers (except Air Florida) could be profitable while charging low fares per mile.

Profits

The low fares that have been offered by the successful U.S. intrastate carriers have benefited their passengers, but have they adversely affected the profits of these carriers? Table 7.1 shows that they have not. This table compares the operating ratios of the Canadian mainline and regional carriers with those of the selected U.S. trunk, local service, and intrastate carriers. Operating ratios are calculated by dividing total operating expenses by total operating revenues. The lower the ratio (due to low expenses relative to revenues) the larger the profits, while high ratios mean small profits with ratios close to or exceeding 100 indicating losses.

It can be seen that during 1977 and 1978 the operating ratios of the federally regulated airlines were quite similar. The simple average of the operating ratios for Air Canada and CP Air was 92.8, compared with 93.0 for the three selected U.S. trunk carriers. During the same period, the five Canadian regional carriers had a simple average of 95.0 while the four selected U.S. local service carriers had an average of 93.1. In contrast to the similarity among the regulated airlines, considerable diversity in profits existed among the low-fare U.S. intrastate carriers. On the high side (indicating losses), fledgling Air Florida radically bettered its performance by reducing its operating ratio from 154.4 in 1977 to 98.1 in 1978. On the low side (indicating high profits), Southwest's superior and improving performance gave it ratios of 79.1 and 73.9. At the same time, the older Air California and PSA had "normal" operating ratios yielding a simple average of 93.6.[17]

It is clear from these data, and those in the previous section, that the successful intrastate carriers were able to achieve low operating costs that were consistent with their low fares per mile. With the exception of Air Florida in 1977, they were at least as profitable as the high-cost federally regulated airlines charging

TABLE 7.1

System Operating Ratios: Canadian Mainline,
Regional, and Selected U.S. Carriers, 1977–78

Carrier	Operating Ratios	
	1977	1978
Mainline		
Air Canada	92.5[a]	93.6[a]
CP Air	94.7[a]	90.6
Trunk		
Trans World	98.2	98.0
Northwest	90.0	91.4[a]
Delta	90.7	89.9
Intrastate		
Air Calif.	90.9	94.4
Air Florida[b]	154.4	98.1
PSA[c]	95.3	93.8
Southwest	79.1	73.9
Regional		
East. Prov.	104.2[a]	96.2
Nordair	89.9[a]	90.7[a]
Pac. Western	96.2[a]	93.3[a]
Quebecair	95.8[a]	97.8[a]
Transair	92.5[a]	92.9
Local Service		
Allegheny	94.8	94.0
Frontier	88.9	95.4
N. Central	92.3	88.4
Southern	95.3	95.9

[a]Service interrupted by strikes. In 1977, a strike by air traffic controllers resulted in a four–day service suspension by all Canadian carriers. The 1978 strikes were also relatively minor except for the 108-day strike by Northwest's pilots.

[b]Fiscal years ended July 31, 1977, and July 31, 1978.

[c]Includes the following subsidiaries in addition to the airline: Pacific Southwest Airmotive (maintenance services), Airline Training Center, and Jetair Leasing. Airline and Airmotive revenues together accounted for around 98 percent of total revenues in 1977 and 1978.

Source: William A. Jordan, Performance of Regulated Canadian Airlines in Domestic and Transborder Operations (Ottawa-Hull: Ministry of Consumer and Corporate Affairs, 1982), p. 22.

high fares per mile. This demonstrates that high fares are not a necessary condition for large airline profits.

Reasons for Cost Differences

It has been said that "necessity is the mother of invention." Apparently the necessity of having to charge low prices in order to compete effectively with the established regulated airlines resulted in the intrastate carriers finding ways to operate that were truly low-cost. The question is, how did they manage to do this?

Canadian airline executives frequently state that their airlines are inherently higher-cost operators than U.S. airlines because of having to fly under relatively adverse weather conditions in a country having a small and dispersed population. [18] This overlooks the fact that during 1975-78 the operating expenses per RTM of the federally regulated Canadian mainline and regional carriers were simi-lar to those of comparable federally regulated U.S. airlines, while being much higher than those of the U.S. intrastate carriers (see Figure 7.2). The large differences in operating expenses, there-fore, were not associated with differences in nationality, but with differences in regulation. Furthermore, both direct and indirect evidence from several analyses of these matters indicates that the lower operating expenses per RTM of the U.S. intrastate carriers were not due to differences in weather or population. [19] Finally, even if weather and population should increase airline operating costs in Canada to some small degree, the fact is that during 1975-78, purely domestic RTM accounted for just 47.0 percent of total system RTM for the seven Canadian carriers! For the same period, transborder RTM equaled 15.0 percent of total, while international RTM was 38.0 percent of total system RTM. [20] This means that for a very large portion of their total operations, Canadian carriers are subject to the weather conditions of other countries and can draw upon the populations of those countries for a significant portion of their traffic.

If country, weather, and population do not account for differ-ences in operating expenses per RTM, what factors do appear to be important within the context of regulatory differences? In 1978, labor expenses accounted for around 39 percent of total system op-erating expenses for the 18 carriers studied, while fuel expenses accounted for around 21 percent. Together, on average these two major inputs comprised just over 60 percent of total operating ex-penses, ranging from 50.5 percent for Air Florida to 66.8 percent for Delta. Therefore, the very large differences in total operating expenses per RTM should be reflected to an appreciable extent in price and/or utilization differences for these two major inputs.

Employee Utilization

Figure 7.3 shows that during 1975-78 the federally regulated Canadian and U.S. airlines (except Northwest) had generally similar labor productivity after adjusting for the effects of distance. Indeed, regressing RTM per employee with average passenger trip length for these carriers (excluding Northwest) yields an R^2 of 0.837 for the best-fit trend line.[21] In contrast, the four U.S. intrastate carriers all had labor productivity above the trend line, ranging from 17 percent for Air Florida, to around 67 percent for Air California and PSA, and on to 118 percent for Southwest.[22] So, again, the performance of the three largest U.S. intrastate carriers was much superior to that of the federally regulated airlines (except for Northwest's 82.5 percent deviation). This maintains the basic pattern of similarity among the carriers operating under regulatory monopolies in contrast to the large differences between those carriers and the three largest intrastate carriers operating under regulatory duopolies.

Labor Payments

Total payments to employees for wages and salaries, benefits, and personnel expenses (mainly covering travel, lodging, and meals for flight personnel) show significant differences among the various carrier groups. The three U.S. trunk carriers paid an average of $30,000 per employee during 1978, while the four U.S. local service carriers paid an average of $27,500. Air Canada and CP Air paid an average of $25,000 per employee (in Canadian dollars) and the five regional carriers paid about $22,000 per employee, or about 17 and 20 percent less than their federally regulated U.S. counterparts (which is contrary to G. B. Hunnings's assertion that factor input prices are higher in Canada—see note 18). Finally, Air California, PSA, and Southwest also paid around $22,000 per employee in 1978, which is about 26 percent less than the U.S. trunk carriers and roughly the same as the Canadian regional carriers (ignoring possible exchange rate adjustments).[23]

Employee Payments per RTM

Dividing each carrier's average annual payments per employee by annual RTM per employee yields employee payments per RTM. These are plotted in Figure 7.4 and the best-fit trend line between employee payments per RTM and average passenger trip length for the federally regulated airlines (again excluding Northwest) yields an R^2 of 0.865.[24] The effects of the differences in average employee payments are indicated by the two Canadian mainline carriers being above the trend line while the lower-paying five regional carriers were all below the trend line. At the same time,

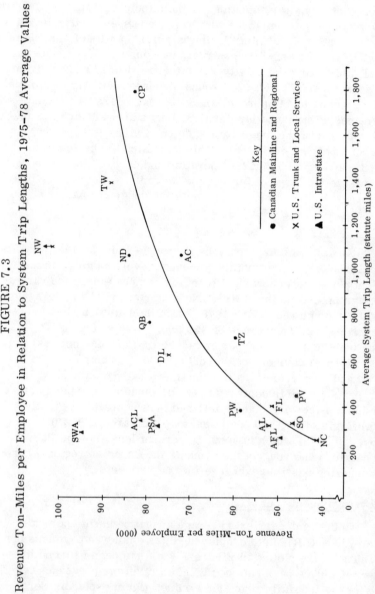

FIGURE 7.3

Revenue Ton-Miles per Employee in Relation to System Trip Lengths, 1975–78 Average Values

Source: William A. Jordan, Performance of Regulated Canadian Airlines in Domestic and Transborder Operations (Ottawa–Hull: Ministry of Consumer and Corporate Affairs, 1982), p. 68.

FIGURE 7.4

Employee Payments per RTM in Relation to System Trip Lengths, 1978

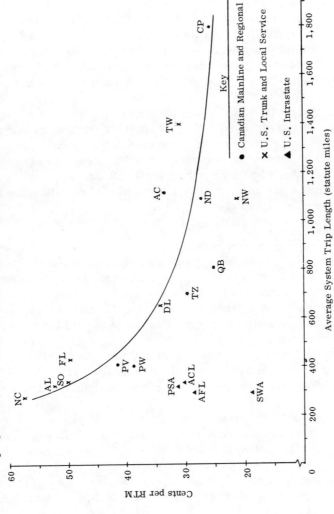

Key

● Canadian Mainline and Regional

✕ U.S. Trunk and Local Service

▲ U.S. Intrastate

Average System Trip Length (statute miles)

Cents per RTM

Source: William A. Jordan, Performance of Regulated Canadian Airlines in Domestic and Transborder Operations (Ottawa–Hull: Ministry of Consumer and Corporate Affairs, 1982), p. 93.

the U.S. local service carriers plus Trans World were all above the trend line, while Delta was slightly below it and only Northwest, with its very high employee productivity counterbalancing its high employee payments, fell well below the line. Thus, there is a tendency toward intercountry differences in this measure, with the Canadian carriers being favored in this respect due to having lower average employee payments.

The performance of the U.S. intrastate carriers, however, was even more significant than the intercountry differences. All four had employee payments per RTM that were much lower than even the Canadian regional carriers—ranging from -38.9 percent below the trend line for PSA on down to an impressive -65.1 percent for Southwest.[25] This was due both to lower average employee payments for these carriers (especially Air Florida) and to very high employee productivity. The fact that the intrastate carriers were so far below the norm in an expense category that accounts for around 39 percent of total airline operating expenses goes a fair way in indicating why they could be profitable while charging regular economy fares per mile as much as 50 percent lower than the federally regulated airlines.

Fuel Prices and Utilization

The U.S. intrastate carriers also achieved low fuel expenses per RTM, thereby having superior performance in an additional 21 percent or so of total operating expenses. This time, however, their favorable performance was not helped by paying lower prices for the input. Actually, the intrastate carriers paid the highest average prices among the U.S. carriers, but the differences were small—their 8.2 to 10.7 cents per liter prices from 1975 to 1978 were only about 2 percent higher than the trunk carriers' system prices and about 1 percent higher than the local service carriers prices.[26]

Much larger differences existed in the fuel prices paid by the Canadian carriers relative to the U.S. carriers. After making exchange rate adjustments for fuel purchased outside Canada, Canadian mainline carriers generally paid between 15 and 20 percent more for fuel than comparable U.S. trunk carriers during 1975-78; and the Canadian regional carriers paid from 15.8 to 43.4 percent higher prices than the U.S. local service carriers, with an average difference of 27.4 percent.[27] It is interesting to note that the higher prices paid by the mainline carriers were due primarily to higher taxes and fuel-related airport fees in Canada than in the United States. Net domestic Canadian fuel prices excluding taxes and airport fees were seldom more than 5 percent higher than net domestic prices paid by Northwest and Trans World. In contrast, the Canadian regional carriers' net domestic fuel prices (except for Transair) were 1.6 to 24.2 percent above those of the U.S. local service carriers, with the larger differences probably due to higher prices paid for fuel purchased in the far north.[28]

Similar fuel prices among the U.S. carriers means that any significant differences in their fuel expenses per RTM would have to come from differences in fuel utilization. One measure of fuel utilization is RTM per liter of fuel, and this measure for the 18 carriers is plotted in Figure 7.5 together with the distance-related trend line for the federally regulated airlines.[29] This figure shows that all the federally regulated U.S. airlines (except Frontier) fell below the trend line, while all the Canadian carriers (except Eastern Provincial and Transair) were above average in fuel utilization. At the same time, in what is by now a familiar pattern, all the U.S. intrastate carriers (except Air Florida) also had high fuel utilization.

Taken together, fuel prices and utilization yield average fuel expenses per RTM, and this measure is plotted in Figure 7.6 together with the distance-related trend line for the federally regulated airlines.[30] It can be seen that there was a tendency for the high prices paid by Canadian carriers to be offset by their high utilization, while the lower prices of the federally regulated U.S. airlines were offset by their lower utilization. As a result, Figure 7.6 shows no consistent intercountry differences in fuel expenses per RTM among the federally regulated airlines, with three federally regulated airlines of each country having above average fuel expenses per RTM and four having below average expenses. At the same time, however, the three largest U.S. intrastate carriers (and Frontier) had expenses per RTM that were -11.5 to -21.4 percent below the trend line while none of the other airlines had expenses more than -9.0 percent below the line.[31] While not as outstanding as their employee payments per RTM, this favorable performance also contributed to the intrastate carriers' ability to profit while charging low fares per mile.

Summary

The evidence presented above is consistent with the hypothesis regarding the effects of regulation by a single independent commission. On the one hand, the performance of the federally regulated airlines in Canada and the United States were similar while, on the other hand, their performance differed appreciably from that of the U.S. intrastate carriers operating under regulatory duopolies. Performance under regulatory monopolies was characterized by coach/

FIGURE 7.5

Average RTM per Liter of Fuel in Relation to System Stage Lengths, 1975-78 Average Values

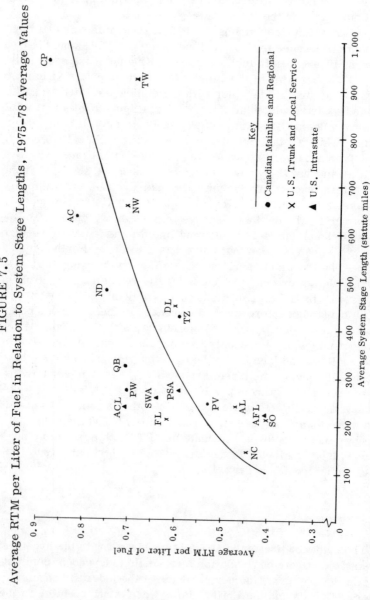

Source: William A. Jordan, Performance of Regulated Canadian Airlines in Domestic and Transborder Operations (Ottawa-Hull: Ministry of Consumer and Corporate Affairs, 1982), p. 115.

FIGURE 7.6

Average Fuel Expenses per RTM in Relation to System Stage Lengths, 1975–78 Average Values

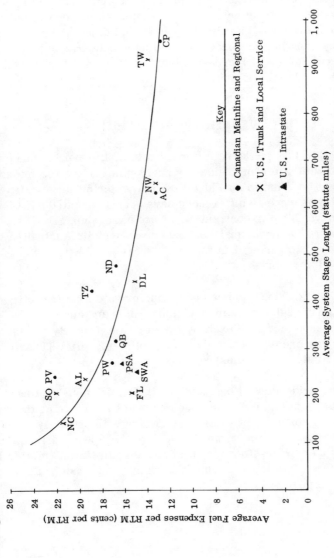

Source: William A. Jordan, <u>Performance of Regulated Canadian Airlines in Domestic and Transborder</u>
<u>Operations</u> (Ottawa-Hull: Ministry of Consumer and Corporate Affairs, 1982), p. 122.

economy fares being from 50 to 100 percent higher than those of the U.S. intrastate carriers operating under regulatory duopolies, by correspondingly higher operating expenses per RTM and, therefore, by profits that were similar to those of the three largest intrastate carriers. The distinguishing operating characteristic of the intrastate carriers was their consistently high utilization of inputs. They also benefited from relatively low employee payments, but not from low fuel prices. Overall, it appears that direct government regulation by a single independent commission does have adverse effects on performance by increasing both the fares and the operating costs of the regulated airlines.

EFFECTS OF GOVERNMENT OWNERSHIP

Now that the large differences in airline performance associated with different regulatory environments have been identified, the next question to be addressed is whether or not significant additional performance differences have been associated with government ownership in contrast to private ownership. David G. Davies compared the performances of the two domestic Australian trunk carriers and, using data for the 16-year period from 1958-59 to 1973-74, concluded:

> The evidence indicates that the private firm [Ansett Airlines], operating under the rules and customs associated with exchangeable private property rights, is more productive than the public enterprise [Trans-Australia Airlines].[32]

Davies' evidence will be examined in detail later, but first let us contrast his findings with those obtained by comparing the performance of government-owned Air Canada with privately owned CP Air, Delta, Northwest, and Trans World. Specifically, within regulatory monopolies, has private ownership in North America been associated with more productive performance than has government ownership?

North American Evidence

It has already been shown that there were no differences in the fares per mile offered by Air Canada and CP Air during 1978 and earlier years, and that their economy fares per mile were very similar to the coach fares per mile of the U.S. trunk carriers.

Thus, as in Davies' articles, the question of performance differences concerns productivity and related operating costs. It has also
been demonstrated that distance plays an important role in airline
operating expenses, employee productivity, and fuel utilization.
Therefore, intercarrier efficiency comparisons should continue to
be undertaken using performance data that have been adjusted for
the effects of distance, that is, by using the percentage deviations
from the distance-related trend lines for the various measures.
These percentage deviations for Air Canada, CP Air, Trans World,
Northwest, and Delta are summarized in Table 7.2, with the airlines listed in decreasing rank order of efficiency for each of seven
measures.

Table 7.2 shows that Air Canada ranked relatively low (fourth
or fifth) among these five large carriers in terms of employee productivity (RTM and operating revenues per employee) and employee
expenses (total employee payments per RTM). In contrast to its
relatively poor performance with regard to employees, however,
Air Canada was the best of the five carriers in terms of fuel utilization and expenses, consistently ranking first in these three measures
while Trans World consistently ranked fifth. Thus, since labor and
fuel together generally accounted for something over 60 percent of
total operating expenses during 1978, it is not surprising to find Air
Canada ranking fourth among the carriers in terms of total operating expenses per RTM, the most inclusive of airline cost measures.

Air Canada's 4.2 percent deviation above the distance-related
trend line for operating expenses per RTM compares with 7.0 percent for fifth-ranking Trans World and 1.6 percent for third-ranking
CP Air. Thus, since Air Canada lies midway between CP Air and
Trans World and since both these latter carriers are privately owned,
there seems to be little reason to attribute Air Canada's above-
average operating expenses per RTM to government ownership.
This conclusion is supported by the fact that the 5.4 percentage-
point interval encompassing the positive deviations of these three
carriers was small relative to the 10.3 percentage-point interval
between CP Air's 1.6 and Delta's -8.7 percent deviation, and the
20.8 percentage-point interval between CP Air and Northwest's
-19.2 percent deviation, with all of these carriers being privately
owned. It appears that factors other than ownership account for the
variations in operating expenses per RTM among the federally regulated airlines.

If the comparison is limited to the two Canadian mainline carriers (similar to Davies' comparison of the two Australian carriers),
it can be said that Air Canada was inferior to CP Air in two of the
three employee measures, and was superior to it in all three of the
fuel measures. Overall, Air Canada's operating expenses per RTM

TABLE 7.2

Efficiency Rankings and Percentage Deviations from Distance-Related Trend Lines for Various Performance Measures: Canadian Mainline and Selected U.S. Trunk Carriers

| | Carrier and Its Percentage Deviation—Average System Values | | | | | | |
| | Employees | | | Fuel | | | |
Efficiency Ranking	RTM per Employee 1975-78	Operating Revenue per Employee 1975-78	Total Payments per RTM 1978	ATM per Liter 1975-78	RTM per Liter 1975-78	Fuel Expenses per RTM 1975-78	Total Operating Expenses per RTM 1975-78
1	NW 82.5	NW 55.6	NW -25.8	AC 16.9	AC 11.7	AC -9.0	NW -19.2
2	DL 14.5	TW 9.0	DL -2.0	NW 15.3	CP 5.5	NW -7.8	DL -8.7
3	TW 6.5	DL 8.5	CP 2.8	CP 0.7	NW -3.8	DL -5.3	CP 1.6
4	CP -5.0	AC -2.1	TW 16.2	DL -5.7	DL -8.7	CP -1.0	AC 4.2
5	AC -6.7	CP -5.2	AC 18.3	TW -12.9	TW -15.2	TW 5.9	TW 7.0

Note: Percentage deviations from distance-related trend lines calculated for the Canadian and U.S. federally regulated airlines in the previous section.

Source: William A. Jordan, Performance of Regulated Canadian Airlines in Domestic and Transborder Operations (Ottawa-Hull: Ministry of Consumer and Corporate Affairs, 1982), pp. 27, 67, 72, 92, 112, 121.

were somewhat poorer than CP Air's but, as indicated above, the deviation difference was just 2.6 percentage points, which is not large enough to conclude that important performance differences are associated with government ownership.

Table 7.3 provides additional information showing that Air Canada did not have unusually poor performance relative to privately owned airlines. To the contrary, it ranked third in RTM load factor (tied with Trans World) and second in revenue passenger-mile (RPM) load factor (with CP Air ranking first in both measures).

TABLE 7.3

Rankings and Average System Values for Load Factor
and Input Price Measures: Canadian Mainline
and Selected U.S. Trunk Carriers

	Carrier and Its Average System Values			
	Load Factor		Payment per Employee	Fuel Price per Liter
Ranking	RTM 1975-78	RPM 1975-78	1978	1975-78*
1	CP 52.5%	CP 64.6%	CP $24,160	DL 8.984¢
2	DL 49.2	AC 62.0	AC 26,460	TW 9.455
3	AC 48.3	TW 59.1	DL 28,445	NW 9.502
4	TW 48.3	DL 58.1	NW 30,432	AC 10.797
5	NW 42.1	NW 48.8	TW 30,601	CP 11.193

*Canadian cents per liter for Air Canada and CP Air, U.S. cents per liter for the U.S. carriers. Estimated fuel purchased by Canadian carriers in foreign countries adjusted for the exchange rates between the Canadian and U.S. currencies. 1975-78 data calculated as the simple average of annual data for the four years.

Source: William A. Jordan, Performance of Regulated Canadian Airlines in Domestic and Transborder Operations (Ottawa-Hull: Ministry of Consumer and Corporate Affairs, 1982), pp. 82, 103, 106, 117.

The overall rankings of the prices paid for labor and fuel were
clearly affected by intercountry differences. Within Canada, however, Air Canada paid about 9.5 percent higher prices for its labor
and about 3.5 percent lower prices for its fuel than did CP Air.
Again, these data do not provide a consistent pattern denoting inherent inefficiency on the part of government-owned airlines, even
though the load factor data for just the two Canadian airlines might
be considered weak evidence in support of this contention.[33]

Australian Evidence

The inconsistency between Davies' findings and the evidence
from North America naturally calls for further analysis. As stated
in the introduction, this inconsistency can be resolved by broadening Davies' analysis through the use of more detailed information
that was not available to him.

It happens that the privately owned firm in Australia (Ansett
Transport Industries) operates through four airline subsidiaries
and Davies' data were for the combined operations of all four rather
than for each individual carrier. Of the four, only Ansett Airlines
of Australia (then named Ansett ANA) was similar to the government-
owned Trans-Australia Airlines (TAA) in providing interstate trunk
operations throughout the country. Indeed, due to the detailed
coordination and regulation of these two airlines through the Rationalization Committee and the Minister for Transport, a majority of the physical attributes of these two carriers have been virtually identical over the years.[34] In contrast, the other three
Ansett Airlines were regional carriers operating smaller aircraft
in largely intrastate service.[35] Therefore, a more appropriate
comparison would have been between TAA and just Ansett Airlines
of Australia (AAA), rather than between TAA and the combined
operations of all four Ansett subsidiaries as was done by Davies.

Davies recognized the possibility that his aggregate data
could be misleading:

> One possible deficiency in the data is that the statistics
> for the private firm include the figures for the Ansett
> Transport Industries' small intrastate airlines as well
> as the big interstate carrier, Ansett ANA. We were
> not able to obtain sufficient separate data for Ansett
> ANA per se.
>
> Should these subsidiaries have higher measures
> of productivity than Ansett ANA's measures of produc-
> tivity, then our statistics presented below will overstate

Ansett ANA's measure and make it appear to be more productive than it is. On the other hand, if the various ratios for the subsidiaries were below those of Ansett ANA, the latter's measures would understate its productivity.

Unfortunately, this is an empirical question and deduction is of little help in settling the issue. Sketchy empirical information, however, would tend to support the assertion that Ansett ANA's productivity for freight-mail and passengers is higher than that of the small intrastate subsidiaries. All but one of Ansett Transport Industries' intrastate subsidiaries operate on uneconomic routes and receive subsidies from the Commonwealth. In the absence of conclusive evidence to the contrary, however, we shall assume that the productivity of the subsidiaries is approximately the same as that of Ansett ANA.[36]

Fortunately, it happens that annual traffic, personnel, and aircraft data are now available for each Australian interstate and intrastate carrier.[37] This more detailed information makes it possible to test Davies' assumption regarding the relative productivity of the various Ansett airlines and, more importantly, to make the appropriate direct comparison between AAA and TAA.

In addition to the above, there are two other problems with Davies' data that decrease their usefulness in providing evidence regarding the performance of privately owned versus government-owned airlines. The first of these is that the output measures Davies used were number of passengers, tons of mail and freight, and revenues.[38] It happens that an airline transporting its passengers and freight/mail an average of 500 miles is more productive in a physical sense than one that carries the same quantities of traffic only 250 miles. Unfortunately, this fact would not be reflected in Davies' first two output measures and would be somewhat obscured in the revenue measure if there were a significant distance taper in prices (see Figure 7.1).[39] Clearly, a better measure of passenger output would be revenue passenger-miles, while freight and mail output would be better represented by revenue ton-miles, both of which incorporate the important distance dimension of airline output.

The final problem with Davies' evidence is that it also ignores the differing relationships between distance and productivity measures for various inputs. Davies used employees as his input measure and compared the airlines' productivity in terms of number of passengers per employee, tons of freight and mail per employee, and revenue earned per employee. He failed to recognize, however, that there is a <u>negative</u> relationship between distance and employee productivity measured in terms of passengers or tons of freight/mail per employee due to the fact that it requires less labor to carry 1,000 passengers (or 100 tons of freight/mail) an average of 250 miles than to carry them an average of 500 miles. In contrast, productivity measured in terms of RPM or RTM per employee yields a <u>positive</u> relationship between average trip length (distance) and employee productivity (see Figure 7.3). Finally, given a balancing fare taper, revenue per employee may vary very little with changes in distance.

Failure to recognize these differing relationships between distance and alternative measures of employee productivity is probably behind Davies' assertion in the above quotation that Ansett ANA's employee productivity should be higher than that of Ansett's intrastate subsidiaries. This would be true in terms of RTM and RPM per employee if Ansett ANA had longer average trip lengths, but not in terms of passengers or tons of freight/mail per employee. Unfortunately, Davies used the latter measures of employee productivity without recognizing that short-haul intrastate carriers are likely to outperform long-haul interstate carriers in terms of passengers and tons of freight/mail per employee.

Differences between the Interstate and Intrastate Carriers

The more detailed data now available for 1974-80 show that appreciable differences have existed between Ansett's smaller intrastate carriers and the two large interstate carriers, AAA and TAA. First of all, during these years their fleets were largely comprised of different types of aircraft (see note 35).

Second, as shown in Table 7.4, there were also significant differences in average system scheduled trip lengths. Ansett Airlines of New South Wales (ANSW) had average passenger and freight/mail trip lengths about one-half those of AAA, while the trip lengths for Ansett Airlines of South Australia (ASA) were less than one-third as long as AAA. At the same time, the average trip lengths of MacRobertson Miller Airlines (MMA) over sparsely settled Western Australia were in excess of 25 percent longer than those of AAA. More importantly, it can be seen that the average passenger trip lengths for all four of the Ansett subsidiaries (the grouping used by Davies) were consistently <u>shorter</u> than those of TAA, while AAA alone had <u>longer</u> trip lengths than TAA. Given the inverse relationship between distance and passengers per employee, this reversal of the relative distances could have had a significant impact on Davies' findings. The same reversal did not apply to

TABLE 7.4

System Scheduled Passenger and Freight/Mail Trip Lengths: Ansett Airline Subsidiaries and Trans-Australia Airlines, 1974–80

| Calendar Year | Passenger Trip Length[a] | | | | | | Freight/Mail Trip Length[b] | | | | | |
| | Ansett Subsidiaries | | | | | TAA | Ansett Subsidiaries | | | | | TAA |
	AAA	ANSW	ASA	MMA	Total	Total	AAA	ANSW	ASA	MMA	Total	Total
1974	539	279	148	667	511	525	592	308	166	758	594	579
1975	548	273	152	693	519	536	613	298	169	777	614	604
1976	517	269	148	669	490	506	576	289	163	722	577	553
1977	514	272	152	669	489	510	559	296	161	690	559	544
1978	531	269	152	659	503	518	577	292	161	705	579	532
1979	540	269	150	681	512	528	551	288	151	736	556	522
1980	548	282	151	695	524	542	556[c]	290[c]	153[c]	747[c]	563[c]	520[c]
Mean[d]	534	273	151	676	507	524	575	295	161	733	577	547

[a]Statute miles—total revenue passenger-kilometers divided by revenue passengers embarked, and multiplied by 0.62137.

[b]Statute miles—total freight plus mail tonne-kilometers performed divided by tonnes embarked, and multiplied by 0.62137.

[c]Calculated from actual freight tons, freight RTM, and mail RTM, plus estimated mail tons (actual freight tons plus estimated mail tons based on percentage increases in mail RTM over 1979).

[d]Weighted average.

Sources: Calculated from data in Australian Department of Transport, Australian Transport, 1974–75 to 1979–80 (Canberra: Australian Government Publishing Service); and International Civil Aviation Organization, Traffic, Commercial Air Carriers, 1976–80 (Montreal: ICAO).

freight/mail trip lengths. The small freight operations of the regional carriers resulted in there being little difference between the average trip lengths of AAA and the total Ansett subsidiaries, with both AAA and Ansett total having somewhat longer trip lengths than TAA.

Third, it happens that the three Ansett regional carriers did not report any maintenance and overhaul personnel in their employee counts. There are three possible explanations for the exclusion of these essential personnel: AAA does all the maintenance/overhaul work for these carriers; the maintenance personnel of the Ansett regional carriers are combined with, and reported by, AAA; outside firms provide all maintenance/overhaul services for these firms. It seems likely that the first of the explanations is the correct one, but if either the first or the second possibility is true, the proper adjustment would be to increase the regional carriers' maintenance/overhaul and total employment figures by appropriate amounts and reduce AAA's figures by equal amounts. This adjustment is calculated in Table 7.5 and is based on the fact that maintenance and overhaul employees comprised at least 20 percent of total personnel reported for Ansett total, Connair, East-West Airlines, and TAA during 1974-80. Therefore, the total reported employee figure for each of the Ansett regional carriers was increased by 25 percent (equivalent to 20 percent of adjusted employees) with the added employees being assigned to their maintenance/overhaul employee category. At the same time, AAA's figures were reduced by equal amounts. The adjusted total figures for the Ansett airlines are given in Table 7.6 (together with TAA's reported figures) and were utilized in all employee productivity measures calculated in this chapter, thereby increasing AAA's employee productivity by about 2.8 percent while decreasing those of the three Ansett regional carriers by 20 percent. Obviously, the resulting measures are partial estimates, but there is good reason to believe they are considerably more accurate than productivity measures based on the reported employee data for the Ansett airlines.

Passenger and Freight/Mail Tons per Employee

The effect of Davies including Ansett's three regional carriers in his passengers per employee and freight/mail tons per employee measures is more clearly seen in Table 7.7. To provide perspective, Davies' employee productivity measures for fiscal years 1971-74 are given for Ansett total and TAA, and then the more detailed information for each of the four Ansett subsidiaries, Ansett total, and TAA are given for calendar years 1974-80.

Looking first at scheduled passengers per employee, it can be seen that during 1974-80 ANSW and ASA were well over twice as high as AAA in this measure, while MMA was generally slightly lower than AAA (all of which is consistent with the differences among these carriers' average passenger trip lengths). On average, the net effect of combining the three regional carriers with AAA is to yield passenger per employee measures for Ansett total that are over 6 percent higher than those of AAA for the seven years from 1974 through 1980. More significantly, it can be seen that TAA's passengers per employee figures consistently fall between those of AAA and Ansett total, that is, they are about 4.5 percent higher than AAA and about 1.5 percent lower than Ansett total. Davies reported that "the average number of passengers carried per employee over the 16 years under observation is consistently higher for Ansett Airlines, the private company."[40] This is quite true for the combined four Ansett subsidiaries due to the very high figures for ANSW and ASA; but it is not true for AAA alone, and AAA is the carrier whose operations are most similar to those of TAA.

The pattern is somewhat different for freight/mail tons per employee. In this case ANSW and ASA had lower tons per employee than AAA while MMA had higher tons per employee, the net effect being figures for Ansett total that were almost identical to those of AAA. Comparing the CY 1974-80 figures with Davies' figures for FY 1971-74, however, shows that there was something of a decline in this measure for Ansett total (and probably AAA) over the 1970 decade. In contrast, the data for TAA show general improvement between FY 1971 and CY 1980 in its freight/mail tons per employee figures. As a result, in 1979 TAA's freight/mail tons per employee exceeded those of AAA and Ansett total. This situation continued through 1980.

Overall, using Davies' own productivity measures, direct comparisons between TAA and AAA (rather than Ansett total) indicate similar employee productivity for combined passenger plus freight/mail operations regardless of differences in ownership. This, of course, is consistent with the North American experience and is quite inconsistent with Davies' findings.

RPM and RTM per Employee

The detailed data for 1974-80 also allow comparisons to be made between the Ansett subsidiaries and TAA using the RPM and RTM measures that incorporate the important distance dimension of airline output.[41] Table 7.8 presents scheduled RPM per employee, freight/mail RTM per employee, and total RTM per employee. It shows that during these years TAA had <u>higher</u> RPM

TABLE 7.5

Average Annual Number of Employees by Category: Australian Domestic Airlines as Reported and as Adjusted to Allocate AAA Maintenance Employees among All Ansett Subsidiaries, 1974–80

Carrier	Pilots and Copilots	Other Cockpit	Cabin Attendants	Maintenance and Overhaul	Traffic and Sales	All Other	Total
				Average Annual Number of Employees[a]			
				As Reported			
AAA	546.3	115.6	783.3	1,898.1	2,232.2	2,782.6	8,358.1
ANSW	67.9	0	61.0	n.r.[b]	33.9[c]	115.8[c]	278.6
ASA	29.2	0	32.4	n.r.[b]	58.9	13.7	134.2
MMA	79.4	0	71.2	n.r.[b]	222.3	142.3	515.2
Total	722.8	115.6	947.9	1,898.1	2,547.3	3,054.4	9,286.1
Connair[d]	30.2	0	12.8	65.9	24.2	21.3	154.4
East–West[e]	90.9	0	72.0	133.5	111.2	78.1	485.7
TAA	577.8	92.1	745.3	1,818.7	2,312.9	2,538.0	8,084.8

188

As Adjusted

AAA	546.3	115.6	783.3	1,666.1[f]	2,232.2	2,782.6	8,126.1[f]
ANSW	67.9	0	61.0	69.7[g]	33.9	115.8	348.3[g]
ASA	29.2	0	32.4	33.5[g]	58.9	13.7	167.7[g]
MMA	79.4	0	71.2	128.8[g]	222.3	142.3	644.0[g]
Total	722.8	115.6	947.9	1,898.1	2,547.3	3,054.4	9,286.1

[a]Simple average of midyear and year-end employment for 1974-80.

[b]None reported—it appears that all maintenance for this carrier is done by AAA or that its maintenance employees are reported with those of AAA.

[c]Data for traffic and sales employees and all other employees appear to be reversed for 1974-75 and 1980. This average calculated after reversing the data for these two categories to be consistent with the values for 1976-79.

[d]Average for 1974-79—data for 1980 are not available as this is being written.

[e]Average for 1975-80—data for 1974 are not available.

[f]Reported figure minus estimated maintenance and overhaul employees allocated to Ansett's three regional carriers.

[g]Estimated by assuming maintenance and overhaul employees equaled 25 percent of reported total employment (or 20 percent of adjusted total employment).

Source: Calculated from data in International Civil Aviation Organization, Fleet Personnel, Commercial Air Carriers, 1974-80 (Montreal: ICAO).

189

per employee than AAA except for 1980, and that TAA exceeded
Ansett Total in this productivity measure for every year except 1978
and 1980. The opposite relationship applied to freight/mail RTM
per employee—both AAA and Ansett Total had higher RTM per employee than TAA for every year except 1979, when they were essentially equal to TAA in this measure.

TABLE 7.6

Average Annual Number of Employees: Ansett Airline
Subsidiaries and Trans-Australia Airlines, 1974-80

| Calendar Year | Average Number of Employees[a] | | | | | TAA Total |
| | Ansett Subsidiaries[b] | | | | | |
	AAA	ANSW	ASA	MMA	Total	
1974	7,905.5	347.5	158.0	635.0	9,046.0	7,855.0
1975	8,149.0	369.5	172.5	640.0	9,331.0	7,904.5
1976	7,970.0	349.5	172.5	620.5	9,112.5	7,869.5
1977	8,036.5	334.5	176.0	631.0	9,178.0	8,001.5
1978	8,281.5	340.0	177.0	642.0	9,440.5	8,180.5
1979	8,340.0	337.0	166.0	657.0	9,500.0	8,226.5
1980	8,200.5	360.0	152.5	682.5	9,395.5	8,556.5

[a]Simple average of midyear and year-end employment for
1974-80.

[b]The data for the individual Ansett subsidiaries are adjusted
as described in the text. The Ansett and TAA totals are as reported.

Sources: Calculated from data in International Civil Aviation
Organization, Fleet Personnel, Commercial Air Carriers, 1974-80
(Montreal: ICAO); and Table 7.5.

Combining these two major segments of traffic into total
RTM per employee again indicates that there has been no consistent
pattern of superiority between the two interstate carriers.[42] AAA
alternated between being slightly higher and slightly lower than
TAA from 1974 to 1980, with these two carriers' simple averages
for the full seven-year period being essentially equal. At the same
time, Ansett Total was higher than TAA for five out of the seven
years, but only by small amounts. Ansett Total's simple average
for all seven years is just 1.2 percent higher than that of TAA, and

TABLE 7.7

System Scheduled Passengers and Freight/Mail Tons per Employee: Ansett Airline Subsidiaries and Trans-Australia Airlines, Fiscal Years 1971-74 and Calendar Years 1974-80

| | Scheduled Passengers per Employee[a] | | | | | | Scheduled Freight/Mail Tons per Employee[a] | | | | | |
| | Ansett Subsidiaries | | | | | TAA | Ansett Subsidiaries | | | | | TAA |
	AAA	ANSW	ASA	MMA	Total	Total	AAA	ANSW	ASA	MMA	Total	Total
FY 71	n.a.	n.a.	n.a.	n.a.	417[b]	399[b]	n.a.	n.a.	n.a.	n.a.	8.75[b]	5.70[b]
FY 72	n.a.	n.a.	n.a.	n.a.	437[b]	414[b]	n.a.	n.a.	n.a.	n.a.	8.82[b]	5.63[b]
FY 73	n.a.	n.a.	n.a.	n.a.	468[b]	449[b]	n.a.	n.a.	n.a.	n.a.	9.07[b]	5.62[b]
FY 74	n.a.	n.a.	n.a.	n.a.	532[b]	496[b]	n.a.	n.a.	n.a.	n.a.	10.02[b]	6.06[b]
Mean[c]	n.a.	n.a.	n.a.	n.a.	464[b]	440[b]	n.a.	n.a.	n.a.	n.a.	9.16[b]	5.75[b]
CY 74	485	1,054	1,238	500	521	515	9.17	6.91	4.80	10.54	9.10	6.65
CY 75	496	1,040	1,218	487	530	530	8.00	5.43	4.26	9.59	7.94	6.41
CY 76	487	1,067	1,233	470	522	512	8.21	5.59	4.16	10.04	8.16	6.55
CY 77	503	1,120	1,246	481	539	536	8.11	5.38	3.95	9.85	8.05	7.34
CY 78	533	1,232	1,291	535	573	552	8.45	5.55	3.65	11.12	8.44	8.14
CY 79	558	1,295	1,348	530	596	595	8.64	6.46	4.09	10.49	8.61	9.20
CY 80	607	1,218	1,399	554	620	600	8.53[d]	5.51[d]	3.95[d]	10.05[d]	8.45[d]	8.62[d]
Mean[c]	524	1,147	1,282	508	557	549	8.44	5.83	4.12	10.24	8.39	7.56

n.a. = Not available.

[a] The Australian Dept. of Transport implies that its data are for scheduled operations, but they may include nonscheduled operations as well. ICAO data indicate that nonscheduled service has been operated only by AAA and TAA, and comprises less than 0.2 percent of total traffic. Freight/mail short tons equal metric tonnes times 1.10232.

[b] Davies does not state whether his data are for scheduled or for scheduled and nonscheduled service.

[c] Simple average of the values for fiscal years 1971-74 or calendar years 1974-80.

[d] Actual freight tons plus estimated mail tons based on percentage increases in mail RTM over 1979.

Sources: Calculated from data in Australian Department of Transport, Australian Transport, 1974-75 to 1979-80 (Canberra: Australian Government Publishing Service); International Civil Aviation Organization, Fleet Personnel, Commercial Air Carriers and Traffic, Commercial Air Carriers, 1974-78 and 1976-80 (Montreal: ICAO); Table 7.6; and David G. Davies, "Property Rights and Economic Efficiency," Journal of Law and Economics 20 (1977):226.

TABLE 7.8

System Scheduled RPM, Freight/Mail RTM, and Total RTM per Employee:
Ansett Airline Subsidiaries and Trans-Australia Airlines,
Calendar Years 1974-80

| Calendar Year | Scheduled RPM per Employee[a] | | | | | TAA Total |
| | Ansett Subsidiaries | | | | | |
	AAA	ANSW	ASA	MMA	Total	
1974	261,421	293,626	183,747	333,450	266,357	270,477
1975	271,572	284,422	185,264	337,305	274,994	284,491
1976	251,646	286,518	182,800	314,110	255,934	259,101
1977	258,902	305,160	188,954	321,597	263,557	273,810
1978	283,141	331,035	196,085	352,656	287,961	285,367
1979	300,820	348,516	202,614	360,843	304,947	313,937
1980	332,905	343,272	211,226	384,731	335,092	325,125
Mean[b]	280,058	313,221	192,956	343,527	284,120	287,473

| Calendar Year | Scheduled Freight/Mail RTM per Employee[c] | | | | | TAA Total |
| | Ansett Subsidiaries | | | | | |
	AAA	ANSW	ASA	MMA	Total	
1974	5,433	2,129	797	7,986	5,404	3,853
1975	4,905	1,618	719	7,450	4,872	3,870
1976	4,733	1,614	678	7,247	4,708	3,620
1977	4,528	1,590	636	6,789	4,502	3,991
1978	4,881	1,618	588	7,840	4,885	4,331
1979	4,757	1,860	619	7,725	4,787	4,800
1980	4,743	1,600	603	7,508	4,756	4,481
Mean[b]	4,854	1,718	663	7,506	4,845	4,135

| Calendar Year | Scheduled Total RTM per Employee[d] | | | | | TAA Total |
| | Ansett Subsidiaries | | | | | |
	AAA	ANSW	ASA	MMA	Total	
1974	31,368	31,260	19,025	41,066	31,829	30,687
1975	31,848	29,835	19,101	40,916	32,154	32,094
1976	29,699	30,040	18,812	38,411	30,099	29,325
1977	30,214	31,865	19,381	38,694	30,649	31,156
1978	32,972	34,459	20,040	42,827	33,453	32,642
1979	34,601	36,436	20,719	43,525	35,041	35,946
1980	37,770	35,656	21,561	45,676	38,000	36,737
Mean[b]	32,639	32,793	19,806	41,588	33,032	32,655

[a]RPM equals revenue passenger-kilometers times 0.62137.
[b]Simple average of the values for 1974-80.
[c]RTM equals metric tonne-kilometers times 0.68495.
[d]Passenger, freight, and mail RTM.
Sources: Calculated from data in Australian Department of Transport, Australian Transport, 1974-75 to 1979-80 (Canberra: Australian Government Publishing Service); International Civil Aviation Organization, Fleet Personnel, Commercial Air Carriers and Traffic, Commercial Air Carriers, 1974-78 and 1976-80 (Montreal: ICAO); and Table 7.6.

even this small performance superiority is due in large part to the high employee productivity of MMA in Western Australia. In general, then, the findings remain consistent with those for the North American carriers—there appear to be no important differences in employee productivity attributable to differences in ownership. [43]

Summary

The finding that performance among the federally regulated airlines is similar regardless of ownership should not be a complete surprise. Davies compared the airlines assuming a dichotomy of private ownership versus government ownership, but this dichotomy fails to recognize the existence of various types of private ownership and various degrees of government control. In his lectures at the University of California, Los Angeles, back in the 1960s, Armen A. Alchian described a range of ownership types, each having the possibility of motivating different performance on the part of individuals and, therefore, by their organizations. The following is a list of some of these types of ownership:

Full private property with unconstrained profits
Private property with profit sharing
Private property with constrained profits
Private property with regulated profits
Nonprofit
Government ownership
Public/communal ownership.

This list in itself implies that the performance differences between government ownership, on the one hand, and private ownership with regulated profits, on the other hand, should not be as large as between government ownership and full private ownership with unconstrained profits. The performance data from both North America and Australia support this implication. Indeed, they indicate that, given a regulatory monopoly, airline performance under private ownership differs little from performance under government ownership.

CONCLUSION

The first part of this chapter has identified large and consistent differences between the performance of the federally regulated airlines of Canada and the United States, on the one hand, and that of the U.S. intrastate carriers operating within regulatory duopolies, on the other hand. In this latter situation, independent state regulation allowed new airlines to enter and to compete with the established CAB-regulated airlines on the basis of both price and service quality (rather than primarily service quality as has been the case in regulatory monopolies). In this environment the successful intrastate carriers charged much lower prices and managed to incur comparably lower operating expenses than the federally regulated airlines, thereby achieving roughly the same profits. That this was due to regulatory differences is supported as much by the performance similarities among the federally regulated Canadian and U.S. airlines as by the differences between their performance and that of the U.S. intrastate carriers.

In contrast, the conclusion of the second part is that ownership is not a relevant factor in airline performance where regulatory monopolies exist. The small and varied performance differences between comparable privately owned and government-owned airlines in both North America and Australia are quite inconsistent with the hypothesis that ownership is an important factor in airline performance under federal regulation.

It is important to emphasize that the evidence regarding ownership does not necessarily apply to performance in a deregulated environment. Indeed, it could well be that the performance similarities among federally regulated airlines, regardless of ownership, are a common response to a dominant environment produced by a regulatory monopoly, and that performance differences due to ownership would develop with the removal of such regulation. For example, in the absence of regulation, would a government-owned airline respond in the same ways as a privately owned airline if it faced bankruptcy because of the competition of rival carriers? Might not the government-owned airline (supported by its employees and suppliers) turn to the government for subsidies (such as direct payments and low-interest loans) or for the allocation of an increased share of government traffic, rather than make the painful adjustments that a small, privately owned airline would tend to make in similar circumstances? If so, the performance of the government-owned airline would diverge from that of the privately owned airline.

The policy implications of the chapter are straightforward. If the objective is to achieve appreciable differences in airline performance, the choice is between a regulatory monopoly with closed entry or an appreciably less regulated environment where new carriers can enter and practice price and service-quality competition. This first of these regulatory environments would yield higher fares, costs, and service quality, while the second would result in much lower fares and costs as well as somewhat lower service quality.

The question of government ownership could be decided on the basis of factors other than economic performance if a regulatory monopoly were in place, but further investigation would have to be given to the effects of government ownership if a much less regulated environment were to be the norm.

NOTES

1. Government ownership is defined as the situation where a corporate entity, operating in the marketplace as an autonomous unit, is owned by a government. In the cases included in this paper there is 100 percent government ownership, but other situations exist where a government owns only a majority or controlling share of the issued stock of a corporation with the remainder owned by private investors.

2. David G. Davies, "The Efficiency of Public versus Private Firms: The Case of Australia's Two Airlines," Journal of Law and Economics 14 (1971):149-65; and David G. Davies, "Property Rights and Economic Efficiency," Journal of Law and Economics 20 (1977): 223-26.

3. William A. Jordan, "Comparisons of American and Canadian Airline Regulation," in Perspectives on Canadian Airline Regulation, ed. G. B. Reschenthaler and B. Roberts (Montreal: Institute for Research on Public Policy, 1979), pp. 17-31. Between 1952 and 1972 large aircraft were defined as those having a maximum certificated takeoff weight of over 12,500 pounds (about 20 passengers). In 1972 this definition was changed by the CAB to mean aircraft having over 30 seats or being able to carry a payload in excess of 7,500 pounds. See William A. Jordan, "Airline Performance Under Regulation: Canada vs. the United States," in Research in Law and Economics, vol. 1, ed. R. O. Zerbe, Jr. (Greenwich, Conn.: JAI Press, 1979), pp. 35-79, n. 5.

4. Air Canada and Trans World both have major transcontinental routes with additional routes extending down to the South and Southwest United States. In addition, their international routes are predominantly transatlantic. CP Air and Northwest have roughly parallel transcontinental routes extending on to Hawaii, with major transpacific international routes. Northeast also serves the U.S. South and Southwest while CP Air operates to California, Mexico, and South America. Allegheny, North Central, and Frontier all had the majority of their routes in northern areas, including Canada. Pacific Western purchased 97 percent of Transair's stock in 1978 and formally merged with it in 1979. Southern was merged into North Central to form Republic Airlines in 1979.

5. Trans-Canada Air Lines Act, S.C. 1937, c. 43. More generally, see John Langford, "Air Canada," in Public Corporations and Public Policy in Canada, ed. Allan Tupper and G. Bruce Doern (Montreal: The Institute for Research on Public Policy, 1981); and John Baldwin, The Regulatory Agency and the Public Corporation (Cambridge, Mass.: Ballinger, 1975).

6. Richard G. O'Lone, "Pacific Western Seeks Area Dominance," Aviation Week and Space Technology 107 (August 8, 1977):33-35. See also Allan Tupper, "Pacific Western Airlines," in Public Corporations and Public Policy in Canada, ed. Allan Tupper and G. Bruce Doern (Montreal: The Institute for Research on Public Policy, 1981).

7. Toronto Globe and Mail, January 20, 1979, p. B6.

8. In December 1978, an average of Canadian $1.179 was required to buy a U.S. dollar. Department of Finance, Economic Review (Ottawa: Minister of Supply and Services Canada, April 1979), p. 217.

9. For an analysis of why it is inappropriate to apply the full exchange rate when comparing domestic prices for domestic goods between two countries, see Jordan, Performance of Regulated Canadian Airlines in Domestic and Transborder Operations (Ottawa-Hull: Ministry of Consumer and Corporate Affairs, 1981), App. B.

10. Ibid., pp. 11-14. The ADA extended CAB jurisdiction to the intrastate carriers and Air Florida's first CAB tariff was effective December 14, 1978. The new CAB-authorized standard coach fares (as plotted in Figure 7.1) were about 11 percent higher than Air Florida's previous coach fares filed with the Florida Public Service Commission. Capacity-controlled economy fares, in contrast, were either unchanged or were decreased by 5 percent from night and weekend fares in effect prior to December 14. Air Florida, "Florida Public Service Commission Tariff No. 1," 16th rev., p. 8, 1978; and Airline Tariff Publishing Co., "CAB Tariff No. 139," 34th rev., 1978, p. 14.

11. Jordan, "Airline Performance Under Regulation," pp. 47-49.

12. Jordan, Performance of Regulated Canadian Airlines, pp. 10-18.

13. Average system trip length is calculated by dividing total system RPM by total system passengers.

14. The six mathematical relationships and each R^2 are as follows:

(1) $Y = 117.689 - 0.041X$ $\qquad R^2 = 0.664$
(2) $Y = 120.409e^{-000*X}$ $\qquad R^2 = 0.701$
(3) $Y = 1,011.356X^{-0.385}$ $\qquad R^2 = 0.823$
(4) $Y = 49.582 + 20,227.564/X$ $\quad R^2 = 0.866$
(5) $Y = 1/(0.008 + 0.000*X)$ $\qquad R^2 = 0.712$
(6) $Y = X/(0.017 - 2.619X)$ $\qquad R^2 = 0.799$

*Designates significant value beyond three decimal points.

Based on the lowest mean squared error, the best fit was equation 4.

15. For a <u>random</u> sample of 14 pairs, the 5 percent level of significance is achieved at an R^2 of 0.283, while the 1 percent level of significance obtains at an R^2 of 0.437. The 14 federally regulated airlines selected for this study do not constitute a random sample. They do, however, comprise more than 50 percent of the 26 federally regulated airlines operating large aircraft in scheduled passenger/cargo service in Canada and the 48 contiguous states of the United States.

16. Jordan, Performance of Regulated Canadian Airlines, p. 27.

17. Air Florida began operating in September 1972 and Southwest in June 1971. Air California inaugurated service in January 1967 and PSA has provided scheduled service since May 1949. Jordan, ibid., p. 24 n.

18. "There are some who will claim that the wide differences between fares in Canada and the 'efficient' cost of production of United States carriers is not explainable by the fact that factor input prices are higher in Canada, that Canada has a Federal Sales Tax; more severe, generally speaking, weather conditions, and that the Canadian market is about a tenth the size and much more randomly distributed than U.S. markets." G. B. Hunnings, "Regulating Canada's Airlines: Where Do We Go From Here?" Paper presented at the National Conference on Airline Regulation, Ottawa, June 27, 1979, mimeographed, pp. 4-5.

19. Jordan, Performance of Regulated Canadian Airlines, chaps. 10 and 11.

20. Ibid., p. 36.

21. Based on the lowest mean squared error, the best fit was obtained from the following equation: $Y = X/(0.004 + 0.000009X)$. The associated R^2 of 0.837 is significant at the 1 percent level. Ibid., p. 79n.

22. Ibid., p. 67.

23. Ibid., pp. 82-83. Air Florida paid only $13,600 per employee in 1978, reflecting the low-price labor pool available in Florida with its large immigrant population plus an across-the-board wage reduction in 1977 in response to the carrier's large loss that year.

24. Based on the lowest mean squared error, the best fit was obtained from the following equation: $Y = 19.272 + 10,205.857/X$. The associated R^2 of 0.865 is significant at the 1 percent level. Ibid., p. 77n.

25. Ibid., p. 92.

26. Ibid., p. 103.

27. Ibid., p. 106.

28. Ibid., pp. 107-8.

29. The logarithmic relationship between average RTM per liter of fuel and average system stage length (flight distance) is: $\text{Log } Y = \text{Log } 0.100 + 0.309 \text{ Log } X$. The associated R^2 of 0.615 is significant at the 1 percent level. Ibid., p. 129n.

30. Based on the lowest mean squared error, the best fit was obtained from the following equation: $\text{Log } Y = \text{Log } 88.206 - 0.281 \text{ Log } X$. The associated R^2 of 0.693 is significant at the 1 percent level. Ibid., p. 130n.

31. Ibid., p. 119. Air California is not shown in Figure 7.6 because only fragmentary fuel expense data are available for it. Partially estimated data for 1978 indicate that its average fuel expense was at least 11.5 percent below a distance adjusted average for that year. Ibid., pp. 121 and 130n.

32. Davies, "Property Rights and Economic Efficiency," p. 226.

33. The input price differences are, however, consistent with the hypothesis that a government-owned airline is subject to paying higher prices for inputs supplied on a monopoly basis (unionized labor), but not for those supplied by an oligopolistic industry (fuel).

34. Davies, "The Efficiency of Public versus Private Firms," pp. 154-61; and Australian Department of Transport, Domestic Air Transport Policy Review Volume I (Canberra: Australian Government Publishing Service, 1979), pp. 33-41.

35. Between 1974 and 1980 the three Ansett regional carriers operated Fokker F-27s and F-28s, plus one or two de Havilland DHC-6s. In contrast, AAA and TAA operated mainly Boeing B-727-100/200s and DC-9-30s, plus some F-27s, Lockheed L-188s, and (for TAA) a few DHC-6s. International Civil Aviation Organization, 1974-80.

36. Davies, "The Efficiency of Public versus Private Firms," pp. 161-62.

37. Data for 1971 were published by the Australian Department of Civil Aviation in Civil Aviation, 1971-1972 (Canberra: Australian Government Publishing Service, 1972), and data for prior years may be available in earlier editions of that publication. Data for more recent years have been published by the Australian Department of Transport in Australian Transport. George Birch, Australian representative to the Council of the International Civil

Aviation Organization (ICAO), was most helpful in making copies of these publications available for use in this chapter. Data for the individual Australian carriers have also been published by ICAO starting with 1974. Reporting deadlines sometimes result in the ICAO data being preliminary while the Australian publications generally contain final figures. Telephone conversation with William Bekunda, Statistical Officer, ICAO, Montreal, August 10, 1981.

    38. Davies, "The Efficiency of Public versus Private Firms," p. 161.

    39. A fare taper has existed in Australia since at least 1969. See C. A. Gannon, "Pricing of Domestic Airline Services: Selected Aspects of Fares on Australia's Competitive Routes," in Australian Department of Transport, Domestic Air Transport Policy Review Volume II (Canberra: Australian Government Publishing Service, 1979), p. 12.

    40. Davies, "Property Rights and Economic Efficiency," p. 225.

    41. Neither the Australian Department of Transport nor ICAO publishes revenue and expense data for domestic airlines. Therefore, it has not been possible to extend Davies' revenue per employee data for the Ansett subsidiaries.

    42. ICAO calculates passenger RTM from RPM by assuming each passenger and baggage weigh an average of 90 kilograms (198.4 pounds).

    43. The RPM and RTM per employee data have one anomaly that deserves to be mentioned. Given the effects of distance on employee productivity (see Figure 7.3), Table 7.4 implies that these measures for short-haul ANSW and ASA should be lower than those for AAA and TAA, while long-haul MMA should be somewhat higher in these measures. This is the case in Table 7.8 except for ANSW in terms of RPM per employee and total RTM per employee. This carrier had higher RPM and total RTM per employee relative to AAA and TAA despite its shorter average trip lengths. This could be due to the possibility that AAA provides services such as ground handling and reservations to the small intrastate subsidiaries in addition to the maintenance and overhaul services mentioned above. If so, then AAA's total employment should be reduced somewhat more than was done in Table 7.6. This would further serve to yield small increases in AAA's employee output while causing larger decreases for ANSW (and probably ASA and MMA as well). Of course, any reallocation of personnel among the Ansett subsidiaries would have no impact on the measures for Ansett Total. It would be desirable to determine the extent that such adjustments should be made, but the similarities among AAA, Ansett Total, and TAA for total RTM per employee make it unlikely that the conclusions of this analysis would be changed by any additional reallocations of personnel.

8

WHAT HAPPENS WHEN SPONSORS AND CLIENTS WANT DIFFERENT SERVICES: THE CASE OF AMTRAK

George W. Hilton

THE DECLINE OF PASSENGER TRAINS

By the late 1960s the passenger train in America was immediately threatened with extinction. The nation had, as of 1890, been about 95 percent dependent on the passenger train for intercity travel, but first relatively and, after 1920, absolutely, the passenger train had declined until by 1970 only a bare network of major intercity trains remained, plus a small scattering of others. The trains were still being operated by the railroads as they had always been. The activity was unusual in being subject to a control over exit. Virtually all state public utility commissions had been vested with authority over discontinuance of passenger trains in the late nineteenth or early twentieth centuries. Beginning in 1958 the Interstate Commerce Commission was granted authority over discontinuance of interstate passenger trains and appellate authority over discontinuance of intrastate passenger trains, the discontinuance of which had been denied by state authorities.[1]

Discontinuance of most passenger trains was controversial. Regulatory authorities were continually confronted with two rival explanations of the decline of the passenger train. First, it was argued that the passenger train had declined for objective reasons. Beginning with the interurban electric railway in the early years of the twentieth century, the economy had provided travelers with alternatives: the automobile, the intercity bus, piston aircraft, and finally, after 1958, jet aircraft. According to this interpretation, the public simply found the alternatives preferable. The automobile provided point to point service at the scheduling of the owner and it provided him with a vehicle for local transportation

200

when he arrived at his destination. The bus provided the lowest-cost means of intercity transport but originally it had few other attractions. After the building of the interstate freeway system the bus could, in general, offer higher speeds than railway passenger trains, a much higher degree of punctuality and lower noise levels, owing to its being a rubber-tired vehicle. Aircraft offered higher speeds than any surface carrier could match and a comfort level which most, but not all, travelers evaluated higher than surface carriers. Its initial disadvantage in safety relative to surface carriers was dealt with very successfully with the introduction of successive generations of aircraft until its safety experience was finally tolerable to any traveler who was willing to undergo the risks of automobile travel at all.

Similarly, on the supply side the train had several disadvantages relative to its rivals. Notably, it was an extremely labor-intensive form of transportation. In a widely cited figure, a Southern Pacific passenger train between San Francisco and Los Angeles in the mid-1960s required approximately 16 employees for a one-way trip. A rival airline with a single crew of seven could produce two round trips per day. In addition, the passenger train had a low productivity of capital. The Boeing 727 aircraft used between San Francisco and Los Angeles cost about $3.6 million, which was approximately the same investment as in the Southern Pacific's passenger train.[2] Alone among the alternatives, the passenger train had a steel-on-steel contact with its running surface that was loud and jarring, especially to passengers who rode directly above the trucks. Moreover, the jarring caused malfunctions of heating, air conditioning, and other on-board service functions. Finally, because passenger trains shared facilities with freight operations that were themselves highly variable in time, it was impossible to provide the punctuality of rival forms of transportation.

As the passenger train declined, in general, the people with highest valuation of time deserted it most readily. The airlines, which became a serious rival to the passenger train after introduction of the DC-3 aircraft in the mid-1930s, typically set their tariffs at the level of first-class rail fare plus a lower berth on the ground that most of the passengers whom they were endeavoring to attract were businessmen who traveled in Pullman lower berths. The airlines' effort was, of course, almost completely successful and by 1970 virtually all such business travel had, in fact, gone to the airlines. Consequently, as the passenger train declined, the demand for Pullman space, dining car meals, and club car service tended to decline more rapidly than the demand for basic coach service.

The airlines did not widely offer rail coach-competitive fares until after 1949. Rail-coach passengers were lost mainly to automobiles and secondarily to buses. By the 1950s, rail passenger service had a strongly negative income elasticity estimated at -0.6.[3] That is to say, the typical American responded to a 1 percent increase in income by reducing his quantity demanded of rail passenger service by six-tenths of 1 percent. As a consequence, as rail passenger traffic declined in the 1950s and 1960s, there was a strong tendency for the remaining travelers to demand a bus-competitive level of service rather than an air-competitive level of service. On the typical passenger train, first the club car would go, then the Pullman car, then the dining car and finally the train would be a coach-only facility by the time the railroad applied for discontinuance. The Southern Pacific's Sunset Limited and the Illinois Central's Panama Limited had histories of this sort.

Although such experiences are readily explained by the presumption that the passenger train was declining for objective reasons—the availability of superior alternatives and the high cost level of rail passenger service—the observed phenomenon gave rise to the second interpretation of the decline. This hypothesis was simply that the railroads were discouraging utilization of the trains. The railroads found rail passenger service less profitable than rail freight service, it was argued, and discouraged utilization of the train by downgrading the quality of the service. In this interpretation removal of club cars, dining cars, and Pullman cars repelled passengers who then turned to alternatives, and finally, after a real or fictional show of unprofitability, the railroad endeavored, usually successfully, to get rid of the passenger train through regulatory proceedings.

In discontinuance actions protestants continually brought in evidence of removal of club, sleeping, and dining cars to buttress arguments that the railroad was discouraging utilization of the train. The examiners report in the case concerning adequacy of service on the Sunset Limited represented rather a high point of such arguments, including a proposal that the Interstate Commerce Commission imposed minimum standards for provision of sleeping, dining, and lounge facilities, even though the commission's statutory authority of 1958 did not appear to grant such powers.[4] On a popular level, Peter Lyon's book To Hell in a Day Coach argued that the railroads' passenger deficit, which amounted to several hundred million dollars per year, was a fiction and that the passenger train had declined unnecessarily because of the railroads' discouragement of patronage.[5]

The discouragement hypothesis was attractive to a minority of travelers who combined a low valuation of time with a desire for a high quality of service. The majority of passengers who had an evaluation of time low enough to be on a passenger train, as stated previously, demanded a bus-competitive level of service: coach seats, vendomat dining facilities or lunch counters, and the like. The affluent elderly, in particular, did not behave in this fashion. A retired person might consistently combine a low valuation of time with a desire for dining car meals, Pullman berths, and lounge car facilities. Similarly, railroad fans and others who enjoyed rail travel as a form of consumption on vacations or otherwise were entirely consistent in demanding a higher quality of service than bus lines provided. People who were afraid to fly might also evaluate rail service more highly than the alternatives and be eager that trains be preserved with a high quality of service. These groups might easily overlap. In particular, fear of flying was highly concentrated in higher age brackets among people whose conception of flying was developed in the early days of aviation when it was, in fact, a highly risky activity.

The hypothesis that the passenger train had declined for objective reasons was, of course, universal within railroad management, and was accepted by most academic specialists on the industry. It was eloquently stated to the Interstate Commerce Commission by its own examiner, Howard Hosmer, in his report on the railroad passenger deficit of 1958.[6] The discouragement hypothesis, however, commanded great popular esteem. The National Association of Railroad Passengers was founded in 1967, providing an effective lobbying group for perpetuation of the passenger train. Peter Lyon had explicitly proposed nationalization of the passenger train in 1968.[7] Support for a national system of rail passenger service came mainly from three sources: first, people who held the discouragement hypothesis and felt that the passenger train could be brought back as a major form of intercity transport by raising the quality of the service; railroad labor organizations that were eager to preserve a major source of employment of their members; and certain railroad managements that had become pessimistic that the Interstate Commerce Commission would ever let them get rid of their remaining passenger trains. By 1970 only a relatively small number of intercity passenger trains covered their variable expenses, and the passenger deficit was typically over $400 million per year for the American railroad system. The Interstate Commerce Commission had been trying to maintain a basic network of at least a single passenger train per day between all major American cities in the apparent expectation that Congress would establish a federal rail passenger system. Spokesmen for the commission had testified on several occasions that it was becoming successively more difficult to find that the public interest required continuance of passenger trains in the face of the deficits that existed by the late 1960s.

THE CREATION OF AMTRAK

Congress responded to these pressures by establishing the National Railroad Passenger Corporation in 1970. The corporation adopted the trade name Amtrak, an acronym for "American travel by track." This enterprise took over operation of American intercity passenger service (with certain exceptions) in the spring of 1971. We now have a full decade of experience to evaluate.

In all respects, the statutory authority of the corporation was an embodiment of the discouragement hypothesis of the decline of the passenger train. It was intended that the administrators of the corporation should have a single-valued incentive to restore ridership of the passenger train through improving the quality of the service. They were, however, initially expected to make money. Although a profit quickly demonstrated itself to be an impossible objective and was, in fact, dropped from the statutory authority, the corporation remained under strong incentives to minimize its losses and to use its annual subsidy in some optimal or at least rational fashion. In addition, the Interstate Commerce Commission's control over the quality of service was an outside constraint on the corporation's decision making that did not necessarily accord with market demands.

THE PERFORMANCE OF AMTRAK

Market demands rather quickly demonstrated themselves to be what the railroads had previously confronted. The demand for sleeping car accommodations and other luxury aspects of the service continued downward relative to the demand for coach travel. The system proved able to attract enough passengers to amount only to about one-fourth to one-third of 1 percent of Americans moving between cities. Such growth as the system had in the 1970s was mainly a consequence of Congress's expansion of the network. In addition, the petroleum shortage of 1974 and the rise in the price of gasoline in 1979 by making the alternatives more expensive resulted in considerable increases in the demand. That is, the demand rose from about one-fourth to one-third of 1 percent of intercity movements. [8]

Amtrak's own research into demand conditions for rail passenger service indicated relatively high price elasticity, about -2.2

for the entire system and an income elasticity that is thought to be insignificantly positive.[9] The change from a negative income elasticity in the 1950s to an apparently positive income elasticity currently probably reflects mainly the highly discretionary and recreational nature of much of the travel on Amtrak. Amtrak's econometric model used for forecasting ridership on its individual routes found that schedule frequency was the principal determinant of ridership.[10] Amtrak's cost inferiority to intercity buses, which was about four to one, made it impractical to rival Greyhound and Trailways in schedule frequency outside of the Northeast corridor. It was this, rather than an absence of luxury, that caused Amtrak to be so unsuccessful in rivalry with buses. Buses also proved to be faster when they could use the interstate freeway system and were more punctual. There was a further matter that the incentive structure that Congress provided in an effort to make Amtrak more punctual resulted in railroads lengthening schedules and providing cushions in time tables so as to assure more punctual arrival at the final terminals.[11]

A further problem for Amtrak was that after 1973 energy was popularly conceived as something uniquely worth conserving. The standard stainless steel or aluminum passenger car that Amtrak had inherited from the railroads was a large heavy vehicle and trains require continual acceleration or deceleration. As a consequence, Amtrak proved to be approximately as energy efficient as the standard American automobile. Amtrak's energy inputs per passenger mile proved to be more than triple those of intercity buses.[12] The luxury aspects of railroading, especially sleeping and dining cars, are particularly bad offenders. Both are heavy, the sleeping cars have low passenger capacities, and the dining cars are nonrevenue equipment that carry no fare-paying passengers per se. The incentive on Amtrak to become more energy-efficient was an incentive to go to lighter weight coaches with more dense seating configurations and to replace dining cars with snack bars in the coaches. This incentive was essentially identical to the incentive the railroads had had—and which Amtrak still has from its market demands—to become more bus-competitive over time.

Adversely, however, Amtrak remained under considerable political pressure from Congress to offer high-quality service. Late in 1973 the Interstate Commerce Commission issued a very restrictive set of rules requiring high quality of service on passenger trains. Remaining passenger carriers were required to provide food and beverage service on all trains operating over two hours and to provide full diners on runs of over 12 hours. Private-room sleeping cars were required on trains operating over six hours between midnight and 8 A.M., and reclining seat leg rest coaches with pillows were required on trains operating four or more hours between 10 P.M. and 8 A.M. Nonrevenue lounge space was required on trains running more than 6 hours and dome cars were required on runs of over 16 hours if clearances allowed such equipment. Temperature had to be maintained between 60 and 80 degrees and separate facilities had to be provided for smokers and nonsmokers.13

Amtrak responded to these divergent incentives in a remarkably consistent fashion. To get rid of steam heating and to reduce maintenance costs, Amtrak's management wanted to reequip the system from the outset. For corridor services and light-density longer runs, the system adopted the so-called Amfleet coaches of light weight and dense seating configurations. It dropped Pullman cars on its Inter-American to Texas and attempted to do so on its Cardinal and Panama Limited but restored such service upon the Interstate Commerce Commission's requests. It eliminated dining cars on trains of the Amfleet type almost entirely. In the northeast corridor only a single train, the Montrealer, retained orthodox dining car service.

On transcontinental trains, which former Secretary of Transportation William T. Coleman claimed are in the nature of cruise ships where the travel is largely an end in itself, Amtrak endeavored to satisfy the political demands for high-quality service and installed high-level coaches of relatively low seating density for comfortable overnight service and also retained sleeping cars. The reequipment of such trains is proceeding on the basis of orders made in the 1970s in spite of Amtrak's greater budgetary stringency under the Reagan administration.

It is difficult to predict which of the trends will be dominant. Amtrak's recent response to its budget cut indicated that the corporation will get rid of all remaining existing orthodox dining car services in favor of cold food or airline-type meal service. This is certainly in accordance with the economic demands on the system, as distinct from the political pressures, which would lead one to expect an atrophy in its support in Congress in the long run. Meanwhile both of the divergent trends identifiable over its history will probably continue.

The size of the system, as distinct from the character of its service, is also subject to conflicting pressures. Since the administrators of Amtrak are dependent on budgetary allotments for the scope of the system, they have an incentive to concentrate their resources on the system's strongest services. The corporation was apparently eager to get rid of its Chicago-Miami train, the Floridian. Anthony Haswell of the National Association of Railroad Passengers accused the corporation of trying to eliminate the train by downgrading the quality of its service—the same argument used against the railroads when they operated American passenger trains.[14]

From the outset, there has been strong political pressure to have a nationwide system. It has been thought that Congressmen from the West and South would be unlikely to vote appropriations for a system restricted to the Northeast. The consequence has been a thin system, mainly operating a single train per day on its long routes. Only on some corridors, mainly under 300 miles, has the system operated multiple daily service. The National Association of Railroad Passengers has accepted Amtrak's evaluation that its principal competitive disadvantage relative to buses is its lower frequencies on all routes but the Northeast corridor. It has favored comprehensive increases in frequency, and efforts to coordinate train and bus.[15] Essentially the association seeks to shift the longer-distance bus passengers to rail and to use bus as a feeder to Amtrak. Since the cost of moving passengers by Amtrak is some four times the cost by bus, this would be a very costly policy. Not surprisingly, funds have never been made available to implement it, beyond some adaptation of Amtrak terminals to house intercity buses. The association interprets Amtrak's problems as largely the consequence of underfunding, and advocates establishment of a trust fund along the lines of those in existence for freeways, airports, and waterways.[16] Partly because such a policy would be hostile to the intercity bus industry, opposition is likely to remain vocal.

In the long run, it is difficult to picture Amtrak's surviving. The secular forces for increase in its costs and for diversion of its passengers to rival forms of transport are probably impossible for the corporation to deal with. Meanwhile, as long as it exists, the political pressures for a high quality of service and expansion of the system will presumably continue to rival the economic incentives for a lower quality of service and contraction of the network.

NOTES

1. George W. Hilton, The Transportation Act of 1958 (Bloomington: Indiana University Press, 1969), pp. 35-38, 97-154.

2. Ely M. Brandes and Alan E. Lazar, Rail Passenger Traffic in the West (Menlo Park, Calif.: Stanford Research Institute, 1966), pp. 19-30.

3. Louis J. Paradiso and Clement Wilson, "Consumer Expenditure-Income Patterns," Survey of Current Business 25 (1955):29.

4. Adequacies-Passenger Service-Southern Pacific Company between California and Louisiana, examiner's proposed report, Docket No. 34733 (1968).

5. Peter Lyon, To Hell in a Day Coach (New York: Lippincott, 1968).

6. Railroad Passenger Train Deficit, proposed report, Docket No. 31954 (1958).

7. Lyon, To Hell in a Day Coach, p. 276.

8. On the experience, see George W. Hilton, Amtrak (Washington, D.C.: American Enterprise Institute, 1980).

9. Ibid., p. 37.

10. Ibid., pp. 41-42.

11. Ibid., pp. 53-57.

12. Ibid., p. 52.

13. Ex parte No. 277, Adequacy of Intercity Rail Passenger Service, 351 ICC 883 (1976).

14. U.S., Congress, Senate, Amtrak Oversight and Authorization, Hearings before the Subcommittee on Surface Transportation of the Committee on Commerce, 93rd Cong., 1st sess., 1973, p. 40.

15. Letter of Thomas C. Crickelaire, assistant director of the National Association of Railroad Passengers, U.S., Congress, Senate, Financial Condition of the Motor Bus Industry, Hearings before the Subcommittee on Surface Transportation of the Committee on Commerce, Science and Transportation, 95th Cong., 1st sess., 1977, pp. 95-96.

16. Statement of Ross Capon, director of the National Association of Railroad Passengers, on a radio program on Amtrak in which the author participated, Station WRC, Washington, D.C., July 26, 1980.

9

TOWARD A POSITIVE THEORY
OF JOINT ENTERPRISE

Catherine Eckel and Aidan Vining

INTRODUCTION

The joint public-private ownership of corporations (hereafter
simply referred to as joint enterprise) is an important, albeit little
studied, phenomenon. Indeed, there has been little analysis of how
these organizations actually behave. There are some unanswered
questions. Why are these hybrids created? What are their advantages and disadvantages relative to complete public or private
ownership? What kind of behavior can they be expected to exhibit
relative to private or public firms? Is this expected behavior consistent with the government-stated objectives of these firms? What
is the performance of these firms?

The majority of the literature on government enterprise is
normative rather than positive in orientation.[1] As R. Mazzolini
points out, the critical weakness of this literature is that "it can
generally be faulted for prescribing principles where the validity
has not been clearly verified" and "it tends to lack a solid empirical
base."[2] It also lacks a clear theoretical base. In particular, the
question of what governs a firm's behavior when it is not forced to
maximize profit remains unanswered. Although there has been
little development of a positive theory of joint enterprise, the
groundwork for such a theory can be found in the recent work of
public choice economists such as W. Niskanen, T. Borcherding,
J. L. Migué and G. Bélanger, E. Furobotn and S. Pejovich, and
C. Lindsay.[3]

The objective of this chapter is to determine some of the
implications of cases where the state owns a percentage of shares
in a regular joint-stock corporation and where the remainder of the

shares are owned by private individuals.[4] Such patterns of ownership are common in Europe and Japan, but can also be found in
North America. Indeed, the United States is one of the few countries where joint enterprise is not pervasive.

There are typically two basic models of joint enterprise: the
government directly owns shares in the corporation, or a state
holding company acquires shares in the company. Canada, Great
Britain, West Germany, France, and Japan all have prominent examples in the former category. Thus, the federal government of
Canada owns 49 percent of the shares of the Canada Development
Corporation (CDC)—a large ($3.5 billion in assets) corporation with
investments in petrochemicals, mining, and oil and gas. Telesat
Canada, though government controlled, is 50 percent owned by the
major telecommunications carriers,[5] one of which (CN/CP Telecommunications) is also jointly owned. The province of Alberta
owns 50 percent of the Alberta Energy Corporation, a large energy
conglomerate. IPSCO, a steel producer, is jointly owned by the
governments of Alberta and Saskatchewan as well as private stockholders.[6]

In Great Britain, British Petroleum, 49 percent owned by the
government, has been the prototype for many of the jointly owned
firms that have subsequently developed around the world. The most
famous example of joint ownership in West Germany is Volkswagen,
which has now been partly privatized (currently the federal government and the state of Lower Saxony each own 20 percent of the
shares, while 60 percent are owned by private shareholders).
Joint enterprise corporations play a prominent role in the Japanese
economy.[7] Firms such as Electric Power Development Company
(Dengen Kaihatsu K.K.), Japan Airlines Company (Nihon Koku K.K.),
and the Japanese Raw Silk Corporation (Nihon Sanshi Jigyōdan) are
all examples of <u>tokushu kaisha</u>, or joint enterprises.

The latter approach—the state holding company—is common
in many European countries including Italy, Great Britain, and
France. In Italy, IRI, ENI, EFIM, GEPI, and EGAM all own
shares in a variety of companies, often less than 50 percent.[8] In
Great Britain the National Enterprise Board holds shares in a wide
range of companies. It is likely that joint ownership will continue
to be attractive if only because it limits the capital requirements
of government.

THE LITERATURE ON JOINT ENTERPRISE

Within the literature on public enterprise, there is almost no
mention of the special qualities of joint ownership. Christopher

Green devotes a paragraph to joint public-private efforts, distinguishing only in a footnote between ". . . 'joint ventures' between government(s) and private corporations and 'joint ownership' where some of the shares are owned by the government and the remainder by numerous relatively small private investors." He states that joint efforts are most desirable when the purpose is "(a) to assure a project is carried out by assisting in the provision of financial capital; (b) having some control over the project's or enterprise's direction; and (c) participating in whatever profits or rents are generated."[9] However, no rationale is given for the appropriateness or empirical validity of these particular conditions.

William G. Shepherd and Clair Wilcox point out that the government's share in the ownership of a public enterprise can range anywhere from zero to 100 percent, but they attach no particular significance to the mix of ownership of the enterprise.[10] They only suggest that the degree of public ownership should match the degree of public interest in the industry, and should be "just enough to achieve the specific aim." Once more the question of whether there are special characteristics of the jointly owned firm is ignored.

Mitnick mentions the "mixed-ownership corporation" as a type of public enterprise particularly useful in rescuing ailing private industry judged socially desirable, and in aiding in the financing of large projects, such as public works, which the private sector would not produce alone.[11] Again, the behavioral impact of partial ownership is not explored.

Why, then, might the government choose joint ownership rather than some other policy instrument? Jointly owned enterprises probably have been created for as many ostensible purposes as other types of public enterprise.[12] The obvious advantage of joint ownership over total government ownership is the increased pressure for financial or commercial viability. Private owners will presumably, through concern for their own well-being, pressure the firm to be efficient and profitable. On the other hand, relative to a completely private firm, government will have a greater say in the conduct of the joint enterprise. We will argue that the key to both the behavior and usefulness of the joint enterprise is likely to be the constraint on government direction of the firm that can be exercised by the private shareholders.

Joint ownership is unique, both in its implication for the value of the firm and therefore stock price, and in its effect on the potential for control of the corporation. A discussion of the stock price effects is included in the next section, followed by a treatment of the ownership rights of the shareholder of a joint firm. A model of public and joint enterprise is then developed. Canadian examples are discussed in the final sections.

JOINT OWNERSHIP AND STOCK PRICE

First let us consider the importance of the path by which joint enterprise is reached. Government may either purchase part of a privately owned firm, or it may create a firm that is eventually partially sold (or otherwise allocated) to the private sector. Thus the government may either acquire or divest shares in the corporation. If the government purchases stock, the expectations of the remaining stockholders as to the expected profitability of the corporation will likely be affected, and the stock price will change accordingly. The direction of the change will depend on the reason for the intervention, and its expected effect on the profitability and risk of the firm. As an example, suppose the government "bails out," by a major stock purchase, a firm that is otherwise facing bankruptcy. The reduction in risk that occurs is likely to be capitalized into the value of the stock, resulting in a capital gain to remaining stockholders.[13] Stock prices would most likely fall, on the other hand, if government purchased stock in an economically healthy corporation in order to influence its behavior toward more socially oriented activities and away from profit maximization. Last, the stock price might be unaffected by a non-control-seeking government purchase for the purpose of capture of rents associated with, for example, oil or mineral extraction. In all cases, the change in the stock price will reflect the expected impact of government ownership on profitability, and can be thought of as an index or measure of the value (positive or negative) of intervention. Each of these cases is analogous to the stock price response to any government action that is perceived to affect the profitability of the corporation.[14]

Suppose, on the other hand, the government creates an enterprise with explicit social objectives, and issues a fraction of the stock to private shareholders. The expected deviation from profit maximizing behavior on the part of the managers subject to government directives (based on the stated social objectives of the firm) will be capitalized into the initial stock price. As long as these objectives are pursued as expected, the stock price, ceteris paribus, will remain stable. If, however, the government changes the objectives of the firm or otherwise increases its intervention, veering the firm farther from profit maximization, the stock price will fall to reflect the expected impact on profitability. Once more the change in stock price constitutes a measure of the value of the marginal deviation from profit maximization.

Before considering the impact that these capitalizations will have on shareholder (and government enterprise) behavior we must first incorporate the impact that government partial ownership has upon the potential for control.

JOINT ENTERPRISE AND CONTROL

When an investor purchases equity in a corporation, the value of that equity depends on two factors—a share in expected profits and a voting share in the control or direction of the company.[15] The importance of the voting attribute of stock ownership depends on the concentration of ownership, i.e., on the probability that the vote will affect the behavior of the firm. The potential for control of the firm is particularly important when management performs poorly, and incentives for takeover are created. Partial public ownership will affect the ability of stockholders to control the behavior of the firm, particularly if the government holds a large proportion of the shares.

In the private sector, "dissident" owners of shares, to paraphrase A. O. Hirschman,[16] have three options: exit (sell); control (specialize in ownership); or voice (complain). In most situations in the private sector where the shareholder is dissatisfied, exit and control dominate as strategies. Of course some shareholders will engage in the voice option—the complaining shareholders at the annual meeting. However, this is unlikely to be a very successful strategy in the private sector, except in terms of cosmetic issues, in either of two circumstances: ownership of shares is concentrated, in which case a majority of shareholder(s) will tend to ignore the voice, or the ownership of shares is dispersed, in which case management will be able to resist the voice. There are two possible exceptions to the impotence of voice: the minority shareholder who is perceived to have the potential to acquire control or the potential to harm share price (by dumping large numbers of shares), and the dissident shareholder who can bring to the attention of other potential owners the opportunity for improving the profitability of the corporation. In general, however, within the private sector the main options facing the unhappy minority shareholder are likely to remain exit or control.

What, then, is the situation of the "dissident" shareholders when the government owns either an absolute majority of the shares or has a controlling interest? The first obvious difference is that control is no longer a viable option. One would expect this information to be (negatively) capitalized in the share price—both because the minority shareholder no longer has the option of control and, perhaps more importantly, no other entrepreneur has such an option (this would apply whether the shareholders would actually sell or not). Of course exit remains an option. The question is then what happens to the value of voice. This can be addressed by first considering the wholly government-owned enterprise.

In a totally government-owned enterprise, voters are, in a sense, the implicit shareholders of the firm, but without the options of control or exit. All they have is voice. The benefits of the government-owned enterprise tend to be concentrated on the users of the firm's product or service. The costs, as with all government programs, are scattered over all taxpayers. A voter, then, bears little of the cost of any deviation from profit maximization by the firm, and so has little incentive to exercise his voice option.[17]

If part of the stock of the firm is privately owned, as mentioned earlier, any changes in the firm's objectives are reflected in the stock price. Costs are now borne by a comparatively concentrated subgroup of the population. Thus, even if control is ruled out as a possibility, existing stockholders have a rather larger incentive to exercise their voice options as an alternative to exit, exerting pressure on the managers or the government to preserve the profitability of the firm.

A MODEL OF JOINT OWNERSHIP

In a world of perfect information and costless income transfers, the problem facing the government is a simple one. If voters value social pursuits and profitability, the government need only choose the combination of the two that maximizes social welfare subject to resource availability. In Figure 9.1, a sort of production possibilities locus $G(\pi, S)$ represents the set of available profit(π)/ social goal(S) combinations. Social indifference curves $(SIC_1, \ldots, SIC_n)$ represent levels of social welfare $W(\pi, S)$. The government would choose combination E, with profits π^* and social goal S*, where the marginal rate of transformation is equal to the marginal rate of substitution.

Government enterprises are generally created to remedy some perceived failure in the private market. Difficulties may arise because, while the arms-length enterprise possesses an advantage over bureaucratic organization in that it faces some (typically breakeven or fixed deficit) constraint, the pressures for efficiency that control private markets are either weaker or absent altogether. Government monitoring is then required. In addition, social output is often difficult to measure, further increasing monitoring cost. In Figure 9.1, both these difficulties may move the enterprise away from E. If the government does not know the location of G, managers of the enterprise can cheat, reducing profits toward π' for a given level of S. If S is costly to measure, slack will be present, and the enterprise may reduce S toward S' for a given level of profit. Monitoring is also costly and uses resources, necessarily shifting G inward toward the origin.

FIGURE 9.1

Public Enterprise

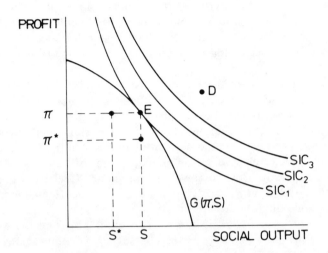

A further difficulty that arises when the location of G is uncertain is that government may set unrealistic or unattainable combinations of π and S as targets, as in point D in Figure 9.1. When
this occurs managers of the firm are faced with impossible objectives, such as earning a market rate of return in a competitive
industry while pursuing unprofitable social objectives. There is
some evidence that managers in these firms develop a form of
"organizational cognitive dissonance." For example, Mazzolini
reports numerous examples of this cognitive dissonance from his
interviews with senior management of joint enterprises. This appears to be particularly problematic when government "instruc-
tions" on social objectives are vague, conflicting (i.e., different
"suggestions" from different ministries), changing, or implicit.
It appears that many joint enterprises resolve the dissonance by
concluding that profitability is not important.

    Partial private ownership lessens the need for monitoring of
the joint enterprise's profitability by government. Since private
shareholders care about the profitability and riskiness of the firm,
and managers of the firm recognize the need to maintain share
price to facilitate raising capital, and so forth, managers have an
incentive to improve efficiency. The share price provides a signal
to government and private investors of perceived efficiency.

Here the appeal to government of partial private ownership is clear. By selling off part of its ownership in a public enterprise, government reduces the monitoring cost to it of moving the firm toward the peak of the profit hill for a chosen level of social output. On the other hand, by buying only part of a privately owned firm, government can move the firm to a higher level of social output without radically reducing the managers' motivation to maximize profit.

As well as affecting the incentives of managers for efficiency in attaining targeted objectives, government ownership also affects the riskiness of the firm. When there is some private ownership, the response of stock price to changes in government intervention provide useful signals to the policymaker. The value of the firm, and so the stock price, depends on expected profit and the riskiness of the enterprise. Government ownership can affect the value of the firm in two ways. First, government intervention generally implies some deviation from profit maximization, reducing expected profit. Government intervention can also affect the expected rate of return, particularly in the case of a government bail-out or takeover of a private firm. In this case the risk of bankruptcy is reduced, and the value of the firm increased. However, the overall change in the value of the firm resulting from an increase in government intervention would be indeterminant. Except perhaps in the case of a government bail-out, the effect on profitability is likely to dominate, and a fall in share price is likely to occur. The effect of a change in government ownership share on risk will not be large except at the initial investment. Since any government ownership implies a willingness to support the firm during bad times, reducing the probability of bankruptcy, marginal changes in government ownership should have little effect on the expected rate of return.

Another source of change in the value of the firm would be a change in the government's objective vis-à-vis the firm. This could occur without altering its share of ownership. In effect, the government could use its share to increase the targeted social output or it could increase its monitoring of social output, forcing the firm to a higher social output level. This might happen if, say, the political party in power changed unexpectedly. The effect of a government-induced change in S on the value of the firm would be to reduce the value of the firm. Changes in the value of the firm resulting from changes in government intervention, as mentioned above, provide a useful signal as to the cost of the intervention in terms of reduced expected profitability.

STOCK PRICE AND GOVERNMENT OWNERSHIP:
CANADIAN EXAMPLES

Two recent Canadian examples provide some empirical support, illustrating the propositions that a perceived incremental
move away from profit maximization by a corporation that has always had government participation will result in a negative share
capitalization, and a purchase of shares in a healthy private corporation by a government or its agent will also result in a fall in
share price.

The Canadian Development Corporation, created by the
Canadian federal government in 1971 as a profit-oriented enterprise
with a mandate to promote Canadian development, provides an example in the former category. Although the federal government
owns 49 percent of the outstanding shares of CDC, it had stressed
repeatedly the importance of profitability, and CDC's stock price
reflected that expectation. By 1980 the CDC had grown to be
Canada's twenty-sixth largest corporation in terms of total revenues.

The firm's independence was short-lived. In late 1980, officials in the Departments of Finance and Industry, Trade, and
Commerce began to consider publicly the possibility of tighter government direction of the CDC or of the government purchase of the
outstanding shares of CDC. It was suggested that government officials would like to see a CDC bail-out of the then ailing Massey-
Ferguson Ltd. CDC directors refused. Finally in 1981 it was
rumored that the government wanted to replace F. W. Sellers,
chairman of the CDC, with its own nominee, Maurice Strong.
Strong, who was subsequently elected a member of the board of
directors, was known to be sympathetic with the federal government's position toward the role of the CDC. The response of the
press (of which the following excerpt is an example) and of the
stockholders was markedly negative. As one columnist stated:

> Ottawa, it would seem, is directing its attention to the
> CDC, not because it is unsuccessful, but because it is
> performing well. The Government, which is seriously
> over-extended in its spending commitments, sees the
> healthy cash flow of the CDC as a convenient source of
> financing for some of its own initiatives and obligations.
> Furthermore, the Government appears to regard
> a federally directed CDC as a potential instrument for
> intervention in the manufacturing sector, comparable
> to the part played in the oil and gas industry by Petro-
> Canada. The Government is said to be developing a

strongly interventionist and nationalist industrial strategy, and it evidently requires a corporate vehicle as the carrier of its policy.

A senior, but unnamed, federal official is quoted as saying there is no reason why the CDC could not be profitable, and still pay "a good deal of attention to industrial, economic and financial strategies." . . . What evidently lies at the root of Ottawa's decision that it needs to have greater influence in the CDC's boardroom was the corporation's refusal last fall to help rescue Massey-Ferguson Ltd. by taking up an interest in the troubled farm machinery manufacturer.[18]

All this publicity was not lost on shareholders. Stock prices fell 8 percent during this period and the stock is still thought to be undervalued.[19] The Toronto Globe and Mail reported the following information four days after the appearance of first story on the government's intentions:

> Since . . . May 12, the common shares have slipped $1.25 to $13.12, the B preferreds are off $11 to $134 and the 1980 preferreds are down $3 to $18.75.[20]

A letter to the paper from J. D. Grant of Sceptre Investment Counsel, Ltd., stated:

> On May 12 . . . , the shares of the company declined in price by about 8 per cent to 9 per cent and the market value of the company was reduced by approximately $85,000,000.[21]

Clearly the possibility of increased government influence on the CDC was perceived as an increased probability of lower profits. The reduction in the value of the firm reflected stockholder expectations that increased interference would bring out an incremental deviation from profit maximization.

An example in the latter cateogry is the announcement that two enterprises wholly owned by the province of Quebec had secretly acquired shares in Domtar Ltd. —a large pulp and paper, packaging, construction materials, and oil and gas corporation with assets over $13 billion in 1980. The news that the two provincial crown corporations had increased the government's interest in Domtar from 23 percent to 42 percent resulted in a $4.62 drop in share price (to $29.87). Again investors feared an increase in government intervention, especially efforts to "persuade" the corporation to invest

in Quebec, at the expense of profitability. The Toronto Globe and
Mail reported that

> Some of these [small, old mills], such as a kraft paper
> mill at East Angus, are borderline operations and need
> a lot of money to upgrade them. They might well be
> closed if profit were the only consideration, but politi-
> cal influence could mean a major investment instead.
>   . . . [T]he uncertainty about who will control the
> company's actions has taken much of the luster out of
> the stock. . . . [22]

Both of these examples suggest that financial markets respond
quickly to perceived increased government intervention.

RESTRICTIONS ON PRIVATE OWNERSHIP OF
SHARES AND THE IMPACT ON CONTROL

As we have already pointed out, part of the value of share
ownership reflects its "vote value" and the potential to capitalize
that value by selling the shares to a control-seeking entrepreneur.
Government legislation often precludes any such capitalization by
limiting the percentage of shares that can be owned either by individuals, certain classes of individuals, or institutions.

Again there are several Canadian examples. Although the
province of British Columbia reduced its holdings in the British
Columbia Resources Investment Corporation (BRIC) to less than
5 percent of the outstanding shares, provincial legislation restricts
individual ownership to 1 percent of the shares and institutions to
3 percent of the shares. Additionally the legislation (following
precedents set by CDC and the Alberta Energy Corporation) allows
BRIC to force "associated members" to reduce their holdings by
selling within 60 days. If they do not sell BRIC can redeem these
shares at the lesser of the issue price, or the stock market price. [23]
These restrictions eliminate the possibility that private individuals
can exercise control over the corporation. The "associated members" legislation precludes shareholders from even acting in concert to influence management. This preemption of the control
option would likely depress stock prices. Ironically, the control
problem is likely to be exacerbated when a government reduces
considerably its share ownership (say, to a small percentage of
shares). In these situations the consequence is that no one external
to the joint enterprise can take control of it, resulting in a management oligarchy. Such regulations also provide strong incentives

for management to finance growth by equity issues to private share-holders rather than borrowing, as external control will be further weakened. Under such legislation the primary control on manage-ment behavior will be the likelihood that, if the firm gets "out of hand" the government will repeal the private ownership restrictions, or exercise more direct control itself over the firm's actions.

Share ownership is also often restricted to certain classes of individuals, with predictable consequences. Speaking of the CDC, one financial analyst concluded:

> Also, the prices of the common and preferred shares
> have been kept low because non-Canadian residents
> are not allowed to own any. "Take away the govern-
> ment interest and give U.S. investors a chance to buy
> and the price of CDC common shares would go to the
> $17 to $20 range overnight."[24]

The implication here is that both government ownership and the re-quirement that only Canadians own shares in the company affect stock price negatively.

CONCLUSION

The analysis presented here constitutes a first step toward a theory of joint enterprise. Several interesting properties of joint enterprises are revealed that help to explain both why governments might choose this form of organization and what the impact of joint ownership is likely to be. The major testable hypotheses that emerge from this research are that jointly owned firms will tend to be more efficient than 100 percent publicly owned firms, but less so than those totally in the private sector, and that expecta-tions about the expected level of government intervention in a joint enterprise's activities will be reflected in the share price of the firm. The three Canadian examples that are given lend support to the implications of the analysis.

An obvious avenue for further research is a detailed empirical analysis of joint enterprises. Both the stock price response to government-announced changes in intervention and the operating behavior of these firms could be examined. Data from countries other than Canada,[25] particularly in Europe, would probably be nec-essary to carry out such a study.

NOTES

1. M. Anshen and W. Guth, "Strategies for Research in Policy Formation," The Journal of Business 46 (October 1973).

2. R. Mazzolini, Government Controlled Enterprise (New York: John Wiley and Sons, 1979), p. 6. Several critics have argued that this is as true of the private corporations as of public corporations. See J. K. Galbraith, The New Industrial State (Boston: Houghton Mifflin, 1967), p. 72; and H. Mintzberg, "Policy as a Field of Management Theory," The Academy of Management Review 2 (January 1977):91.

3. W. Niskanen, Bureaucracy and Representative Government (Chicago: Aldine Atherton, 1971); T. Borcherding, "Towards a Positive Theory of Public Sector Supply Arrangement," Simon Fraser University Discussion Paper 79-15-3, 1979; J. L. Migué and G. Bélanger, "Towards a General Theory of Managerial Discretion," Public Choice, Spring 1974; E. Furobotn and S. Pejovich, "Property Rights and Economic Theory: A Survey of Recent Literature," Journal of Economic Literature 10 (December 1972); and C. Lindsay, "A Theory of Government Enterprise," Journal of Political Economy 84 (December 1976).

4. Thus we do not consider cases (common, for example, in Italy) where several government enterprises hold all the stock in a corporation.

5. Christopher Green, Canadian Industrial Organization and Policy (Toronto: McGraw-Hill Ryerson, 1980), p. 262.

6. Ibid., p. 274.

7. C. Johnson, Japan's Public Policy Companies (Washington, D.C.: American Enterprise Institute for Public Policy Research, 1979).

8. Mazzolini, Government Controlled Enterprises, p. 11.

9. Green, Canadian Industrial Organization, p. 262.

10. William G. Shepherd and Clair Wilcox, Public Policies Toward Business, 6th ed. (Homewood, Ill.: Richard D. Irwin, 1979), pp. 406, 415. Editors' note: See also Chapter 1 in this volume.

11. Barry M. Mitnick, The Political Economy of Regulation (New York: Columbia University Press, 1980), p. 401.

12. For some of the reasons, see Shepherd and Wilcox, Public Policies Toward Business, chap. 6; Green, Canadian Industrial Organization, chap. 9; and Chapter 2 in this volume.

13. Of course, ownership is not necessary for a bail-out by government. The recent U.S. loan guarantees to Chrysler did wonders for its share price.

14. See, for example, R. Ruback, "The Effect of Price Controls in Equity Values," Graduate School of Management, University of Rochester, Working Papers Series No. MERC 79-06, December 1979.

15. Henry Manne, "Mergers and the Market for Corporate Control," The Journal of Political Economy 75 (April 1965).

16. A. O. Hirschman, Exit, Voice and Loyalty (Cambridge, Mass.: Harvard University Press, 1975).

17. S. Peltzman, "Pricing in Public and Private Enterprises: Electric Utilities in the United States," Journal of Law and Economics 14 (April 1971).

18. Ronald Anderson, "Plan Subverting CDC Would Be a Betrayal," Toronto Globe and Mail, May 13, 1981, p. B2. Also see Roger Newman, "Directors of CDC Return Sellers, Hampson to Posts," Toronto Globe and Mail, May 22, 1981, p. B7; and "The Seedy Assault on the CDC," MacLean's, June 1, 1981, pp. 46-47.

19. F. W. Sellers, "The Canadian Development Corporation: What Happens When the Government Owns 49%," paper delivered to the Institute for Research on Public Policy/UCLA Conference on Managing Public Enterprises, Vancouver, B.C., August 14, 1981.

20. Dan Westell, "Ottawa Gets Offer for CDC Shares," Toronto Globe and Mail, May 16, 1981, p. B1.

21. J. D. Grant, "The CDC," Toronto Globe and Mail, May 19, 1981, p. B6.

22. David Stewart-Patterson, "Domtar Drops as Investors React to Control Attempt," Toronto Globe and Mail, August 20, 1981, p. B10.

23. Editors' note: See Chapter 4 in this volume.

24. George Linton, "CDC Shares Drop Sharply After Report of Lobbying," Toronto Globe and Mail, August 20, 1981, p. B1. Prior to the threat of government interference, CDC shares were selling for about $14 to $15.

25. For case studies of the formation and growth of most Canadian joint enterprises, see Marsha Gordon, The Government in Business (Montreal: C. D. Howe Research Institute, 1981).

III

MANAGEMENT STRATEGY OF PUBLIC ENTERPRISES

10

STRATEGIC PLANNING AND THE TENNESSEE VALLEY AUTHORITY

Allan G. Pulsipher

BACKGROUND AND HISTORY

The intellectual and political roots of the Tennessee Valley Authority (TVA) reach back to before World War I, but it is the institutional experimentation that characterized the early New Deal era that is especially evident in the TVA charter. In reporting the TVA Act out, the conference committee was almost poetic in defining their purpose:

> We have sought to set up a legislative framework, but not to encase it in a legislative straitjacket. We intend that the corporation shall have much of the essential freedom and elasticity of a private business corporation. We have indicated the course it shall take, but have not directed the particular steps it shall make. We have given it ample power, and tried to prevent the perversion and abuse of that power. We have set bounds to prevent its liberty from becoming license.

The TVA Act, passed by the Congress on May 18, 1933, established the Tennessee Valley Authority as an agency of the federal government. Under the act, all powers of the corporation are vested in a three-member board of directors, one of whom is designated as chairman. Board members serve for nine-year terms, during which they are prohibited from engaging in any other business. Moreover, they must be persons who "profess a belief in the feasibility and wisdom of the initial TVA Act." Any member of the board may be removed from office by concurrent resolution

of the Senate and House of Representatives. Congress regularly
reviews TVA's nonpower activities through the appropriatons process and periodically conducts general oversight hearings. The
TVA board, however, has full responsibility for setting power rates
and otherwise managing the agency. Because TVA is a federal
agency, its power system is not subject to review by the public
utility commissions in the seven states it serves.

THE TENNESSEE VALLEY'S ENERGY ADVANTAGE

Energy has played an important role in the economic development of the Tennessee Valley since TVA was created in the 1930s.
The 1940s, 1950s, and 1960s were years of rapid economic growth
in the valley. During this period, the region made impressive
economic gains—per capita income rose from about 48 percent of
the national average to 75 percent—gains that were accompanied by
even more rapid growth in electric consumption, about 10 percent
annually in the 1940s and 1950s.

During these years, the cost of generating electricity and its
real price to users fell steadily throughout the United States. It was
an era of cheap energy. In the 1940s natural gas in many areas was
a waste product that was flared simply to get rid of it. Domestic
oil supplies were so plentiful that an elaborate system of production
limitations was instituted and import quotas were imposed to limit
penetration by even cheaper imported oil. The price of coal purchased by utilities to generate electricity actually declined by 9
percent between 1950 and 1965. As the costs of producing and dis-
tributing electricity fell, the "battle" in the state public utility
commissions was over how much rates ought to go down and, occasionally, over whether utilities were being aggressive and far-
sighted enough to keep their capacity expansion programs ahead of
a relentlessly growing demand.

But the valley continued to enjoy a cost advantage compared
to almost all other regions of the country. There were several
reasons for this. First, the valley's energy needs were supplied
almost entirely by inexpensive hydroelectric power. Second,
TVA's early capital facilities were still being financed by interest-
free funds appropriated by the federal government. And, third,
TVA virtually alone enjoyed the efficiencies and economies of
scale associated with building a large, integrated power system
and pioneering the industry's largest coal-fired plants.

But, by the 1970s, some fundamental changes had taken place.
The valley's energy demands had long before outstripped the generating capacity of its rivers, and, today, cheap hydroelectric

power is providing only about 15 percent of the total power consumed in the region. Moreover, TVA's power system had been totally self-supporting since 1959, and the technology that TVA had pioneered in the 1950s and 1960s was now shared throughout the industry. The net effect of these changes was to erase TVA's earlier cost edge; the TVA power system no longer differs technologically or economically from other large integrated utilities.

Then, in 1973—just when TVA and its ratepayers were beginning to feel the full effects of these changes—the embargo-induced energy-cost explosion hit the electric utility industry. In retrospect, the year 1973 was a true historic watershed—economic as well as political. It was the end of an era of cheap energy and the beginning of an era of increasingly expensive energy. We all know what happened. By the mid-1970s, natural gas was in such short supply that some factories were actually relocated in gas-producing states to secure necessary supplies and others were forced to close. The world price of oil increased from a pre-OPEC embargo rate of about $3 per barrel to over $30 per barrel today. And average coal prices paid by TVA increased from $7.43 per ton in 1973 to over $30 per ton today.

Soaring energy costs were accompanied by record-high inflation, skyrocketing interest rates, and major unforeseen changes in power demand. The historical pattern of steady and predictable growth in electricity consumption suddenly seemed to stagnate, but it was not clear whether this signaled a pause in the old trend or the beginning of a new one and, therefore, whether the extensive capacity expansion programs that for many utilities were the legacy of the 1960s should be continued, stretched out, or simply abandoned.

TVA'S NUCLEAR CONSTRUCTION PROGRAM

Like many other utilities, TVA began its program of nuclear construction in the late 1960s when estimates of future demand growth were much higher than they are now. Figure 10.1 compares a recent TVA load forecast with the forecast made in 1974 when the last two nuclear units now under construction were authorized. Load and load forecasts vary substantially from year to year in response to changes in weather and economic conditions, making it difficult to distinguish short-term fluctuations from changes in the long-term trend. But it is the long-term trend in load growth that determines the optimum construction plan and schedule. Moreover, since it takes 10 to 15 years to bring a modern generating plant from the drawing board to production, load must be estimated at least that far in the future. This means that decisions about changing the construction schedule inherently and inescapably involve more uncertainty than most investment decisions.

In 1979 the TVA board decided that there had been a change in the long-term growth trend of future load: it would grow substantially slower than was predicted when TVA's 17-unit nuclear construction program was finalized. As a consequence, the board deferred construction on four units. In August of 1981, the board further adjusted the schedule by deferring an additional unit and slowing down the schedule for the other three units furthest from completion.

FIGURE 10.1

TVA Energy Requirements: Historical Growth and
Long-Term Outlook

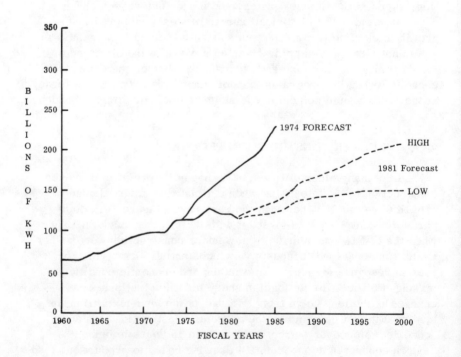

SOME SIMPLE ANALYTICAL PRINCIPLES FOR ANALYZING CHANGES IN THE CONSTRUCTION SCHEDULE

Changes in TVA's nuclear construction schedule are based on careful analysis of their anticipated effect on power rates and supply. The effects on rates varies with the actual demand or load that develops in the future, and the operational methods used to adjust should either surpluses or shortages in capacity occur.

Canceling or deferring units lowers revenue requirements in the near term by reducing the financing costs otherwise required to bring the units into operation. Part of the savings is offset, however, by the additional revenue required to cover expenditures already made, cancel existing contracts, and reclaim the sites. Moreover, because of inflation, the costs of providing capacity in the future will be higher than the costs of continuing to build capacity now. If canceling a nuclear unit means increased reliance on coal, future operating costs will be substantially higher because fuel costs are a larger proportion of the total costs of using coal-fired rather than nuclear generation. Hence, rates in the future are likely to be higher than they otherwise would be.

Two different types of risks are involved when a utility modifies its construction schedule. The first is the "high-load risk" of canceling units and then subsequently experiencing a high rate of load growth. This could result in shortages of generating capacity, the use of expensive imported power and combustion turbines to meet load, and, consequently, higher rates in the future. The second type of risk is that low rates of load growth will result in excess capacity and, as a consequence, rates will be higher than if plants had been canceled.

To compare the option of lower costs and rates in the near term with the option of higher costs and rates in the long term requires some method of taking into account the differences in the value of dollars available at different points in time, i.e., the fact that a dollar available 10 years from now is not worth as much as a dollar available for use today. The standard method of making such comparisons is to use a discount rate to calculate the present value of dollars available in the future.

Table 10.1 shows the present value of 1 kilowatt-hour of electricity for 30 years using a discount rate of 15 percent for each of three alternative construction schedule options under two alternative load growth scenarios. This is a cumulative, discounted measure of the impact of changing the construction schedule on rates. As is evident from Table 10.1, the differences between construction scenarios expressed as a percent of future rates are remarkably small.

TABLE 10.1

Present Value of the Cost of Purchasing 1 Kilowatt-Hour
Annually for 30 Years

Load Growth	Construction Schedule	Present Value	
		Absolute	Difference from Reference Case
High	Restart deferred units in 1984	38.54	(Reference case)
	Cancel the four deferred units in 1984	38.60	+0.2%
	Defer two more units now; cancel all six in 1984	38.67	+0.3% to 1.3%*
Low	Restart deferred units in 1984	38.81	+0.7%
	Cancel the four deferred units in 1984	38.62	+0.2%
	Defer two more units now; cancel all six in 1984	38.29	-0.6%

*Substantial power purchases from other power systems would be required to meet system load if six units are canceled and load growth turns out to be high. This calculation assumes power would be available at "economy rates." However, if TVA was "caught short," it is doubtful that sufficient power would be available for purchase. If TVA had to build combustion turbines to meet the load, the cost would increase sufficiently to make the difference about 1.3 percent higher than the reference case.

Source: Compiled by the author.

A second analytic step in determining the appropriate and prudent construction schedule is to examine the remedies available if one has to "live" with a choice that turns out to be a mistake. Put differently, are there ways to provide the ratepayer some "insurance," given the inherent uncertainty of forecasting future loads? The deferral strategy, itself, is a form of insurance, but one with probably a limited "protection period." A second form of insurance available to a utility should excess capacity develop is to substitute low-cost nuclear energy for higher-cost energy from coal. By shutting down older coal-fired plants and thus avoiding coal, operating, and a considerable proportion of the maintenance costs, the upward pressure of any excess capacity on rates can be reduced. For example, the difference between the capacity required to meet the high and low loads in 1990 is about 17 percent. However, if TVA had planned capacity to meet the high load but experienced the low load, rates in 1990 would need to be only about 7 percent higher than they would be if TVA plans had been exactly on target. This insensitivity of rates to excess capacity is largely due to the ability of the system to "back out" coal.

A third form of insurance against the possibility of an excess or a shortage of capacity is the ability to exchange power with neighboring utilities. While the amounts of power that could be available for exchange are not known, TVA's studies show that exchanges with utilities that burn significant quantities of oil and natural gas would benefit customers of those utilities as well as the TVA ratepayer.

A TIME OF TROUBLES FOR ELECTRIC UTILITIES

The strategic situation, or dilemma, described is very similar to that in which many large private utility systems found themselves as the country entered the new energy economy after the oil embargo era of the Organization of Petroleum Exporting Countries (OPEC). Paradoxically, the principal difference between TVA's plight and the rest of the industry was that TVA, as a public entity, apparently had much more managerial discretion and control. Unlike TVA, almost all public and privately owned utilities are subject to regulation and, as costs escalated, the state regulatory system soon not only dominated managerial discretion but defined the parameters for strategic planning and policy development as well. Some utilities responded to the energy cost explosion that began in 1973 by voluntarily canceling large coal and, especially, nuclear units because of the long lead times and regulatory uncertainty they entailed. But other utilities had little choice in deciding what to do. In effect, the decision was made by state public utility commissions—suddenly transformed from sleepy repositories of political patronage and ambition into emotional battlegrounds where one of the hottest issues of the day was to be decided and where the stakes quickly reached the billions. In many states, the utility commissions simply refused to approve rate increases adequate to attract the capital necessary to keep the increasingly expensive construction programs going.

In retrospect, it is apparent that the regulatory system that had evolved in the earlier era of technological progress, growing demand, and declining costs simply could not adjust to an era of energy-led inflation and high interest rates. For many private utilities, simple financial survival—not an analytical exercise of the sort outlined above—"drove" the decision to curtail or abandon their construction programs. But it is important to keep in mind that it was regulatory failure, coupled with the messages from the market, that produced the financial realities to which private utilities responded.

TVA's unique charter, placing all power to set rates with the board, freed TVA from the regulatory failure side of the equation but not from the new realities prevailing in the marketplace. For the historical reasons discussed above, a highly energy-intensive economy had developed in the valley. As indicated in Table 10.2, the cost advantage enjoyed by the region up until the 1970s had the predictable effect of attracting to the valley a disproportionate share of energy-intensive industries such as primary metals, chemicals, and paper.* Moreover, electric heating—actively promoted by TVA historically—was much more pervasive in the Tennessee Valley, in both the commercial and the residential sectors. As a consequence, the unrest and dissatisfaction that developed among TVA's consumers as costs and rates rose was, if anything, more intense than elsewhere. TVA's rate increases and anything that could be associated with them—the agency's management, its nuclear construction program, its energy conservation program (also among the nation's largest and most aggressive), and its nonpower activities—became significant regional political issues. The dissatisfaction was so intense that major changes in TVA's organic act—creating a regional regulatory commission, expanding the number of members on the board from three to five or seven, selling TVA plants to private utilities, and many more—all found a hearing and many found serious champions.

---

*Column 5 of Table 10.2 relates employment in the industry in the Tennessee Valley to how much employment one would "expect" in the region if its industrial composition were identical to that of the nation as a whole. To illustrate, the most electric energy-intensive industry is primary aluminum. Twelve percent of the jobs in this industry are in the TVA region (column 4). Since only 3.2 percent of the total nonfarm labor force is employed in the valley, 375 percent more people are employed in this industry in the valley than one would "expect" based on the national norm (100 percent representing the norm).

TABLE 10.2

Electric Energy-Intensive Industries

SIC	Industry	(1) 1974 Electric Energy per Employee (1,000 kwh)	(2) 1976 Electric Energy per Employee (1,000 kwh)	(3) Percent Change 1974–76 Electric Energy per Employee	(4) Percentage of U.S. Employment in TVA Region	(5) Column 4 as a Percentage of the Percentage of Total Nonfarm Employment in TVA Region
3334	Primary aluminum	2,794.8	2,234.9	-20.0	12.0	375
2813	Industrial gases	1,254.2	1,389.6	10.8	3.2	100
2812	Alkalies and chlorine	1,140.1	953.6	-16.4	1.2	38
3313	Electrometallurgical products	989.3	950.6	-3.9	10.2	319
2819	Inorganic chemicals	659.2	769.5	16.7	23.5	734
3339	Primary nonferrous metals	427.0	466.0	9.1	3.0	99
2873	Nitrogenous fertilizers	452.5	439.5	-2.9	7.2	225
3241	Hydraulic cement	334.2	325.3	-2.7	3.3	103
2911	Petroleum refining	251.0	258.4	2.9	0.2	6
2874	Phosphatic fertilizer	186.2	220.1	18.2	0.7	22
2869	Organic chemicals	269.2	203.8	-24.3	1.2	38
2611	Pulp mills	381.5	183.8	-51.8	5.5	172
2865	Cyclic crudes	163.2	176.7	8.3	0.3	9
2621	Paper mills	241.8	163.9	-32.2	4.4	138
2631	Paperboard mills	305.0	156.9	-48.6	2.4	75
	Total nonfarm employment				3.2	

Source: Compiled by author.

TVA had clearly entered the third stage of its life—the stage of "conflict and challenge"—or in Toynbee's more literary term, its "time of troubles." In effect, TVA faced the prospect of the public sector equivalent of bankruptcy—such major changes in its organization, mandate, and character as to imply irreparable institutional failure.

To survive as a viable institution, TVA had to explain the strategy that directed its planning and management to a hostile and restless public. This strategy was explicitly formulated as part of the process of preparing for a series of congressional hearings in 1980 and 1981. Testifying before the Senate Subcommittee on Energy and Water Development in December 1980, then Chairman S. David Freeman defined his agency's two major goals:

> For TVA, the job today boils down to, first, helping the Valley maintain and extend its energy advantage in a world of rising energy costs, energy shortages, new energy technologies, environmental concerns, and regulatory uncertainty. This energy advantage will be vital in achieving TVA's second major objective of helping keep open the door to economic prosperity for the Valley in a world of stiff foreign and domestic competition. . . .
> TVA's future "energy advantage" will lie in having an ample supply of reliable power at competitive prices when other regions may well be short of capacity.

Underlying these broad corporate goals was an essentially technical and analytical argument that can be outlined as follows. First, how much energy and electricity will be demanded 10 or 20 years in the future is inescapably uncertain. Hence, although a utility must try to improve its forecasting capability, the basic uncertainty will remain. The problem is how to deal with the uncertainty prudently and intelligently. Subjective factors necessarily play an important part in any major decision characterized by uncertainty. Second, the prudent way to deal with an inherently uncertain future is to base planning on a range of future demand bordered by a high and a low forecast. Third, the construction schedule should be designed to meet the high forecast rather than low or "midrange" forecast because of the following reasons:

> Future rates, in TVA's case, would be only 2 or 3 percent higher for a few years if using the high forecast did result in maximum "overbuilding." Eventually, the rate impact of overbuilding would reverse itself and rates would be lower than they would be if plants were canceled.

Backing out old coal-fired plants and exchanging power with neighboring oil- or gas-burning utilities were valuable forms of insurance against excessive costs to ratepayers from overbuilding.

The knowledge that TVA was taking firm steps to ensure that adequate power would be available would be an economic advantage that would make the valley more attractive for industrial expansion and recruitment. Conversely, the perception that TVA was planning for slow growth would become a self-fulfilling prophecy.

TVA established a corporate planning system late in 1979 and those responsible for it were active participants in the articulation of the strategy formulation process, but the strategy itself was clearly the result of the essentially political process of preparing for congressional hearings. This does not imply that the strategy was created for the hearings. In my view the strategy was clearly an articulation of an implicit strategy that had guided TVA for decades—simply adapted to the peculiar circumstances of TVA's "time of troubles." Despite the recent surge of popularity in strategic planning for public agencies and private enterprises, I doubt whether TVA's experience is unusual.

CONCLUDING OBSERVATION

The institutional attribute that differentiates TVA's power program from that of other electric utilities is the ability of the TVA board to change rates solely at its discretion without review or approval by state public utility commissions. Such freedom undoubtedly gives TVA considerably more operational control and protection against risk than other utilities enjoy. However, in TVA's recent time of troubles reviewed above, this freedom from outside review may well have been an exacerbating rather than ameliorating factor. Review by a public utility commission is a formal, open process in which all interested parties can gain access to the same basic factual data, the utility's interpretation of the data's implications, and the plans and proposals they derive from it. The review process provides both a focus for criticism, dissent, and contrary interpretation as well as an eventual ruling by an independent and objective body.

Prior to the energy price explosion that followed the 1973 oil embargo, the function that utility commissions performed was largely a technical one relevant to the industry itself. After the embargo, when rapidly rising energy costs became a major national political issue, public utility commission review probably served a new role: that of diluting and decelerating public discontent. Without such an institution in the Tennessee Valley, TVA's rapid rate increases and their causes became general political issues of intense interest. This meant that TVA's "strategic situation" became a part of the regional (and to a lesser extent, national) political environment and issue structure; conversely, TVA's strategic situation became much more politicized.

TVA had to respond to this alteration in its environment or situation, as did the relevant regional political leaders and entrepreneurs. However, since the technical and analytical issues involved in the modification of TVA's nuclear construction schedule are complex and difficult to articulate to the general public, they did not provide an effective vehicle for the political participants to react to and to respond to their concerned constituents. The public dialogue evolved into a discussion of either the appropriateness of TVA's broad goals—growth and no growth, nuclear power, conservation, and so forth—or a review of historical issues—public versus private power, the contribution of TVA to the development of the valley, the role of individual states in the control of the agency—a discussion to which both the elected officials and their constituents could relate. This may have tended to make the hand of the past weigh somewhat more heavily on TVA's strategy formulation process than might have been the case had TVA's time of troubles been less politicized. Changes in strategy threatened traditional sources of understanding and support became riskier as did changes in strategy that might have built new constituencies and sources of support.

If one were to generalize this experience, one might speculate that when the time of troubles for private enterprises intensifies the probability of departures from past patterns of behavior tends to increase—either through changes in management or ownership. For public enterprises, however, as the time of troubles intensifies and the strategic situation becomes more politicized, the tendency is to attempt to return to traditional sources of support and ways of doing business.

11

CANADIAN NATIONAL: DIVERSIFICATION AND PUBLIC RESPONSIBILITIES IN CANADA'S LARGEST CROWN CORPORATION

John Gratwick

INTRODUCTION

In this chapter I am concerned with Canadian National Railways (CN), the oldest as well as Canada's largest federal crown corporation. Although my intent is not to provide a lesson in Canadian history or politics, I shall focus on those circumstances and personalities that contributed to Canadian National's becoming a modern, diversified, and profitable crown corporation.

This process was an evolutionary one. Canadian National (CN) began diversifying in the 1920s, modernizing in the 1950s, and recording profits in the mid-1970s. (See Tables 11.1 and 11.2.) The company is still active on all these fronts, but now they are synchronized. Throughout CN's evolution, it has been restructured, refined, and redirected in response to changing economic, political, and social realities. But then, as now, the company pursued its mandate to operate on a commercial basis.

I believe the company's adherence to this mandate is the single most important reason for its success today. To be sure, Canada has had its share of political leaders making bold statements about transportation—and transportation people trying desperately to make them into realities. But over the years, the twin threads of competition and commercialism have repeatedly taken precedence over political rhetoric and campaign promises.

It is unlikely, however, that the company will be able to meet the transportation challenges of this decade and remain financially sound unless some changes are made in policy, if not in principle. More will be said about this a little later, but first more should be said about who CN is and where it came from.

TABLE 11.1

Chronology of Major Events in CN History

Year	Issue	Action	Policy Response
1916	Excess rail capacity threatens to bankrupt some 200 rail lines.	Appointment of the Smith-Drayton-Ackworth Royal Commission.	Formation of CN with mandate to operate as "one united system, on a commercial basis under its own politically undisturbed management for benefit of Canada."
1923	Political interference (government overrules company's refusal to permit employees to seek political office while working for company).	CN president, D. B. Hanna, resigns.	First and last instance of political interference.
1932	CN losses; CP criticism of CN expansion.	Appointment of the Duff Royal Commission.	Reaffirmed principle of competition, but recommended replacement of board of directors with three trustees.
1933	Duplication of CN and CP rail services.	CN-CP Act.	Legislated recommendations of Duff Commission—more cooperation between two railways in eliminating wasteful and duplicate service. Replaced CN board with board of trustees. Board of directors reinstated in 1936.
1937	CN debt burden.	Government forgives loans and interest from 1923 to 1937.	Partial recognition of long-term debt as impediment to fiscal soundness.
1948	Railway freight rates.	Appointment of the Turgeon Royal Commission.	Profits possible, but rates should cover cost and help economic development.

Year			
1952	CN debt burden.	CNR Act cuts company's indebtedness in half.	Partial recognition of long-term debt as impediment to fiscal soundness.
1959	Rail's survival.	Appointment of the MacPherson Royal Commission.	Reaffirmed principles of competition, rate-making freedom, and financial compensation for providing nonprofitable services in national interest.
1967	Fragmented and inequitable transportation policies.	National Transportation Act.	Enshrined above principles into law governing all modes.
1976	Company's organization.	Reorganization of company into profit centers.	Businesslike approach to pursuing commercial mandate.
1978	CN debt burden.	Recapitalization Act forgave $808 million debt in exchange for future self-financing and dividend payments.	Full recognition of long-term debt's effect on debt-equity ratio.
1980	Future directions of company.	Corporate policy statement.	"The management of Canadian National sees no conflict between a profit-oriented role for the Corporation and a responsibility to serve national purposes. Indeed we believe that the principle that CN should seek a commercial return on all its activities will lead to a clearer definition of the national tasks to be performed and to more efficiency and less cost in the performance of these tasks."

Source: Compiled by the author.

TABLE 11.2

Chronology of CN's Major Acquisitions

Year	Acquisitions
1919-23	Some 200 publicly and privately owned rail lines and associated properties (hotels and real estate) and services (express and telegraph).
1923	CN (France) S.A. (hotel and rental property).
1925	Canadian National Steamship Company (west coast ferry service, inactive).
1927	Canadian National West Indies Steamship Company (inactive).
1923-75	Various east coast marine ferry services entrusted to company.
1931	Canadian National Transportation Limited (nonrail transportation; trucking, 1959; pipelines, 1966).
1947	CN-CP Telecommunications (pooled telegraph services et al.).
1949	Newfoundland Railway (condition of province joining confederation).
1954	CN Hotels, Inc.
1969	HALTERM (rail-ship, port facility; owned jointly by CN, Province of Nova Scotia, and Clarke Traffic Services Limited).
1971	CANAC Consultants Limited (international transportation consulting).
	AUTOPORT (automobile storage and servicing facility in Nova Scotia); owned jointly by CN and the province; in 1976 CN became sole owner.
1972	CN Tower (communication facility and tourist attraction).
1976	Divisional organization: CN Rail, CN Telecommunications, CN Trucking and Express, CN Hotels and Tower, CN Marine, Grand Trunk Corporation (U.S. rail subsidiaries—Central Vermont, Grand Trunk, and DW&P).
	COGEMA (rail-ferry link in northern Quebec; CN owns 49 percent).
1977	VIA Rail Canada Inc. (rail passenger services, became separate crown corporation 1978).
	Terra Transport (Newfoundland ground transport services).
1978	CNT (noncommercial telecommunications services provided for all CN divisions) and Terra Nova Tel (telecommunications for Newfoundland) and NorthwesTel (telecommunications for Northwest Territories).
	CNM Inc. (all marine-related activities, except east coast ferry services).
1979	CN-CP Telecommunications (formal partnership agreement).
1980	Northern Alberta Railway (purchased outstanding 50 percent from CP).
	Detroit, Toledo & Ironton Railway Company (U.S. rail line).
1981	CN explorations (mining and drilling).

Source: Compiled by the author.

ORIGINS AND POLITICAL CONTEXT

Let me emphasize at the outset that the involvement of successive Canadian governments and political leaders in railways has not been based on any political belief in the virtues of state ownership over private enterprise. It is merely a recognition of the realities of the Canadian situation. The rail facilities that exist in Canada today would never have come into being if it had been left up to private enterprise alone.

In the first place, the building of railways in Canada—with its vast empty spaces, its very small and widely distributed population, and its rigorous climate—was not likely to provide a secure and reasonable return on investment. In the second place, a rail network built purely by private enterprise would have developed along north-south lines following the geography of the land and the flow of commerce with the more populous United States.

The fathers of Canadian confederation realized that if they were to accomplish their dreams of an independent dominion stretching from sea to sea, north of the United States, it was essential that there be a complete and Canadian-owned transportation link across the country. That is why when the first four provinces and former colonies—Ontario, Quebec, New Brunswick, and Nova Scotia—joined in the confederation known as Canada in 1867, with an intercolonial railway one of the essential points of the agreement.

The next province to join the confederation was British Columbia in 1876 and a railway was part of the price of its joining. So the Canadian Pacific Railway (CPR) was built between Montreal and Vancouver—a distance of some 3,000 miles.[1] The CPR was built and operated by a private company. But there was a tremendous input by the government of Canada in both financial outlays and land grants.

With the completion of the CPR it might have been felt that the need for a Canadian transcontinental railway had been met. But Canadians have always abhorred a monopoly situation, so there were soon moves to have another line built across the prairies. Railway construction then proceeded at a frenetic pace and just about the time of the First World War the country ended up with not one but three transcontinental systems and a great number of short lines in Eastern Canada. A painful fact soon became apparent. There just was not enough traffic to keep these and many of the other smaller lines in business.

The government was faced with a dilemma. The private companies could not be allowed to go bankrupt in the usual way. This would have deprived the nation of rail services which, although not immediately viable, were required for the economic development of

Canada. Furthermore, a collapse of this nature that involved large numbers of foreign investors would have damaged Canada's reputation on international money markets. Besides, Canadian taxpayers already had a sizable investment in many of the railways through various forms of government support.

In moments of crisis, Canadian governments appoint Royal Commissions of Inquiry—and that is what was done in 1919. This commission investigated the railways that had difficulties—almost all of them, except the CPR and its affiliates. From experience, Canadians had learned that a railway system operated directly by government was not the answer. The history of the Intercolonial Railway tells of efforts by politicians to control the hiring and firing of staff—and equally determined efforts by the officers in charge to run a railroad without political interference. Private enterprise had not proved to be the answer either. Entrepreneurs had a habit of launching many high-risk ventures, taking the profits if they were successful, and leaving the government to pick up the pieces if they were not.

In a typical Canadian compromise, the commission investigating the railway situation decided to combine the virtues of both systems in an effort to avoid the vices of each. The commissioners recommended that control of some 200 rail lines, both publicly and privately owned, "be transferred to a new body and be operated as one united system on a commercial basis under its own politically undisturbed management on account of, and for the benefit of, the people of Canada."[2] The new body came to be known as Canadian National. (An overview of the major events in CN's history is given in Table 11.1.)

THE PERIOD 1923-69

The principle of operating "without political interference" was challenged in the early history of the company's existence when its first president, D. B. Hanna, interpreted that to mean no personnel could run for political office and remain with the company. He was overruled by the prime minister, MacKenzie King, and promptly resigned. That was the first and last direct act of political interference in the company. It occurred in 1923.

Hanna's successor, Sir Henry Thornton, American by birth and British by title, made it clear he expected to have a free rein in company affairs when he said "there is as much chance of politics getting into CN as there is of an elephant walking a tightrope." Operating on a commercial basis, however, was another matter. In addition to the physical assets of the railways that became part of CN, the company also inherited their long term debts of $1.5 billion (in 1920 dollars). Although Sir Henry had all he could do to pay the interest on the debt, let alone eradicate it, he did make some solid achievements in galvanizing the disparate equipment, management styles, and practices of the companies that comprised CN into a single operation with its own identity.

In the process some lines were eliminated, track was upgraded, and new equipment was purchased. The new organization competed effectively with privately owned CP not only in rail operations, but in hotels and steamship services as well. (See Table 11.2.) Sir Henry even introduced a network of radio stations so that rail passengers could be entertained while traveling. This radio network, incidentally, later became part of today's Canadian Broadcasting Corporation, another crown corporation.[3] Sir Henry divested the railway of redundant lines, services, and personnel and diversified its activities in other spheres. Unfortunately, Sir Henry's timing was off. His expansionary pursuits during the Depression compromised the railways' commercial mandate and invited criticism from the privately owned CP.

In keeping with Canadian tradition, another Royal Commission was established in 1933 to study the situation. The commission report reaffirmed the principle of competition between the two railways, but did recommend replacing CN's board of directors with three trustees who would work with CP in eliminating duplicate services.[4] This was done, but proved to be unworkable and control of CN was returned to a seven-member board of directors. The commission also broached the subject of CN's historic debt burden and, as a result of its findings, the company's capital structure was revised in 1937 by forgiving government loans and accrued interest since 1923.

During this period of retrenchment, the railways experienced the initial erosion of their passenger monopoly as automobiles and airplanes began to attract travelers.[5] However, the railways enjoyed a last hurrah as a transportation monopoly during the Second World War when they assumed the main burden of carrying supplies and personnel to support the war effort.

Following the war, the railways requested a freight rate increase—their first in some 25 years. The freight hikes were necessary to pay for the rapidly growing wage and materials bills and to rehabilitate the plant that had been neglected during the war years. The increases were opposed by most of the provinces so another Royal Commission was appointed in 1948 to study the issue. This commission concluded that the railways were to make a profit if they could, but that the objective of rate setting should be to both cover costs and help the country's economic life.[6] In summary, the commission advocated a transportation policy that was neither socialistic nor capitalistic, and it clearly deviated from the free enterprise doctrine of the two previous Royal Commissions.

Although the commission gave muddled guidelines, Donald Gordon, the company's new president, had a clear vision of what direction the company should take. He left an indelible mark on the company for innovations in both railway technology and management. He spearheaded the transition from steam to dieselization (not completed until 1960) and introduced the first study that helped shape a geographic organization of the company into five regions.

Despite these advances, labor strife, increased competition from highway carriers, and an unrealistic freight rate structure made it clear to the government that drastic changes would be needed if the railways were to survive. Such changes could only be suggested by a Royal Commission, so one was set up in 1959. It recognized the changing environment of transportation in Canada and its findings heralded a complete break with tradition. The commission's major recommendations included a total relaxation of control over the rate-making policy of the railways to give free play to competitive market forces.[7] It also proposed that compensation be paid to the railways for services provided in the public interest and required by national policy. These recommendations, in turn, formed the cornerstone of the country's National Transportation Act of 1967.[8] With very few exceptions, both the industry and its customers acknowledge that the act has served the country well to date.[9]

The guidelines set forth in the act represented a challenge as well as an opportunity for both CN and CP. If, as the act stipulated, the railways were to be treated like the other modes of transportation and enjoy the same rate-making freedom, then they would have to be more responsive to customer needs in such a competitive environment. At CN this meant new services, modern technology, and a more flexible management style to better meet the demands of the marketplace.

DECENTRALIZATION, RECAPITALIZATION, AND DIVERSIFICATION

The move to decentralize the company was accelerated in the mid-1970s when Robert A. Bandeen took over as president.[10] Under his stewardship, day-to-day decision making was shifted to the regional level so that long-range planning and development would be the principal concern at corporate headquarters. Bandeen gave new meaning to the company's commercial mandate by making words like "bottom line" and "profits" respectable and desirable. To that end, he reorganized the company into profit centers. This gave management—and shareholders—a yardstick for measuring the success of the company.

There were some who claimed making money was not the role of a crown corporation, but Bandeen argued it would be socially irresponsible for Canadian National to provide services without any concern for their economic viability and expect the taxpayer to bear the ever-increasing load.[11] By linking responsibility to fiscal solvency, he reconciled the company's vigorous business orientation with its obligations to meet Canada's growing transportation requirements. He also reiterated that government, not CN, should make decisions or choices on the allocation of benefits to sectors or regions of the country. CN wanted to stand up and be counted like any other business: that is, provide efficient services for a reasonable rate of return and be self-financing.

The National Transportation Act provided the mechanism for the railways to establish levels of service and rates, but it was not until the Recapitalization Act of 1978 that CN obtained a blueprint to become self-financing. This statute converted some $800 million of debt to equity. As a result, CN's debt-to-equity ratio decreased from 60 percent to around 42 percent. This is more in line with other successful railways of its size. In return, the government was no longer obliged to purchase each year preferred shares that were pegged to gross revenues. Furthermore, CN was required to pay a dividend to its shareholder, the government, of not less than 20 percent of net earnings. In 1980 this amounted to $38.5 million, and was about the same in 1981.

Concurrently with the Recapitalization Act, implementation of the profit center concept began to identify which divisions were profitable and which ones were losers. Of all the divisions, only two are in the latter category. They are CN Express, which now carries larger, multipiece shipments by rail and truck, but traditionally had been in the small package business, and Terra Transport, which provides transportation services in Newfoundland, Canada's largest island province. However, measures have been taken to improve both operations, with those introduced for CN Express already having favorable financial results. The Terra Transport program may begin to have a positive effect by the end of 1981; a significant step was for the federal government to take some financial responsibility for the losses in Newfoundland. Other divisions like the Grand Trunk Corporation, which includes the company's subsidiary rail lines in the United States, reversed their historic loss patterns and began recording profits.

In addition to singling out winners and losers among divisions, the profit center concept also helped to identify those service components that hampered even greater returns for profitable divisions. For example, CN Rail was the largest and most profitable division, yet the provision of intercity passenger services, commuter trains in Montreal, and the movement of grain at rates set in 1897 all represented a severe drain on its profit level.[12] Progress has been made in all these issues.

For the last three years passenger service has been the responsibility of another federal crown corporation, VIA Rail Canada Inc., which contracts for service with both railways. The money-losing commuter service in Montreal appears headed for resolution some time in 1982 and action on the statutory grain rate is likely to become a priority in the West now that an energy agreement has been reached by the federal government and the province of Alberta.

CURRENT STRATEGIC ISSUES

It was noted above that CN would probably be unable to meet the transportation challenges of the future unless there were some changes in policy. Foremost among those is the need to resolve the statutory grain rate so that CN and CP can receive a fair return for hauling this commodity. Grain represents about 17 percent of CN Rail's traffic yet accounts for only 3 percent of its revenue. Translated into dollars, it means that CN Rail lost $130 million hauling grain in 1980. CP loses even more. Meanwhile, other western traffic of coal, potash, and sulphur is growing at an unprecedented rate and requires billions of dollars of investment in new track and equipment during the coming decade. If the rate remains unchanged, Canada's two major railways could lose up to $8.5 billion in needed revenue over the next ten years.

The solution I favor in resolving this issue is contained in David Harvey's book on the grain rates entitled Christmas Turkey or Prairie Vulture. Harvey suggests a one-time payment by the federal government to the producer. It would cost about $2 billion and be distributed in the form of a bond, on the basis of acreage. The bond could be cashed at face value, placed in an interest-bearing account, or transferred when the farm changes hands.[13]

If the government fails to come up with a solution to the projected shortfall from the statutory rate, CN will have to either decelerate its plans for expansion to remain fiscally sound or broaden its access to equity financing by issuing shares in the company to the public. At this time, there is more likelihood of the former than the latter. Of course, CN could always borrow the extra money needed to meet all its requirements for good customer service. But that would probably raise its debt to equity ratio from 40 to 50 percent and leave the government with the possibility of a further refinancing by the early 1990s.

These fiscal concerns highlight what I believe to be another serious policy dilemma that affects CN but occurs at the federal government level within the Department of Transport itself. I am referring specifically to the difficulties the department has in recognizing its responsibilities in representing CN to Parliament as owner as well as operator. As owner, the department should be confined to concern for the financial affairs of the company, and for its directors and top management—just as the shareholders of any company do. Meanwhile, its functional relationship with CN should be identical to that of transport companies in the private sector. Over the years the Department of Transport has given CN more direction as operator than as owner. Perhaps the government should consider having someone other than the Minister of Transport represent crown corporations as owners—such as the Minister of Finance or even a new Minister of State for transport industries. I believe the government should show more interest in discharging its ownership responsibilities to the company as it approaches the crossroads of its evolution.

Despite some unresolved issues that have been outlined, CN can declare that its original mission has been accomplished. Now the company believes it can play an even larger role in the economy. And it has identified a number of growth opportunities—all based on the principle of putting the company's existing resource of talent, materials, and property to wider use. Presently, about 13 percent of CN's net profit comes from non-rail related activities, but the company sees that level rising to at least 25 percent in the years ahead.

CN's approach to diversification and new business is to require that a proposed venture meets one or more of the following criteria:

It supports or augments existing services.
It preserves or develops the assets vested in CN by the nation.
It maximizes the use of the corporation's human resources.
It makes a significant and supportable contribution to the achieve-
   ment of the corporation's social and environmental responsibilities.

For instance, CN has already set up a company to manufacture and distribute an electronic identification system for locomotives and rail cars and is planning a retail operation to supply and service add-on communication equipment for the home and office, based on the expertise it already has in its two telephone companies. It also expanded its rail operations in the United States with last year's purchase of the Detroit, Toledo & Ironton Railway. CN has extensive real estate holdings that it is developing, including some western oil acreage. The company is also prepared to take a leading role in launching a Canadian Merchant Marine, based on its experience in running marine services on the east coast and the Great Lakes, and its financial interest in CAST, a leader in transatlantic shipping.

CN is seeking ways to make new business ventures complement the company's social commitment to its employees and the country. By expanding the company's base of activities, it might be possible to offset layoffs in some of its operations with job opportunities in new ventures. The company is currently pursuing this in Newfoundland, where some of its laid-off rail workers are being integrated into its shipbuilding facility in that province.

New business must be undertaken with minimum use of new capital and maximum prospects for generating earnings and improving the asset base of the company. With that in mind, the company has participated in, and is still actively seeking, joint ventures with both the public and private sectors. For instance, the company is partners with the government of Nova Scotia and a privately owned transportation company in the container terminal at Halifax. And the company's trucking subsidiary recently acquired a trucking firm in Quebec in partnership with the provincial government.

I do not want to leave the impression that CN has neglected its social responsibilities while pursuing its business or economic goals. Like most companies operating on a national and international scale, it works hard at being a good corporate citizen to its employees, customers, and neighbors in the communities where it has a presence. Similarly, the company's day-to-day operations are subject to the same government regulations as its competitors in the private sector. As a crown corporation, however, CN is more visible and, therefore, comes under closer public scrutiny in the way it conducts its business than its competitors. On most counts, CN's record is quite good; and where improvement is required, corrective action is taken. In short, CN is just as concerned about its rating by society as it is by Moody's—and scores equally well with both.[14]

NOTES

1. The origins and construction of the CPR are described in Pierre Berton, The National Dream: The Great Railway, 1871-1881 (Toronto: McClelland and Stewart, 1970).

2. [Drayton-Ackworth] Royal Commission to Inquire into Railways and Transportation in Canada, Report (Ottawa: King's Printer, 1917). Generally, see L. T. Fournier, Railway National-ization in Canada (Toronto: Macmillan, 1935).

3. See Frank W. Peers, The Politics of Canadian Broad-casting, 1920-1951 (Toronto: University of Toronto Press, 1969).

4. [Duff] Royal Commission to Inquire into Railways and Transportation in Canada, Report (Ottawa: King's Printer, 1932).

5. In 1937 another federal crown corporation, Trans Canada Airlines, was established as a subsidiary of CN. Renamed Air Canada in the 1960s, the airline's total revenues in 1980 exceeded $2 billion. A discussion of its performance can be found in Chapter 7 of this volume.

6. Report of the Royal Commission on Transportation (Ottawa: King's Printer, 1951); and Report of the Royal Commission on Agreed Charges (Ottawa: King's Printer, 1951).

7. Report of the Royal Commission on Transportation (Ottawa: Queen's Printer, 1961), 2 vols.

8. See F. W. Anderson, "The Philosophy of the MacPherson Royal Commission and the National Transportation Act: A Retro-spective Essay," in Issues in Canadian Transport Policy, ed. K. W. Studnicki-Gizbert (Toronto: Macmillan, 1974), pp. 47-80. See also Howard J. Darling, "Transport Policy in Canada: The Struggle of Ideologies versus Realities," in Issues in Canadian Transport Policy, ed. K. W. Studnicki-Gizbert (Toronto: Macmillan, 1974), pp. 3-41.

9. See Trevor D. Heaver and James C. Nelson, Railway Pricing Under Commercial Freedom: The Canadian Experience (Vancouver: University of B. C. Centre for Transportation Studies, 1977). See also Chapter 5 in this volume.

10. Editors' note: Robert A. Bandeen has a Ph.D. in Eco-nomics from Duke University and has published an article on railway cost functions in Econometrica.

11. Robert A. Bandeen, "A Business and a Responsibility," address to the Vancouver Board of Trade, January 17, 1977.

12. See D. R. Harvey, Christmas Turkey or Prairie Vul-ture? An Economic Analysis of the Crow's Nest Pass Grain Rates (Montreal: The Institute for Research on Public Policy, 1980).

13. Ibid., p. 43.

14. Editors' note: Another view of CN's purposes and per-formance can be found in Garth Stevenson, "Canadian National Rail-ways," in Public Corporations and Public Policy in Canada, ed. Allan Tupper and G. Bruce Doern (Montreal: The Institute for Research on Public Policy, 1981).

12

HYDRO-QUÉBEC AND THE JAMES BAY PROJECT: THE FINANCING STRATEGY

Georges Lafond

INTRODUCTION

It is no secret that things have changed for utilities over the last few years. Government guidelines are more and more putting restraint on them, and the public increasingly wants to get involved in such crucial decisions as investments selection and rate increases. This new situation makes it more difficult than ever for public corporations' managers to respond to such expectations. Before focusing on the financing strategy of the James Bay Project, it will be useful to describe a number of characteristics of Hydro-Québec.

HYDRO-QUÉBEC

Hydro-Québec operates one of the major systems in Canada for the generation and distribution of electric power, serving the largest province in Canada in terms of land area and the second largest in terms of population. A provincially owned corporation created in 1944, Hydro-Québec is a multifaceted company.

First of all, it generates, transmits, and distributes virtually all the electric power consumed in the province of Quebec. Total sales exceeded 100 billion kilowatt-hours in 1980, of which 8 billion were exported to the United States. In fact, total electricity consumption is about the same in Quebec and California. At the same time, Hydro-Québec, through one of its subsidiaries, carries on a sustained construction program in anticipation of future demand for electrical power. This program should translate into investments worth $16 billion over the next five years.[1] A third aspect of the corporation is that it operates through its Research Institute high-voltage and high-power laboratories. It has entered into contracts with other organizations in Canada, the United States, and abroad for use of the facilities for special research and testing. Finally, through Hydro-Québec International, another subsidiary, the company acts as an advisor and consultant in the fields of generation, transmission, and distribution of electricity on a worldwide basis.

The company's growth over the last 15 years has just been phenomenal. Such growth was induced by the rapid increase of electric demand in the province: since 1965, demand has tripled for an average growth rate of 7.3 percent, while assets have been multiplied by 7 and net income by 20 (see Table 12.1). For three years the Financial Post has listed Hydro-Québec as the largest commercial and industrial enterprise in Canada in terms of assets and net income. According to the Canadian Business ranking, Hydro-Québec became, in 1980, the most important crown corporation in Canada in terms of assets, ahead of the Bank of Canada.[2] And according to Fortune, only two telephone companies among all public utilities in North America have assets larger than Hydro-Québec.[3]

TABLE 12.1

Total Assets and Net Income of Hydro-Québec
(millions of dollars)

Year	Total Assets[a]	Net Income[b]
1965	2,593	35
1970	3,890	70
1975	7,068	230
1978	12,886	523
1979	15,505	746
1980	18,012	746

[a]As at December 31.
[b]For year ended December 31.
Source: Compiled from Hydro-Québec Annual Report 1965-80.

Today, Hydro-Québec's production is 99 percent hydroelectric. This situation, which is unique in the world, offers enormous advantages principally related to the fact that water is a free, renewable resource. And this also means that Hydro-Québec is able to offer rates that are among the lowest in North America. Electricity bills for Quebec home owners are four times lower than in New York and about half those paid in cities like Philadelphia, Detroit, San Francisco, Houston, or Chicago (see Table 12.2).

TABLE 12.2

Monthly Electricity Bills for Residential Customers
(U.S. Dollars per 1,000 kwh)

City	Monthly Bill
Montreal (Hydro-Québec)	30.40
Edmonton, Alberta	33.60
Portland, Oregon	34.50
Toronto, Ontario	35.70
Vancouver, B.C.	37.50
Chicago	52.90
Houston	54.80
Detroit	61.60
San Francisco	66.30
Philadelphia	79.30
Boston	94.50
New York	130.00

Note: As of March 1981, excluding sales tax.
Source: Hydro-Québec, Annual Report, 1981.

Since the beginning of the energy crisis, oil costs have risen faster than electricity prices and so, in recent years, electric heating has made greater inroads into the residential and commercial sectors. The percentage of Quebec households using electric heating climbed from 12 percent in 1974 to 38 percent in 1980.[4] Moreover, more than 80 percent of new dwellings have electric heating.

Hydro-Québec's installations now include some 50 hydroelectric power stations, with a total capacity of about 15,000 megawatts. But in 1971, when the corporation decided to go ahead with the

James Bay Project, its generation capacity just exceeded 10,000 megawatts. In itself, the James Bay Project was designed to double that figure by 1985.

THE JAMES BAY PROJECT

The James Bay Project is one of the largest in the world.[5] Built at a cost of $15 billion, the La Grande Complex—Phase 1, as it is called, has attracted more than a bit of attention, earning such nicknames as the "Arabs with a French accent" and the "Sheiks of the far North." Objections were raised from all sides when the project was announced in 1971. Many feared that it would prove impossible to finance such a huge investment or, alternatively, that other important projects would have to be sacrificed. Environmentalists expressed concern about the consequences of inundating large wildlife areas, while the natives used the project as a lever to defend their trapping and fishing territories.[6] And to top it all, some experts were urging to build immediately some nuclear plants, so as not to fall behind with that technology for the future.

But economic studies showed that the cost per kilowatt-hour delivered from James Bay would be lower than that from any other alternative thermal plant. Soaring fossil fuel prices during the following years were to make the edge even more comfortable. Furthermore, the economic fallout on the province would be the most important with the James Bay Project, since the industrial and labor structures were already in place to supply the resources required by this hydroelectric development. In fact, it is now evaluated that 85 percent of the project's expenditures are for goods and services supplied by Canadian firms and that the Quebec content is equivalent to about 77 percent.

Construction of the La Grande Complex required the development of a vast nordic territory of some 125,000 square miles that had hitherto remained in its natural state. Until recently, practically the only signs of human activity were the snowshoe tracks of the Cree Indians that would melt away each spring. The La Grande River flows some 600 miles north of Montreal. When the project was announced, the only way to reach this region was by helicopter or float plane. Today, there are some 900 miles of roads, five permanent airports, and temporary villages that accommodated 18,000 people in 1980 during the peak period of construction.

The project includes, in its first phase, three powerhouses totaling about 10,300 megawatts, five transmission lines running for a total of 3,000 miles, and the diversion of two adjacent rivers into the La Grande River, which doubles its natural flow. Eight dams and more than 200 dikes are to be built, requiring a total of some 5 billion cubic feet of fill, that is, moraine, sand, gravel, and riprap. These structures can attain quite impressive dimensions. The longest dam is nearly 2.5 miles long and the tallest 500 feet high. If placed end to end, the dams and dikes would form a wall some 80 miles long.

Construction, which is now entering its ninth year, is quite far advanced. Almost all the infrastructures are in place and some have already been dismantled. As far as the permanent structures are concerned, one underground powerhouse has been in service since 1979 and the last unit will provide its first deliveries of electricity in 1984.

All of this work was accomplished ahead of schedule despite labor unrest that at one point completely paralyzed the work sites for 50 days, harsh climatic conditions that limited the working period to 90 days for certain structures, such as the dams and dikes, and all the unknown and unexpectable elements involved in a project of this magnitude. Moreover, the final cost of the project is now anticipated to be around $14.6 billion, as compared to a 1976 budgeted cost of $16.2 billion. This was done in a period of time marked by rising inflation and interest rates. These elements bring about one of the main problems Hydro-Québec had to deal with during the construction of the La Grande Complex: financing.

THE FINANCING STRATEGY

Hydro-Québec, like other utilities, has to rely heavily on financial markets to pay for its capital expenditures. External financing makes up 80 percent of the corporation's total investment needs, the remainder being financed directly out of its accumulated surplus. During the last decade, in light of the James Bay Project, Hydro-Québec's capital expenditures rose dramatically. In fact, for the last five years only, the project accounted for 70 percent of the corporation's capital investment.[7]

Correspondingly, annual borrowing needs were multiplied by six during the 1970s, as they jumped from $335 million in 1971 to over $2 billion in 1980.[8] Without doubt, this has put a tremendous pressure on the corporation's ability to meet its financial requirements.

If we look at the figures another way we find that during the first five years of the 1970s, Hydro-Québec's borrowings averaged $600 million a year and during the last five, $1.6 million a year. Looking up at the next five years, they should average $2.8 million a year. This is the kind of arithmetical progression that requires a well-formulated financial strategy.

The first major element of Hydro-Québec's financing strategy was to reject the project financing technique for the James Bay Project. That approach would have implied making in advance credit agreements covering the total cost of the project when work started in 1972. However, the duration and size of the project, along with all the unknown factors surrounding it, militated against such a long-term commitment on the behalf of either the investors or the corporation. Therefore, the serial financing technique was adopted. This meant that the James Bay Project would be financed on an annual basis along with the other projects carried on by Hydro-Québec.

The second element of Hydro-Québec's strategy, considering the huge sums it would have to borrow, was to ensure a comfortable "fall-back" position. This included, among other precautionary measures, a major revision of its liquidity policy. At the end of the 1960s, Hydro-Québec was one of Canada's major issuers of commercial paper. During the 1971-73 period, it reduced its commercial paper operation to an annual outstanding average of $25 million. This was an amount that was considered adequate at the time to maintain a reasonable degree of visibility as an "A1," "P1" rated issuer of commercial paper.

For the following three years, Hydro-Québec's plan looked to short-term investment positions of $150 million, $400 million, and $500 million. At the end of 1974 and 1975, it was practically on target, but ended up 1976 clearly above target. Its liquidity position was $1.08 million. At the end of 1978, it had managed to reduce this position around the $500 million level, which it had originally planned to maintain until completion of the James Bay Project in 1985.

The third element of Hydro-Québec's strategy emerged when it became evident that stable historical yield curves were on the verge of becoming a phenomenon of the past and that volatility was going to be one of the most important factors with which it would have to reckon. Then the overall liquidity policy of Hydro-Québec was reviewed. It was decided to ensure that at least ten months of its construction program would be taken care of in advance at all times. Also, the short-term investment position target of $500 million was revised downward to $200 million.[9]

Covering the borrowing program for almost a full year in advance is designed to provide Hydro-Québec with: flexibility in execution of its borrowing program, greater independence toward financial markets, and confidence in the investors' mind. Flexibility in execution of the borrowing program is proving especially crucial in periods of volatile exchange and interest rates such as the ones since the fall of 1979. When interest rates reach 20 percent or more, the corporation that binds itself with 25- or 30-year bonds must have some elbowroom to wait for better times.

The fourth element in Hydro-Québec's financial strategy was to adopt a modified approach to rate making. This was done to assess more accurately its internal cash flow financing. Until recently, Hydro-Québec used to propose annually tariff increases, subject to government approval, a process well-known to most public enterprises. Such an annual exercise has proven in many cases to expose the utilities to the "too little too late" treatment and to the "revolving door" process. In order to minimize this exposure and, more important, to improve the quality of its financial projections and strategies, Hydro-Québec managed with the full support of the governmental authorities to secure preset, annual rate increases for a three-year period. The company is not aware of any other utility in North America that has used such a technique.

Of course, fixing rates three years in advance may prove at times to be risky as inflation rates reached unexpected high levels, thus eroding the corporation's real income more than it was anticipated. However, the new policy was intended to procure for Hydro-Québec greater assurance concerning its sources of revenue. In turn, this would allow the corporation better planning of its borrowing strategies.

Besides setting up precautionary measures, the financial strategy of Hydro-Québec had to respond, in the end, to one tough reality: year after year, it would have to find always more money on the bond market to finance the investment program.

Therefore, the fifth element of its financing was market diversification (see Tables 12.3 and 12.4). During the first five years of the 1970s, the Canadian and U.S. public bond markets supplied about 80 percent of the funds borrowed by Hydro-Québec. But this share dropped to only 50 percent during the next five-year period as it strove to diversify both the source and the form of its long-term external financing. As Table 12.3 indicates, syndicated loans in U.S. dollars and Eurodollars contributed 27 percent of Hydro-Québec's borrowing needs in 1976-80 but were nonexistent in the previous five-year period. Investors as yet untapped, like the Alberta Heritage Fund and the Japanese market, contributed almost $600 million from 1976 to 1980. Finally, bond issues in Eurodollars, Swiss francs, and German marks also increased slightly their share in Hydro-Québec's debt financing.

There are, of course, limits to such a diversification of its debt. Borrowings in foreign currencies result in important exchange risks. These can increase significantly the cost of redemption for the corporation. Moreover, many nonconventional markets simply cannot meet the company's needs in terms of the volume and

maturity of financing. Nonetheless, exploring all sources available
can take out some of the pressure on the conventional markets,
thereby reducing the risks of saturation on such markets, and at the
same time increase the flexibility in Hydro-Québec's debt management. Flexibility is exactly what it will need entering the 1980s.
As emphasized previously, the next five years will bring new financial challenges to Hydro-Québec when annual borrowing requirements
will average nearly $3 billion.

TABLE 12.3

Sources of External Financing for Hydro-Québec
(percent)

Source	1971-75	1976-80
Conventional Markets	90	64
Canada	32	26
U.S. public	47	24
Eurodollar	4	6
Switzerland	4	6
Germany	3	2
Other Sources	10	36
Middle East	8	1
U.S. private	—*	16
Eurodollar credit agreements	—	11
Japan	—	3
Alberta Heritage Fund	—	4
Miscellaneous	2	1
Total	100	100

*Nil.
Source: Compiled by the author.

Looking further down the road in terms of financial strategy,
the next five-year period looks somewhat different than what Hydro-
Québec has been used to during the past ten years. From now on,
financial officers will need a lot of creativity to ensure the success
of the borrowing program. For the time being, Hydro-Québec is
well positioned from a liquidity standpoint. However, its liquidity
policy will have to be reviewed in light of the financial environment
that has prevailed since the fall of 1979.

TABLE 12.4

Yearly Capital Expenditures, Borrowings, and Sources of External Financing for Hydro-Québec

	1971	1972	1973	1974	1975	1976	1977	1978	1979	1980
Yearly Capital Expenditures and Borrowings (millions of dollars)										
Capital Expenditures	389	424	551	616	1,142	1,267	1,950	2,588	2,817	2,589
Borrowings	335	375	430	690	1,080	1,765	1,083	1,537	1,766	2,156
Sources of External Financing (percent)										
Conventional Markets										
Canada	30	59	44	20	25	7	20	24	41	38
U.S. public	44	26	48	38	60	14	–	7	36	44
Eurodollar	13	–	–	4	5	7	12	4	5	5
Subtotal	87	85	92	62	90	28	32	35	82	87
Switzerland	–	5	–	2	7	9	17	5	–	3
Germany	9	8	8	–	–	–	16	–	–	–
Subtotal	96	98	100	64	97	37	65	40	82	90
Other Sources										
Middle East				35						5
U.S. private						61	21			
Eurodollar credit agreement										
Japan							8			
Yen										
U.S. $								4	7	
Alberta Heritage Fund										
Miscellaneous	4	2		1	3	2	6		11	5
Total	100	100	100	100	100	100	100	100	100	100

Source: Compiled by the author.

Hydro-Québec is also in a good position to examine new formulas and to find new ways and means for the financing of its construction program. It will continue its search for new pools of savings that could be tapped at a reasonable cost on an overall basis. Such an objective has been already achieved twice in May and September 1981 when the corporation borrowed £40 million in London and 40 million in European currency units in Brussels by way of public bond issues. Still more important, Hydro-Québec must be prepared to resort to fall-back positions that will have to be maintained accessible at all times, such as the international syndicated loan market.

Within the present context of skyrocketing interest rates,[10] shortening of maturities, and crowding out of markets by deficit-ridden governments and capital-intensive energy contractors, Hydro-Québec plans to continue the implementation of its most important guiding rules: to borrow as much as possible in Canadian dollars, to borrow for the longest possible term, and to borrow as much as possible at fixed rates.

NOTES

1. Unless otherwise indicated, all amounts are in Canadian dollars. In 1981 the Canadian dollar traded at between U.S. 80 and 85 cents.

2. The Financial Post 500 (June 1981) and the Canadian Business (July 1981) lists of large firms do not completely coincide. But the following can be reported. First, the Financial Post ranked Hydro-Québec first in assets ($18.01 billion), first in net income ($746 million) and twenty-sixth in operating revenues ($2.44 billion) in 1980. Second, Canadian Business ranked Hydro-Québec ahead of the Bank of Canada in terms of assets ($17.3 billion) and Ontario Hydro ($15.6 billion). Ontario Hydro's revenues ($2.82 billion) exceeded those of Hydro-Québec. Third, on the Financial Post list the largest private firm, in terms of assets, was Canadian Pacific Limited ($13.04 billion) and the second largest was Bell Canada ($11.45 billion). In terms of revenues, neither Hydro-Québec nor Ontario Hydro ranked in the top 15 in 1979/80. The largest firm on that dimension was Canadian Pacific Ltd. ($9.985 billion). General Motors of Canada was second ($9.45 billion). The tenth largest firm was the Hudson's Bay Co., a retailer, with sales of $3.8 billion in 1979/80.

3. These are AT & T, with assets of $125.5 billion, revenues of $50.8 billion, and net income of $6.1 billion, U.S. dollars; and GT & E, with assets, revenues, and net income of $19.7, $9.8,

and $0.5 billion respectively. Among the largest utilities, Hydro-Québec would rank third in assets, twentieth in revenues, second in net income, tenth in the number of employees, and first in net income as a percentage of net worth in 1980. See Fortune, July 1981.

4. In 1966 only 2 percent of Quebec dwellings were heated by electricity. In 1970 the comparable figure was 6 percent.

5. Outside the Soviet Union, only the Aswan High Dam is larger.

6. See, for example, Boyce Richardson, James Bay: The Plot to Drown the North Woods (Toronto: Clarke Irwin, 1972).

7. Hydro-Québec's actual and estimated capital expenditures and borrowings for the period 1971-85 (in billions of dollars) were as follows:

	1971-75	1976-80	1981-85 (estimated)
Total capital expenditures	3.1	11.2	16.3
of which James Bay	0.9	7.8	5.9
Total borrowings	2.9	8.3	14.0

8. Annual borrowings (in millions of dollars) by Hydro-Québec between 1971 and 1980 were as follows: 335, 375, 430, 690, 1,080, 1,765, 1,083, 1,537, 1,766, and 2,156.

9. For example, for 1980/81 Hydro-Québec's overall liquidity was $2,000 million consisting of $1,100 million in unused term loans, $250 million in regular credit lines, $450 million in potential issues of commercial paper, and $200 million in short-term investments. Its borrowing program for 1980/81 was $2,200 million.

10. Editors' note: This chapter was prepared in September 1981. In October and November interest rates began to fall some-what—more so in the United States than in Canada. However, short-term rates fell more than long-term rates.

13

IMPLEMENTING A PRODUCT MARKET STRATEGY: THE CASE OF THE U.S. POSTAL SERVICE

Christopher H. Lovelock and Charles B. Weinberg

INTRODUCTION

Prior to the 1970s, marketing was virtually unheard of as a management function in postal services. The following criticisms made of Canada Post in 1969 by consultants could well have been applied at that time to the United States Postal Service (USPS) and other national postal systems:

Officers in the [Post Office] Department lack the marketing orientation essential for an efficient service. They see the market as users of mail rather than of communications, transportation and banking services. The services that the Department is permitted to provide under the Post Office Act have been interpreted precisely and have been offered in an administrative and unimaginative manner. . . .

This chapter is primarily derived from an extensive study of the USPS commissioned by the Aspen Institute as part of its Task Force on the Future of the Postal Service and reported on in more depth in Joel L. Fleishman, ed., The Future of the Postal Service (New York: Praeger, 1982). In addition, we have had the benefit of a paper by Gordon C. Morison, Assistant Postmaster General, Customer Services Department, United States Postal Service, and the discussion of Larry Sperling, Assistant Deputy Minister, Marketing, Canada Post, at the UCLA/IRPP Conference on Managing Public Enterprises, Los Angeles, September 10, 1981.

> Employees who serve customers lack the discretion necessary to deal with them: the rate system is not sufficiently flexible . . . retailing facilities leave something to be desired from the point of view of hours, lobby layout, and graphic design; promotion and community relations policies reflect a lack of customer orientation; and communication with large customers is presently inadequate.[1]

In the past decade, considerable progress has been made in the use of marketing by postal services in various countries whether in the context of a government department or a public enterprise. Marketing organizations have been established, new services (products) have been developed and introduced based on analysis of customer needs and competitive offerings, and programs for the various products have increasingly been subject to the rigor and discipline of formal marketing plans.

The survival of North American postal systems in the 1980s and 1990s will depend on their ability to maintain and even expand their revenue base in the face of threats posed by competition using existing and developing technologies. Postal services will not only have to work harder to serve existing markets, but they also will have to initiate searches for new products and new markets. As the postal services become less dependent on government subsidies and derive more of their funds directly from user revenues, both the opportunity and requirement to lessen the restraints of regulation increase. This, in turn, demands a strong marketing orientation, involving careful attention to the needs and concerns of both present and prospective customers in such areas as product features, pricing and payment procedures, delivery and retailing systems, and all forms of customer communications. In brief, success requires that a marketing viewpoint be pervasive throughout the organization.

This chapter examines the role of marketing in improving postal service effectiveness. Four main areas will be covered. First, we shall describe the nature and scope of marketing. We will show marketing to be a broad-based management function that extends from the fundamental strategic question of what the organization does—what products are provided to which markets—to tactical issues such as preparing advertisements and designing brochures. Problems arise when marketing is defined narrowly and confined to very limited tactical areas and not included in strategic development.

Second, we shall examine the interrelationship between marketing management and operations management. In many large service organizations, operational concerns are often emphasized to the detriment of <u>customer</u> desires and convenience. At the operating level, issues such as setting the opening hours of post offices illustrate the conflict. At the strategic level, both marketing and operating management need to be involved in product line decisions. New services cannot be restricted to those which it is "easy" for the systems to add, but must include needs of customers who will go elsewhere if their requirements are not met. On the other hand, new products must be confined to those that the system is capable of providing at present or with the addition of obtainable resources.

The third section continues this theme and examines the question of the stature of the marketing department in a postal service. We show that the responsibilities of the USPS's Customer Service Department, its marketing department, have been narrowly defined, but that the marketing departments in the Canadian and British postal systems have wider scopes. We also show some of the difficulties that have resulted from this narrow definition of marketing.

In the fourth section, we examine the impact of postal regulations on the ability of USPS to compete effectively in the marketplace. Elsewhere, we[2] and others[3] have commented on the differences between marketing in businesses as compared to public sector organizations. In this section we consider the impact of just one of these differences, the regulatory environment that USPS faces.

Postal services are impressive in their size and scope. In the United States, for example, USPS's revenues of over $18 billion would rank it among the top 15 of the Fortune 500 companies, and its more than 500,000 employees would rank USPS as the third largest employer behind American Telephone and Telegraph and General Motors.[4] The mere size of national postal systems makes the marketing challenge these organizations face considerable, but the rewards from successfully meeting such a challenge will benefit vastly users, the general public, and the organization.

TOWARD A DEFINITION OF MARKETING

Marketing, to be properly understood, must be viewed as a broad management function that permeates the organization.[5] Marketing can be defined as the management function that links the organization to its external environments—its customers, funding sources, regulatory agencies, and other relevant publics.

Many organizations view marketing as essentially a tactical activity designed to help the organization improve its effectiveness in attracting resources and customers. They think that this job is accomplished

by adding a marketing director and a small staff who
carry out the necessary planning and doing. They think
that this staff can be added and be effective without
making any changes in the rest of the organization.
The organization continues to produce the same products and services for the same customers and the job
of the marketing staff is to help promote or sell them.
    This view of marketing is of course wrong. If
marketing is to be effective, it calls for more than a
new function or department. It calls for a new orientation of the organization. Marketing is more than a
set of add-on activities. It amounts to a whole new
attitude toward the organization's various publics and
missions. It is the thoroughgoing adoption of this new
orientation that produces the major benefits of better
survival and growth for the organization and satisfaction for its customers.[6]

This customer orientation then translates into marketing
strategy. However, one should not infer that the marketing strategy
is based solely on the needs of the user. Successful marketing
strategy draws on the strengths and objectives of the organization
in the context of a competitive environment. But the marketing
strategy adopted is the key element in:

Guiding organizational decisions to reach objectives in the face of
    difficult and uncertain environments;
Developing and executing the chosen strategy; and
Maintaining a management control and information system to identify
    emerging threats and opportunities, determine whether marketing
    plans are being properly implemented, and measure the results
    achieved against planned targets.

Effective Marketing Management

    In a very useful article, Philip Kotler and Sidney J. Levy
identify nine key features of effective marketing management that
we will review briefly in the context of national postal services.[7]
    The first key feature identified by Kotler and Levy is a
generic product definition, which emphasizes the basic customer
needs being served as opposed to the physical form of the product.
A task force report on the Canadian Post Office identified three
different perceptions of the post office:

The operating role. The Post Office is in the
business of aggregating, transporting, diffusing, and
delivering to the door through one distribution network—small, individual items of any kind.

The communications role. The Post Office is
in the business of transmitting documented messages
between individuals, relatively slowly and with inconsistent speed, at low transmission cost but high transformation cost.

The customer role. The Post Office is in the
business of serving five types of customers: (i) businessmen, who use the mails primarily for formal
financial transactions; (ii) professional mailers who
use the mail system to help them advertise and sell;
(iii) government, which employs the Post Office as a
unifying force in addition to using the mail system as
any business does; (iv) urban householders, who use
the mail system for personal and institutional contacts,
and for the convenience of mail order shopping; and
(v) rural householders, who use the mail system to enable them to participate in a consumer society. [8]

Second, not all customers need the same services or generate
the same level of usage. Target group definition is necessary if an
organization is to focus its efforts and use its limited resources
wisely. As Gordon C. Morison, the Assistant Postmaster General,
Customer Services, of USPS points out:

While we recognize that the number and type of recip-
ients we serve are our strength, it is business and
Government which generate about 83 per cent of our
total mail volume, and their action in connection with
households produces another 11 per cent. Householders are directly responsible for only 6 per cent of
total mail volume.

Business, non-profit and Government mailers—
about six one-hundredths of one per cent (or about
4000 customers)—send 45 per cent of all the mail.
About one third of these largest mailers are mail
service companies; another 20 per cent are companies
providing financial services; 10 per cent are publishers and mail order houses combined; and 7 per cent
are manufacturers. The Government accounts for
about 14 per cent. These are the customers with whom
we have a major franchise. [9]

Postal service managers need to be particularly careful here, however, because postal services also have a mandate to serve the entire public. In fact, in 1977 a review committee criticized the British Post Office for overemphasis on large commercial customers.[10] But the requirement to serve the general public can be looked on as an opportunity rather than an albatross around the postal neck. The British Post Office, for instance, has been adding services needed by people living in rural areas in an effort to maximize the utility of its extensive distribution system.

Third, because customer needs differ, differentiated marketing is required. For example, the British Post Office has a wide range of parcel delivery services to meet the needs of different users. However, in service organizations, the impact of increasing the variety of services on operating efficiency must also be kept in mind: there are financial and operational limits to any organization's ability to tailor products to fit individual customer's needs. Marketing's role is not to provide endless variety, but to bridge the gap between the organization and the environment. The breadth of the product line reflects a blend of customer variation and organizational capability.

Fourth, because impressionistic evidence is insufficient, understanding of customer behavior must be based on formal research and analysis. Indeed, marketing research should be pervasive throughout management, providing both insights and feedback to all managers concerned about the organization's relationships with its environment, customers, and performance in a variety of competitive marketplaces. For example, consumer analysis helps to develop an understanding of motivations and decision making at the level of the individual commercial or household user or prospect. What product characteristics are most important to the consumer and how are they evaluated? How, when, and where are decisions made? Who influences these decisions? These are some of the questions that can be helpful in developing a marketing program, and in which answers can be obtained by monitoring customer behavior and conducting market research studies.

Fifth, a sound marketing strategy requires a differential advantage that will appeal to the target segment being addressed. Unless the national postal services can develop products with a differential advantage to customers, they will find that their user base will consist of the least attractive, most costly customers to serve. This appears to have happened to the USPS in parcels as aggressive competitors developed differential advantages for selected customers (typically urban-based businesses shipping to consignees who were also located in urban areas). A similar threat appears plausible with the development of electronic transmission as an alternative for certain types of messages that now move by first-class mail.

Sixth, an organization has available multiple marketing tools that should be used in concert to achieve marketing objectives. Relying too heavily on advertising to build demand or naively claiming that "if a product is good, it doesn't need advertising, and if it's bad, advertising won't help" are two tactics doomed to failure. As the growth in philatelic programs demonstrates, it is the combination of marketing elements—an attractive product, priced at acceptable levels, conveniently available, and effectively promoted through carefully targeted communication efforts—that is crucial.

Seventh, an organizational structure that provides for integrated marketing planning is required. As the definition of marketing employed here implies, marketing has a broad range of responsibilities. Setting up an appropriate organizational structure in service organizations generally has been problematic and this has been particularly so in postal systems where operations management retains control over virtually all aspects of customer contact and product delivery. In addition, senior marketing executives need to have as important a role in the organizational hierarchy as their colleagues in other functional areas.

Eighth, successful marketing requires continuous marketing feedback to monitor both the environment within which the service is being supplied as well as the organization's performance within this environment. By undertaking market analysis, one can gain a sense of the nature and extent of consumer demand for a particular product category. The quality and value-for-money of an organization's own product, as perceived by prospective customers, contribute to determining market share relative to directly competing offerings. Understanding the nature of the direct competition may provide insights into why a specific institution is doing particularly well or particularly badly. Likewise, an understanding of environmental trends (such as population shifts, developments in technology, and changes in the economy) may enable managers to recognize why the total market for a specific product category is growing or declining, so that they can plan accordingly.

Ninth, just as organizations require periodic accounting audits to check on the state of their financial health and the appropriateness of their accounting and control procedures so, too, do they need marketing audits to provide a systematic review of the organization's marketing objectives, strategies, organizational structure, and performance in the marketplace.

Marketing as a Postal Management Activity

During the past decade, marketing efforts have achieved some real successes. For example, the British Post Office has developed a wide range of services geared to the needs of different segments of shippers to move parcels within the United Kingdom, so that the Royal Mail parcel service is now profitable for the first time in many years. According to Morison, the U.S. Postal Service "will achieve the goal Congress established in 1970—self sufficiency by 1984. How? By placing greater attention than ever before in the history of a public enterprise to the functions normally associated with the discipline of marketing."[11]

But, of course, the adoption of marketing has not been an unmitigated blessing; there have been failures as well as successes. With any innovation there are bound to be difficulties, and especially with an innovation such as marketing, which challenges traditional operating procedures. Furthermore, marketing is an ongoing management activity, not just an abstract concept. Consequently, the manner of implementation has much to do with its actual and perceived success. Marketing programs have not always adequately considered the needs of the operating areas and in the words of one manager "have sometimes been devoted to problems which are susceptible to marketing approaches, not necessarily problems which are critical to the Postal Service." Beyond these and other problems of implementation that could be cited, two more fundamental issues stand out.

First, when compared to the size of the organization, and the magnitude of the problems being faced, the resources devoted to marketing by postal systems have been minimal. This is particularly crucial because sound marketing usually involves substantial amounts of "up-front" investment in market analysis, product development, and market planning. Resources are available to develop relatively few programs and these programs often cannot be planned, implemented, and monitored in sufficient depth.

Second, at least in the United States, there is still insufficient understanding of what marketing is, both by managers within the post office and by government officials charged with regulating the USPS. Many congressmen (who seem, parenthetically, to have no difficulty in voting for federal funding to advertise political candidates) have a narrow view of marketing postal services; some postal officials claim that congressional pressures limit paid advertising by USPS to an unrealistically low level. Within USPS itself, it appears that many managers continue to see marketing largely as a selling activity—that is, to convince people to use whatever services the post office chooses to offer. While marketing does encompass promotion of current services, that is only one aspect of it. In the next section, we explore the need for balance between marketing and other management functions, particularly operations management.

BALANCE BETWEEN MARKETING AND OPERATIONS

Successful service organizations require a balance between operating and marketing orientations. As with many large service organizations, the operations perspective still seems to be dominant in the USPS. Market needs and customer convenience are often relegated to second place behind operational considerations. For instance:

The interiors of most retail post offices are bleak, cheerless, and poorly designed, reflecting a least-cost-per-square-foot mentality, rather than a welcoming impression that says "we want your business!" (The only thing most post offices seem to want is persons sought on charges of mail fraud.)

Pickup times on street mail boxes are often illegible. This is an irritation to customers who need to know box collection times, but of little concern to operating personnel who already know when to pick up the mail.

The opening hours of post offices are at variance with the shopping habits of the nation, closing before many people leave work in the afternoon and only open limited hours on Saturdays in certain locations.

Credit cards are not accepted by USPS for purchase of postal services (although Amtrak will accept them for rail services). Even expensive services sold to large volume mailers do not operate on a credit or billing basis; instead, checks, cash, or a deposit account must be used.

Over-the-counter express mail services are only available at a limited number of post offices, some of which do not seem to have been selected with customer convenience in mind. They are often main postal stations, located at some distance from the types of customers most likely to use this service on a walk-in basis. This may result in diversion of business to Federal Express and other competitors which promote their pickup services and set less restrictive conditions for these pickups than does USPS.

These examples raise some important questions for postal management. Have customer needs and preferences been considered in designing new services? Should long-standing postal operating procedures be reevaluated in light of changing customer needs and new competitive alternatives? Does the potential for increasing sales revenues by changing procedures outweigh the increased operating costs involved? Would greater convenience for household mailers generate an improved image for USPS that might translate into political support for regulatory changes desired by the postal service?

Two Perspectives

Marketing and operations should be seen as mutually supportive functions. Developing customer demand for a service that cannot be produced at a price acceptable to the market is as pointless as efficiently producing a service that nobody needs. Successful products are those that make sense from the vantage points of both operations and marketing.

Nevertheless, there are fundamental differences in orientation between marketing and operations that only superior management can bridge. Marketing management is oriented externally to the needs of the customers and to the threats from competition. In response to this environment, it tends to want to offer a wide range of services and to want to update them frequently. Success is defined in terms of customer satisfaction, sales, and market share. Operations management, on the other hand, is internally oriented. It prefers to offer only a few standardized services, in order to maximize operating efficiency, and is reluctant to make changes. Operations managers tend to believe that if the system is well run according to internal standards, then the public will use it; they tend to measure success in terms of cost minimization and high performance against internally defined efficiency standards that may have no relationship to customer concerns.

The gains from a marketing orientation that pervades the entire organization include the following:

Improved customer satisfaction, achieved by providing services that perform well on dimensions that are relevant to users. This is particularly important in postal services, which are dependent on public (and thus political) goodwill as well as customer satisfaction.

Improved net operating performance, achieved by tailoring services to the needs of major market segments, and offering sufficient value to customers so as to command commercially viable prices.

Improved productivity, achieved by implementation of programs that require customers to modify their behavior. Such service innovations as standard size envelopes, moved mail, zip codes, and presort all require gaining customers' cooperation in changing established behavior patterns so that productivity gains may be achieved.

As is readily apparent, these gains are available to an organization regardless of whether it is a business, a government agency, a public enterprise, or a nonprofit society.

Some managers argue that only a publicity campaign is required to get the public to adopt a required form of behavior.
Although lack of consumer information can result in the failure of
an otherwise sound program, massive publicity by itself is not sufficient—as indicated by the widespread violations of the 55-mph
speed limit in the United States and the failure of many consumer
energy conservation programs. There is a tendency to confuse advertising with marketing. Advertising is but a part of marketing,
and the fact that the Canadian federal government is the largest
spender on advertising in Canada does not make it the leading marketing organization.

Measuring Postal Service Performance

The contrast between a customer and producer orientation can
be illustrated by looking at a key service measure used by USPS.
Service is measured in terms of postmark date to delivery (for
"eligible stamped first-class mail"), a production standard quoted
in the 1978 annual report as a measure of customer service. This
measure may be extremely useful for those who manage the mail-
processing system, but it leaves much to be desired from the standpoint of mailers who are sensitive to the speed of delivery. Similar
measures employed in Great Britain were strongly criticized by the
1977 Carter Commission, whose report noted:

> . . . the standards used are to some extent "self-
> adjusting" in that they measure performance against
> what the Post Office sets out to achieve rather than
> what its customers may be expecting. Thus, for ex-
> ample, when Sunday collections were abolished and
> first-class letters posted between Saturday lunch-
> time and Sunday afternoon were delayed by 24 hours,
> the effect on quality of service as measured by the
> Post Office was nil. This was because the letters
> concerned were collected on Monday and postmarked
> with Monday's date so that, provided they reached
> their destination by Tuesday morning (in the case of
> first-class letters), the Post Office had achieved its
> target and the item concerned would have been recorded
> as a "hit." But to the customer it was delivered 24
> hours later than previously and he would have recorded
> it as a "miss." From the customer's viewpoint, the
> best measure of quality of service would be the number
> of hours from dropping a letter in the post box (or

otherwise delivering it into the care of the Post Office)
to the arrival at the addressee's premises: but this
statistic is in practice hard to obtain. The next best
measure is the number of nights elapsing between deposit in a post box and arrival. This measure, which
would be a great deal more satisfactory than the measure actually used (the number of nights elapsing between the date of the postmark and the date of arrival)
could be derived with use of statistical sampling methods, and we recommend that its adoption be given
serious consideration. It really does not help the public image of the Post Office when the organization
appears to be manipulating the figures to the extent
that a deliberate and obvious worsening in the quality
of service given in practice to customers, such as
the abolition of Sunday collection or the withdrawal
of late evening collections, has had no effect whatever
on the quality of service recorded.[12]

Although the approaches suggested represent a considerable
advance over the present one, they are only the beginning of an
improved system of service measurement. It is necessary to determine what customers in specific market segments mean by service.
Do they mean speed, reliability, or something else? And do they
apply the same definition of service to all types of mail they send or
receive? Most fundamentally, service must be determined by the
benefits that users want. This requires an extensive market research program to identify customer needs, a systematic analysis
of the resulting data, development of market segments based on the
benefits that users desire and other factors, design of appropriate
service programs, and finally the measurement of service provided.

Conclusion

For a postal service to retain existing business and win new
business requires that a balance be maintained between marketing
and operations. At the same time, it should be recognized that a
marketing orientation can play an important role in helping to obtain new operating economies.

But a distinction must be drawn between developing a marketing
orientation throughout the organization and formalization of marketing tasks and responsibilities through the medium of a professional
marketing department. If a government agency or public enterprise
as a whole lacks a strong marketing orientation, it is in part because

operating managers do not always appreciate the nature and role of the marketing function. In the case of USPS, this, in turn, reflects the limited scope of the marketing department. For insights on why this is so, we now turn to an examination of the evolution of the marketing function at the U.S. Postal Service over the past decade.

THE EVOLUTION OF MARKETING AT USPS

The role of USPS's marketing department, encompassed in the Customer Services Department, appears to have been deliberately limited to advertising, sales, and marketing research. Although the Customer Services Department contains a number of experienced managers who combine expertise in marketing with a good understanding of the postal service, they have virtually no input to decisions on pricing or retailing and delivery systems, and only a limited role in new product development. The end result is that marketing expertise is not being brought to bear on one of the service's most critical challenges: developing a stronger competitive posture that will result in increased revenue generation.

There are a variety of reasons for this situation; some of them reflect the way in which the marketing function evolved at USPS during the late 1960s and early 1970s.

Early Marketing Efforts

In reviewing the nature of postal operations in the United States, the 1968 Kappel Commission noted:

> The Post Office has always been operated as if it were an ordinary Government agency. In what it <u>does</u>, however, the Post Office is a business: its customers purchase its services directly, its employees work in a service industry environment, it is a major communications network, it is the means by which much of the nation's business is conducted.[13]

The commission's report explicitly recognized the need for a marketing function. "Only a Post Office quick to identify and meet market needs," it stated, "can successfully serve a changing economy."[14]

The first steps in reorganization preceded passage of the Postal Reorganization Act of 1970 by more than a year. In June 1969, the Bureau of Planning and Marketing was established. This comprised three formerly independent divisions of the Post Office Department and allowed for a more coordinated management effort, while also providing a vehicle for long-range planning. During the past century, the post office had offered new services or expanded existing ones by simply adding them to the structure that existed at the time. This lack of planning or coordination from the top resulted in the development of an uncoordinated conglomerate of parts and contributed to the operational problems experienced in the mid-1960s.

The Customer Services Department

In 1971, following passage of the Postal Reorganization Act, the Customer Services Department was established with responsibility for most marketing functions, although pricing decisions were placed in the Rates and Classification Department. In 1973, Customer Services was stripped of its responsibility for the delivery function, which was transferred elsewhere. Among the early appointments were a number of managers from firms well known for their expertise in marketing consumer goods.

One of these executives, who was appointed director of product management in 1973, described the department's perception of the services offered by USPS as follows:

> Starting from the mandate in the [Postal] Reorganization Act that said we should provide services based on customer needs, have flexible pricing, and take into consideration value of services and market demand, we have asked ourselves: what is the proper business of the Postal Service?
>
> And our answer is that, first, we are in the communications business with our message transfer services like first-class mail. Secondly, we're in the media business by using the mails to deliver advertising messages. Thirdly, we're in the materials handling business with products and services like parcel post. Fourth, we're in the financial business. We're the number one money order brand in the United States, and have a very high cash flow and a lot of financial expertise. And, of course, very clearly, we run a large retail business. I think our number of outlets is ten times greater than the A & P chain's, for example. [15]

Acting on these insights, several separate divisions were established in 1974, each organized around different "product categories"—groups of related services. These divisions included Letter Mail, Parcel Mail, Special Services (subdivided into two groups, one for registered, certified, and COD mail, and the other for advertising mail), and Electronic Mail. The last included the new Mailgram service and was charged with looking ahead at how USPS might participate in the development of electronic mail.

Since the postal reorganization, a number of innovative services have been successfully introduced and several existing programs redesigned. In several instances, the development of specific services has been refined with the aid of market research and testing, which are new management concepts for the postal service (examples include express mail and postal money orders). On the other hand, many of the new managers hired by USPS have felt frustrated by the bureaucracy of the postal service, by the lack of understanding of marketing demonstrated by executives in other functional areas, and by their own lack of clout in the organization. For instance, one manager commented retrospectively:

> Just because there is a law written, it does not change the inertia of operating in a certain way and the value systems that are present in any large, established organization.
>
> I think that people coming from the outside, like I did, really didn't appreciate that. I think there was some confusion between a legislative act and a divine miracle. There's a great gap between the two.[16]

Marketing Difficulties

An important criticism of early marketing efforts was that they were too often directed at "peripheral" issues that were seen as likely to be responsive to marketing solutions—such as an advertising campaign to encourage letter writing—rather than directed at the tougher task of solving key management problems. This led to disenchantment with marketing among many career postal executives.

One early marketing effort, developed in 1973 and targeted at household rather than commercial mailers, quickly ran into political difficulties and was eventually scuttled. USPS marketing managers had developed a range of postal-related goods and services—including packaging materials, postal scales, postage stamp dispensers, photocopying facilities, and self-inking stampers—that were intended to make postal service more convenient for the individual user and to contribute to both the efficiency and profitability of the postal system. This broadened product line was made available in a number of large post offices across the nation.

But representatives of small business interests soon exerted pressure on Congress to terminate what they perceived as "unfair" competition by a public agency and made statements such as "this country was built on free enterprise, and the last thing it needs is to have private business forced to compete with a subsidized entity such as our own Postal Department."[17]

Faced with this opposition (and needing congressional approval for an increased budget), the postal service agreed in 1975 to remove its photocopying machines and to discontinue sales of most postal-related items. Later, after receiving 12,000 letters (an enormous number by usual standards) protesting the discontinuance of photocopying services, copying machines were reintroduced in selected locations.

The new marketing managers were also criticized by old-time postal employees, who felt that the newcomers were trying to change things too fast in an organization they did not fully understand. More thoughtful observers believed that the packaged goods backgrounds of some of these managers did not suit them for jobs that required the marketing of services, a task that demanded different working relationships with operations managers than they might have encountered in a manufacturing industry.[18] It was also pointed out that their past experience had generally involved marketing to household purchasers, whereas the great bulk of postal services were purchased by business mailers.

Nevertheless, the executives imported from consumer goods marketing (some of whom have since left the organization) made some important and lasting contributions to USPS. Most significantly, they scrutinized the various individual services making up the postal product line and emphasized the need for research so that USPS might anticipate and respond to customer needs.

Between 1975 and 1978 a series of reorganizations took place, during the course of which the structure of the marketing organization was revised (and effectively downgraded) several times. A career postal executive with experience in customer services at the regional level was appointed Assistant Postmaster General-Customer Services in 1975, but the continuing reorganizations—one of which resulted in loss of responsibility for the retail function—made it difficult for the department to consolidate its position within the postal service, coordinate its efforts with those of other departments, and achieve demonstrable results.

By the time a new APMG-Customer Services, a former business executive, was appointed in 1978, the original scope and authority of the Customer Services Department had been sharply narrowed. This meant that marketing expertise at the postal service was confined to advertising, personal selling, and marketing research, being almost completely excluded from such customer-related areas as pricing, retailing, and delivery services and, even more importantly, from the strategic planning process. But even in the areas of advertising and personal selling, the effectiveness of marketing at USPS has been severely constrained. As an example, we will briefly review some of the limits placed on advertising at USPS.

Constraints on Advertising

Prior to postal reorganization, the Post Office Department restricted itself to public service advertising. Since the advent of USPS, postal management has been willing to make a moderate commitment to the use of paid media advertising.

In fiscal year (FY) 1979, the total advertising budget for USPS was $11.7 million, which included $10.4 million for media, production, research, and travel. By the standards of most national advertisers, this is a very small amount. Moreover, USPS's advertising expenditures as a percentage of sales (0.06 percent in FY 1979) are much lower than in the British Post Office (0.36 percent) or Canada Post (0.25 percent).[19]

Yet USPS receives both internal and external criticism for even its existing, modest level of paid media advertising. Some postal managers appear to doubt the need for any advertising, while many government officials and legislators question the appropriateness of spending "postal ratepayers' dollars" on advertising, which they seem to regard as wasteful. Such viewpoints display ignorance of the purposes of current postal advertising efforts.

The USPS advertising budget for FY 1979 was $11.7 million, which included $10.4 million for media, production, research, and travel. The USPS Customer Services Department lists the following major advertising programs at USPS in 1979:

PAID MEDIA

Express mail. The objective of this advertising is to generate revenues through increased awareness, trial, and use of express mail services with primary emphasis on next-day service.

Philatelic. The objective of this program is to generate revenues by expanding the number of collectors of U.S. Mint stamps and by increasing the number of U.S. Mint stamps purchased and saved by these collectors. Advertising focuses primarily on U.S. commemorative stamps, with special seasonal support given to other stamp collecting products (e.g., Starter Kits, Mint Sets, and Stamps & Stories, a paperback catalogue) at Christmas time.

Presort first-class mail. Program advertising is directed toward commercial mailers to convince them to presort their first-class mail by making them aware of the advantages of presorted mail.

PUBLIC SERVICE (DONATED) MEDIA

Mail early for Christmas. The objective of this advertising is to remind people to properly prepare and deposit their Christmas mail early for delivery by Christmas day.

Moved mail. The objective of this advertising is to convince people who are moving to notify mail sources well in advance, using the free change-of-address kit.

Zip code. The objective of this advertising is to remind people to include the zip code in all addresses.

It should be noted that two of the three paid media campaigns are intended to increase postal revenues. In a very real sense, advertising represents an investment that, if properly planned and executed, will yield a significant return and more than pay for itself. In the case of Presort, the objective is to encourage customers to behave in ways that will result in cost savings for USPS; so advertising can be viewed as an investment that will pay off in the form of an improvement in net revenue.

USPS's public service advertising (PSA) campaigns are basically reminders to encourage people to continue to behave in ways that will yield benefits for both themselves and the service. But the problem with PSA is that USPS has very little control over where, when, and how frequently these advertisements will be run, or even their exact format where print media are concerned.

Effective advertising requires tight control over media selection, scheduling, and format to make sure that ads reach their target audiences with the intended degree of impact. Otherwise, members of the target audience may not be exposed to the message in ways that will cause them to remember and act upon it.

We suspect that testing of alternative advertising expenditure levels would show that, in many instances, increased budgets for paid media advertising would yield a substantial net improvement in postal revenues. Advertising budgets should be set with this objective in mind, rather than being artificially constrained by internal and external pressures based on misunderstanding or prejudice.

Identifying and Evaluating New Product Opportunities

New products can be developed in a variety of ways: first, responding to external requests; second, solving internal operational or resource allocation problems; third, copying competitors or comparable organizations in other countries; and fourth, identification of unmet market needs through market analysis. Prior to postal reorganization, no new postal products had been introduced for many years. Since then, a number of new products have been developed. Express mail originated in response to requests by the Federal Housing and Mortgage Authority for guaranteed overnight delivery to banks of time-sensitive financial documents. Mailgram resulted from meetings between postal and Western Union executives when the latter became concerned about the high cost of maintaining their hard-copy delivery services. Presort was developed as a solution to the problem of improving the efficiency of postal sorting operations.

Although these three new products have been quite successful, there was an element of happenstance in the development of each. Up to now, market and competitive analysis have played a relatively minor role in new product development at USPS. The widespread perception of marketing as simply advertising and selling tends to delay involvement of marketing specialists until late in the process. The critical question for the postal service is: are profitable product development opportunities being overlooked because of insufficient emphasis on exploring market needs? Although some successful ad hoc systems have been devised, long-term growth requires a systematic process for the generation, development, evaluation, and introduction of new products.

Clarifying the Role of Marketing

To a much greater degree than at USPS, the British and Canadian postal services have achieved a balance between marketing and operations. In both organizations marketing managers are more involved in areas such as pricing and retailing, and they play a more significant role in both policymaking and strategy formulation than is the case at USPS. In part, we believe that the greater acceptance of the marketing function in Canada Post and the British Post Office reflects some of the early appointments made to senior marketing positions—executives who were skilled in the marketing of services, especially to institutional buyers, and who were also sensitive to the dynamics of the public sector.

In both instances, efforts were also made to clarify the role of marketing to other postal managers. For instance, in 1976, as part of an effort to improve understanding of marketing's role at the British Post Office, a booklet titled An Appreciation of Postal Marketing was produced and disseminated quite widely within the organization. Under the heading "Market Objectives," the booklet stated:

> Within the overall task of contributing effectively to the financial prosperity of the business, it is the objective of postal marketing to develop policies which meet the present and future needs of business and private customers, maintain existing traffic and secure new traffic, at prices which people will pay, and which will meet system and operating costs. [20]

Also in 1976, Canada's Assistant Deputy Postmaster General-Marketing stated his perception that the contribution "of marketing can be summarized in six words, to improve the net financial position." [21] He then moved quickly to develop roles for marketing appropriate to the expected performance of the entire organization. These included:

Support for financial and operational aims through productivity selling, revenue generation, and promotion of the postal code and of standards and procedures facilitating mechanization.

Showing the "marketing concept" in action by developing useful linkages between major mail users (and their associations) and the operating units of Canada Post.

Leadership in Canada Post's overall planning process by developing marketing studies and strategies that could serve as the point of departure for overall departmental planning.

An in-depth evaluation of Canada Post in 1979 by external researchers concluded as follows:

> Marketing is emerging as the primary future oriented unit and the chief advocate for organizational change in a Department otherwise overwhelmed with present practices, immediate problems, and past procedures. [22]

Conclusion

The U.S. Postal Service now limits professional marketing management inputs to decisions on advertising, personal selling, and marketing research. There has never been any significant marketing involvement in pricing decisions at USPS and there is no formal new product development process. Indeed, the scope of responsibilities assigned to marketing managers has been deliberately narrowed in recent years, with the Customer Services Department being stripped of its previous responsibilities for delivery and retailing. This situation contrasts with the broader role assigned to the marketing departments at the British Post Office and Canada Post.

Not surprisingly, many operating managers at USPS tend to limit their definition of marketing to the communication element of the marketing mix. Even within this narrowly defined sphere, further constraints have been imposed that serve to restrict the effectiveness of postal advertising. However, not all of the constraints on marketing at USPS are internal in nature. As will be shown in the next section, the forces of regulation also have a significant impact.

THE IMPACT OF REGULATION

The postal service, like many transportation and communication businesses in the United States, is under the jurisdiction of a national regulatory commission established by federal legislation. But there are two important differences. First, the regulatory body in question, the Postal Rate Commission (PRC), regulates only USPS—competitors are regulated by other agencies. Second, the PRC has yet to be touched by the growing trend toward deregulation.

The commission conducts administrative hearings on requests by the postal service for changes in postal rates, fees, and mail classifications, then issues decisions based on these hearings. The PRC is also empowered to issue advisory opinions regarding proposed mail service changes having potentially nationwide impact. In addition, it may review appeals on proposed post office closings and entertain certain complaints by mail users.

One impact of the current regulatory and political environment that USPS faces has been to make the introduction of new products and the abandonment of old ones more difficult. Morison asks us to imagine that you, as a businessman, were about to introduce a new product and found that:

You had to obtain the permission of an independent agency
that invited a number of potential competitors—say 50
or 60 interested parties in all—to evaluate your product
and cost data, and then stretched out its deliberations
so long that any competitor wanting to could beat you to
the market!

You had to establish your pricing before conducting
market tests and that if the tests showed the need for
different pricing you had to go the regulatory route all
over again!

You had run an ad announcing your product was
coming out and then saw the congress pass a law post-
poning its implementation for 26 months!

You had set the price for your product and seen
a Federal court rule that intangible factors such as
value of service could not be factored in, that only
your costs of service could be reflected in your price!

You would have to sell the product in stores you
could not close (even if they were unprofitable)!

Or try this one. You had found that you would
have to set your price much higher than you wanted to
because your competitors were held to have the right
to undersell you! [23]

PRC hearings add considerably to the time and cost of intro-
ducing new products and changing pricing strategies, as Morison's
comments suggest. Moreover, plans are laid bare before competitors in plenty of time for them to react effectively if they so
desire.

Nor does the PRC seek only to be a watchdog. As the commissioners stated in 1973, ". . . this Commission has no intention
of limiting itself to being a mere umpire, calling balls and strikes
only on the proposals of [the] parties."[24] The PRC's authority to
review classifications of service, the institution of an officer of
the commission to represent the "general public," and congressional
permission to consider "such other factors as the Commission may
deem appropriate" in rate hearings made it inevitable that the PRC
would play a substantial role in policymaking.

It is possible that the PRC, having only one organization to
regulate, may play a different role in policy setting than do the
bodies that regulate the postal service's largest competitors, e.g.,
the Interstate Commerce Commission (ICC) for United Parcel
Service and the Federal Communications Commission (FCC) for
American Telephone & Telegraph. Additionally, the impact of
having different regulatory agencies with different standards and

objectives oversee organizations that compete in the same market
needs to be investigated. For example, should not parcel post be
regulated by the ICC in the same manner in which that agency regulates the services provided by United Parcel Service?

Dependence on Cost Criteria

Congress established nine criteria to be observed by the PRC
in considering a postal service request for a change in rates. These
criteria include, in informal terms: value of service actually provided, available alternative means of sending and receiving mail,
effect of rate increases on the general public and other user groups,
degree of mail preparation done by the mailer, and the value (educational, cultural, and scientific) of the mail. The predominant
criterion has been the requirement that "each class of mail or type
of mail service bear the direct and indirect postal costs attributable
to that class or type plus that portion of all other costs of the postal
service reasonably assignable to such class or type."[25] In part,
this emphasis reflects the fact that the other criteria are relatively
"fuzzy," being ill-defined, they are therefore hard to measure. As
a result, the largest part of the commission's time and energy is
devoted to the cost criterion. Many of the PRC's hearings are consumed by the testimony of vested interests among both user groups
(e.g., publishers and greeting card manufacturers) and competitors,
who spend much time arguing that costs should be attributed in ways
that turn out to be favorable to them.
    In defense of the PRC, it must be admitted that this agency
has prodded the postal service into gaining a better understanding
of its costs and how these should be attributed among the different
classes of mail. On the other hand, the commission's emphasis on
costs (along with court interpretations of the law) has sometimes
played into the hands of USPS competitors.
    In contrast, the British Post Office has far more control over
its pricing decisions than does USPS. This flexibility has allowed
it to relate prices to the realities of the marketplace and to compete vigorously for contract business from large corporate mailers.
    While subject to government review, postal pricing decisions
in Great Britain are the responsibility of the marketing department,
which recognizes them as a key element of marketing strategy.
The post office is required by the government to set prices at levels
that will ensure that total postal income meets total expenditure plus
a target return of 2 percent on turnover. But the general approach
adopted is to gear prices to individual services, so that while all
services meet at least their direct costs, the contribution they make

individually to overheads and profits varies in accordance with marketing and other considerations.[26]

In Canada, it is significant to note that when Canada Post was made a crown corporation late in 1981, no body corresponding to the PRC was created. However, Canada Post Corporation's rates will be subject to review by the federal cabinet.[27]

Competition and the Regulatory Process

Some observers seem to visualize USPS as a large, resource-rich organization with the ability to bring subsidies to bear on any market. This visualization is often then followed by a lecture on the private firm's inability to compete against such a colossus. On the other hand, USPS has a public service mission and an organizational history that other observers claim make it a helpless giant. Neither extreme is, of course, true. But USPS does have special problems in competing, as illustrated by its performance against United Parcel Service (UPS) in the small parcel market. Of particular note is the way in which the regulatory process has constrained USPS's ability to compete effectively.

In the early 1960s, UPS delivered about 25 percent of the fewer than 1 billion packages sent annually. By 1978, UPS alone delivered more than 1 billion packages, more than three times as many as the postal service. How did UPS manage to grow so rapidly? It is an aggressive competitor that has specialized in the business sender market and has provided a service to this market so superior to parcel post that even the PRC (Docket R74-1) remarked that "UPS success has been built on providing a better combination of speed, service, lower damage, and price than the Postal Service can offer."[28]

Although UPS accepts parcels from individuals, it concentrates on the business market. By charging a nominal fee for regular pickup service, it effectively screens out most individuals, since UPS has far fewer drop-off stations than does USPS. These locations are not always convenient to residential areas, and telephone directory listings do not always provide street addresses. In contrast, USPS must serve the general public and thus is not in a position to adopt many of the restrictive strategies open to UPS.

If the postal service is to become an effective competitor in the large markets presently dominated by UPS, then pricing and service strategies must be developed that satisfy consumer needs and are superior to competitive offerings. However, United Parcel Service has aggressively argued before the PRC for cost attributions to fourth-class mail that would raise the costs of parcel post. It has also sought injunctions in the courts to halt USPS service tests.

Regulation and Market Testing: The Local Parcel Test Plan

The difficulty of competing under the present regulatory system—especially with a competitor such as UPS so ready to use the courts to protect its position—is illustrated by the court injunction that halted a parcel post experiment called the Local Parcel Test Plan. In October 1977, USPS instituted a 12-month bulk mailing experiment to test the cost and service feasibility of charging a fixed fee per item, based on average weight, for mailings by large shippers, rather than calculating the amount of postage by weighing each individual parcel. This fixed-fee postage payment system eliminated the need to calculate postage individually on each parcel, thus simplifying procedures for both the customer and USPS. This new product was to be tested by 20 shippers in limited geographical areas.

UPS immediately took the postal service to court—which ruled against the postal service, stipulating that even test changes in rates and classifications involving as few as 20 customers must be first heard by the PRC. The Third Circuit Court of Appeals upheld this decision 2 to 1. The majority decided that approval of this small experiment would set a precedent for larger experiments and that if Congress had wanted to exempt experiments from PRC regulation, it would have done so explicitly. Consequently, according to the majority opinion, this experiment involved a rate change as defined by the act.

The dissenting judge's opinion vigorously condemned such a ruling for so constraining managerial initiative:

We have the paradox of the United Parcel Service (UPS)—one of the United States Postal Service's (Postal Service) major competitors—preventing the Postal Service from undertaking on its own a modest and limited experiment which is a relatively small threat, if any, to the plaintiffs, involving not more than twenty selected shippers in no more than five metropolitan areas. As I view the applicable statutes, the Postal Service need not be shackled and prevented from pursuing such modest experimentation. It has some latitude to experiment, without indulging in further bureaucratic processes, and to determine whether a plan can be devised to provide the American public with better service and their major competitor with more robust competition. The learned trial judge below, in his customarily thorough fashion, noted that "as a matter of pure policy the result advocated by the Postal Service is more desirable."[29]

However, in subsequent appeals (going as far as the Supreme Court), the majority decision was not overturned.

Conclusion

It is hard to avoid the conclusion that something is wrong with the way in which the U.S. Postal Service is regulated. Few would deny the need for some form of impartial body to oversee the activities of a public agency whose revenues exceed $18 billion. But the wording of the legislation establishing USPS and the Postal Rate Commission, and the way in which both the PRC and the courts have chosen to interpret that legislation, have combined to produce results that are not, in our view, in the public interest.

We contend that postal regulation has had a damaging impact on USPS's ability to understand and respond to market needs in a highly competitive environment. Although it is beyond the scope of this chapter to propose a new approach to postal regulation,[30] we believe that, at a minimum, new legislation is needed to revise substantially the present system and that serious consideration should be given to abolishing the Postal Rate Commission.

SUMMARY

National postal services have never before had to operate in such a competitive environment as they now face. This competition threatens every class of mail, either directly or by substitution, and requires a new approach to postal management. Even first-class letter mail, which is de jure a monopoly, is increasingly subject to de facto competition from the telephone and emerging electronic technologies.[31] Nothing illustrates better the danger of being complacent about competition and the market than the fate of parcel mail in the United States.

National postal services should recognize that the privileges conferred by statute are not an inalienable right but only make sense to the extent that the postal system continues to provide good quality service and to seek new ways of improving that service. One of Canada Post Corporation's first major actions was to challenge the right of city-owned utilities to deliver their own bills or to use private delivery services.[32] In the long run, however, postal systems should plan to defend the first-class letter mail monopoly in the marketplace, not the courts.

Postal managers at all levels must not think of themselves as a government-protected monopoly; they need to think in market terms. Managers and other employees should be made aware of how direct and indirect competition threaten both their jobs and the future viability of their organization.

In the United States, we believe that strong measures must be taken to correct two weaknesses that continue to plague the postal service and detract from its ability to compete successfully in the marketplace. The first is the lack of a strong market orientation within the organization, especially in such areas as pricing, new product development, retailing, and strategic planning. The second is the climate of regulation and political interference that surrounds the postal service, hobbling management's ability to act boldly and effectively.

In Canada, the new crown corporation Canada Post started life late in 1981 with a stronger marketing orientation and function and with a freer regulatory environment than did USPS in 1971. However, the path for Canada Post will not be easy. Just prior to its creation, the federal cabinet boosted first-class letter rates (effective January 1, 1982) by more than 70 percent (from 17 cents to 30 cents). Perhaps more importantly, its predecessor agency has been bedeviled by poor labor relations, resulting in frequent strikes and slowdowns.[33] This illustrates a key point: strong marketing management is not enough. The other management functions must perform well, too. In particular, a service organization must be capable of meeting, consistently, the operational standards required to create and deliver the product, otherwise customers will quickly become disenchanted. Canada Post is better off than previously now that it has a strong marketing group to help chart the future direction of the organization and tailor its strategies to reflect market conditions. But it can never achieve its full potential unless all management functions pull together. As this chapter has argued, marketing is one—but just one—of the vital management activities that public sector managers must master to achieve success.

NOTES

1. From a consultants' report, cited in Stanley J. Shapiro and J. A. Barnhill, "The Post Office in the Market Place: A Ten Year Retrospective," in Macromarketing: A Canadian Perspective, ed. D. N. Thompson et al. (Chicago: American Marketing Association, 1980). [Note: The original draft of this paper reproduced both paragraphs of the quotation from the consultants' report given in the text, but the version printed in the proceedings volume contained only the first paragraph.]

2. Christopher H. Lovelock and Charles B. Weinberg, "Contrasting Public and Nonprofit Marketing," in 1974 Combined Proceedings, ed. Ronald C. Curhan (Chicago: American Marketing Association, 1975).

3. J. A. Barnhill and Stanley J. Shapiro, "Comparative Public Sector Marketing: Contrasting Two Canadian Programs," in Government Marketing: Theory and Practice, ed. M. P. Mokwa and S. E. Permut (New York: Praeger, 1981).

4. "Fortune's Directory of the 500 Largest Industrial Corporations," Fortune 103, no. 9 (May 4, 1981):324 and "The Fortune Directory of the 50 Largest Industrial Corporations," Fortune 104, no. 1 (July 13, 1981):114-27.

5. Christopher H. Lovelock and Charles B. Weinberg, Marketing for Public and Nonprofit Managers (New York: John Wiley & Sons, forthcoming).

6. Philip Kotler, Marketing for Nonprofit Organizations (Englewood Cliffs, N.J.: Prentice-Hall, 1975), pp. 37-38.

7. Philip Kotler and Sidney J. Levy, "Broadening the Concept of Marketing," Journal of Marketing, January 1969, pp. 3-13.

8. J. Allison Barnhill, "Developing a Marketing Orientation: A Case Study of the Canada Post Office" in 1974 Combined Proceedings, ed. R. C. Curhan (Chicago: American Marketing Association, 1975), p. 204.

9. Gordon C. Morison, "Organizing to Implement a Product Market Strategy: The Case of the U.S. Postal Service," address at the UCLA/IRPP conference on Managing Public Enterprises: Strategy and Structure, Los Angeles, September 10, 1981.

10. Report on the Delivery Performance and Potential of the Post Office's Mail Services, London, Post Office Users National Council, Report No. 17, January 1979.

11. Morison, "Organizing to Implement a Product Market Strategy," p. 2.

12. C. F. Carter (chairman), Report of the Post Office Review Committee, London, Her Majesty's Stationery Office, Cmnd 6850, July 1977, p. 50.

13. Towards Postal Excellence, Report of the President's Commission on Postal Reorganization, Washington, D.C., June 1968, p. 1.

14. Ibid., p. 3.

15. "Now the 'Postman' Hustles for His Piece of the Business," Government Executive, October 1974, p. 17.

16. Christopher H. Lovelock and L. Frank Demmler, "United States Postal Service," in Cases in Public and Nonprofit Marketing, ed. C. H. Lovelock and C. B. Weinberg (Palo Alto, Calif.: The Scientific Press, 1977), p. 156.

17. Subcommittee on Postal Service of the Committee on Post Office and Civil Service, Report on Postal Service Sales of Postal Related Items, Committee Print No. 73-26 (Washington, D.C.: U.S. Government Printing Office, January 1975), p. 9.

18. Christopher H. Lovelock and Charles B. Weinberg, "The Role of Marketing in Improving Postal Service Effectiveness," in The Future of the Postal Service, ed. Joel L. Fleischman (New York: Praeger, 1982).

19. Ibid., Table 1.

20. An Appreciation of Postal Marketing (London: Postal Headquarters, October 1976), p. 3.

21. Barnhill and Shapiro, "Comparative Public Sector Marketing," p. 63.

22. Ibid., p. 76.

23. Morison, "Organizing to Implement a Product Market Strategy," pp. 4-5.

24. Postal Rate Commission, Docket No. MC73-1, April 1973.

25. 39 U.S. §3622.

26. Personal interviews and correspondence with N. N. Walmsley, Director of Marketing (Posts), Postal Headquarters, London.

27. This practice is not unique in Canada. For example, the rates of Saskatchewan Telephones and Saskatchewan Power, both provincial crown corporations, must be approved by the provincial cabinet. In general, regulatory agencies in Canada are less independent than those in the United States. In most cases their decisions may be appealed to the federal or a provincial cabinet. See Hudson Janisch, "Policy Making in Regulation: Towards a New Definition of the Status of Regulatory Agencies in Canada," Osgoode Hall Law Journal 17, no. 1 (1979):46-106.

28. Postal Rate Commission, Docket R74-1, August 1975.

29. United Parcel Service v. United States Postal Service, U.S. Court of Appeals 3d circuit, 3/26/79, Dissent—Circuit Judge S. Leon Higginbotham, Jr., pp. 22-23.

30. This issue is discussed in Roger Sherman, ed., Perspectives on Postal Service Issues (Washington, D.C.: American Enterprise Institute, 1980).

31. John F. McLaughlin et al., "Telephone-Letter Mail Competition: A First Look," unpublished working paper, Harvard University Program on Information Resources Policy, W-79-4 (July 1979).

32. R. James, "Couriers Fear Future," Toronto Star, January 14, 1982, p. D19.

33. Michael Warren, "The Performance of the Canadian Post Office: Will Becoming a Crown Corporation Make Any Difference?," address at the UCLA/IRPP conference on Managing Public Enterprise: Purposes and Performance, Vancouver, B.C., August 14, 1981.

INDEX

ABOUT THE EDITORS
AND CONTRIBUTORS

W. T. STANBURY is a professor of policy analysis in the
Faculty of Commerce and Business Administration at the University
of British Columbia. Between June 1978 and November 1979 he
was director of the regulation reference for the Economic Council
of Canada and was responsible for preparing its Preliminary Report (November 1978) and its Interim Report (November 1979).
Dr. Stanbury then became director of research for regulation and
reference until August 1980. Since November 1977 he has been
director of the Regulation and Government Intervention Program of
the Institute for Research on Public Policy.

Dr. Stanbury received his B. Comm. from the University of
British Columbia (1966), and his M.A. (1969) and Ph.D. (1972)
degrees in economics from the University of California at Berkeley.
In 1976 and 1977, he acted as a consultant and researcher for the
Royal Commission on Corporate Concentration. He has also been
a consultant to the Bureau of Competition Policy of the Federal
Department of Consumer and Corporate Affairs. Dr. Stanbury is
the author or coauthor of more than 80 articles appearing in journals and in a number of books, and has authored or edited ten books,
including Government Regulation: Scope, Growth, Process.

FRED THOMPSON is an associate professor of public policy
and management and associate director of the Canadian Studies
Program in the School of International and Public Affairs of Columbia University. He has been a visiting professor at the Graduate
School of Management at the University of California at Los Angeles
and at the University of British Columbia, and has served as a staff
consultant to the Economic Council of Canada's Regulation Reference,
participating in the preparation of its Interim Report.

Dr. Thompson received his B.A. from Pomona College (1964)
and his Ph.D. from Claremont Graduate School (1972). He is the
author or coauthor of more than 20 publications in such journals as
Public Choice, Policy Analysis, Policy Sciences, and The American
Political Science Review.

DOUGLAS CAVES is a senior economist in the Social Systems
Research Institute, University of Wisconsin, Madison.

LAURITS CHRISTENSEN is a professor of economics, University of Wisconsin, Madison.

CATHERINE ECKEL is an assistant professor of policy analysis, Faculty of Commerce and Business Administration, University of British Columbia.

JOHN GRATWICK is executive vice-president, Canadian National Railways, Montreal, Quebec.

TREVOR D. HEAVER is a professor and chairman of the Division of Transportation, Faculty of Commerce and Business Administration, University of British Columbia.

GEORGE HILTON is a professor of economics, University of California, Los Angeles.

W. A. JORDAN is a professor of economics, Faculty of Administrative Studies, York University.

GEORGES LAFOND is vice-president of finance, Hydro-Québec, Montreal, Quebec.

ARIE Y. LEWIN is a professor of business and international studies, Fuqua School of Business Administration, Duke University.

CHRISTOPHER H. LOVELOCK is an associate professor, Graduate School of Business Administration, Harvard University.

T. M. OHASHI is senior vice-president and director of planning, Pemberton Securities Limited, Vancouver, B.C.

LARRY PRATT is an associate professor of political science, University of Alberta.

ALLAN PULSIPHER is chief economist and director of strategic planning, Tennessee Valley Authority.

W. G. SHEPHERD is professor of economics, University of Michigan.

JOSEPH SWANSON is professor of economics, Northwestern University.

MICHAEL W. TRETHEWAY is a research associate, Social Systems Research Institute, University of Wisconsin, Madison.

AIDAN VINING is an assistant professor of policy analysis, Faculty of Commerce and Business Administration, University of British Columbia.

W. G. WATERS II is an associate professor of transportation, Faculty of Commerce and Business Administration, University of British Columbia.

CHARLES B. WEINBERG is a professor of marketing, Faculty of Commerce and Business Administration, University of British Columbia.

ABOUT THE INSTITUTE FOR
RESEARCH ON PUBLIC POLICY

Founded in 1972, the Institute for Research on Public Policy is a national organization whose independence and autonomy are ensured by the revenues of an endowment fund that is supported by the federal and provincial governments and by the private sector. In addition, the institute receives grants and contracts from governments, corporations, and foundations to carry out specific research projects.

The raison d'etre of the institute is threefold:

To act as a catalyst within the national community by helping to facilitate informed public debate on issues of major public interest.

To stimulate participation by all segments of the national community in the process that leads to public policymaking.

To find practical solutions to important public policy problems, thus aiding in the development of sound public policies.

The institute is governed by a board of directors, which is the decision-making body, and a council of trustees, which advises the board on matters related to the research direction of the institute. Day-to-day administration of the institute's policies, programs, and staff is the responsibility of the president.

The institute operates in a decentralized way, employing researchers located across Canada. This ensures that research undertaken will include contributions from all regions of the country.

Wherever possible, the institute will try to promote public understanding of, and discussion on, issues of national importance, whether they be controversial or not. It will publish its research findings with clarity and impartiality. Conclusions or recommendations in the institute's publications are solely those of the author, and should not be attributed to the board of directors, council of trustees, or contributors to the institute.

The president bears final responsibility for the decision to publish a manuscript under the institute's imprint. In reaching this decision, he is advised on the accuracy and objectivity of a manuscript by both institute staff and outside reviewers. Publication of a manuscript signifies that it is deemed to be a competent treatment of a subject worthy of public consideration.